BEST
BACKPACKING
TRIPS IN
UTAH, ARIZONA,
AND NEW MEXICO

MIKE WHITE AND DOUG LORAIN

BEST

BACKPACKING

TRIPS

IN UTAH, ARIZONA, AND NEW MEXICO

UNIVERSITY OF NEVADA PRESS   RENO & LAS VEGAS

University of Nevada Press, Reno, Nevada 89557 USA
Copyright © 2016 by Mike White and Doug Lorain
www.unpress.nevada.edu
All rights reserved
Manufactured in the United States of America

LIBRARY OF CONGRESS CATALOGING-IN-PUBLICATION DATA
Names: White, Michael C., 1952– | Lorain, Douglas, 1962–
Title: Best backpacking trips in Utah, Arizona, and New
Mexico / Mike White & Douglas Lorain.
Description: Reno, Nevada : University of Nevada Press, [2016] | Includes index.
Identifiers: LCCN 2015046484 (print) | LCCN 2016004104 (ebook) |
ISBN 978-0-87417-996-5 (Paperback : alk. paper) | ISBN 978-1-943859-13-9 (e-book)
Subjects: LCSH: Backpacking—Utah—Guidebooks. | Trails—Utah—Guidebooks. |
Utah—Guidebooks. | Backpacking—Arizona—Guidebooks. |
Trails—Arizona—Guidebooks. | Arizona—Guidebooks. | Backpacking—New
Mexico—Guidebooks. | Trails—New Mexico—Guidebooks. | New
Mexico—Guidebooks.
Classification: LCC GV199.42.U73 W55 2016 (print) | LCC GV199.42.U73 (ebook) |
DDC 796.5109792—dc23
LC record available at http://lccn.loc.gov/2015046484

∞ The paper used in this book meets the requirements of
American National Standard for Information Sciences—Permanence of Paper
for Printed Library Materials, ANSI/NISO Z39.48-1992 (R2002).
Binding materials were selected for strength and durability.

FIRST PRINTING

Disclaimer: The authors have made a reasonable attempt to ensure that the
information contained in this book was accurate at the time of publication.
However, a guidebook cannot guarantee the safety of any individual or group
while hiking on trips described within its pages. Be aware that conditions may
change at any time. You are responsible for your own safety and health while in
the backcountry, which may include such precautions as attention to road,
trail, terrain, and weather conditions, as well as the capabilities and competence
of your companions. Staying well informed and exercising common sense and
good judgment will assist you in having a safe and enjoyable experience.

To Dal and Candy,
two of our oldest Reno friends
and favorite hikers

Thousands of tired,
nerve-shaken, over-civilized people
are beginning to find out
going to the mountains is going home,
that wilderness is a necessity.

—JOHN MUIR

Contents

Illustrations   xi
Acknowledgments   xv
Introduction   xvii
Trail Etiquette, Wilderness Ethics, and Safety   xix
Using this Guide   xxi

PART I — UTAH

1. Highline Trail   5
2. Under-the-Rim Trail   21
3. Zion Park Traverse   37
4. Coyote Gulch and the Escalante River Country   55
5. Salt Creek Canyon and Chesler Park Traverse   73
6. Grand Gulch and Bullet Canyon Traverse   97

PART II — UTAH AND ARIZONA

7. Buckskin Gulch and Paria River Canyon   113

PART III — ARIZONA

8. North Rim to South Rim: North Kaibab and Bright Angel Trails   131
9. Tonto Trail: Grandview to Hermits Rest   151

PART IV — NEW MEXICO

10. Pecos Skyline Trail   173
11. Gila River Canyons Loop   191

Best Trips by Season   207
Index   209
About the Authors   215

Illustrations

Photographs

Human-sized cairn on the Highline Trail 11
Along the Highline Trail 12
Descent from Red Knob Pass 17
Ebenezer and Mary Bryce 27
Scene above Right Fork Swamp Canyon 33
Scene near Yellow Creek Camp 34
Kolob Canyons View 44
On the descent into Zion Canyon 51
Hikers at Coyote Natural Bridge 68
View from above Crack in the Wall 70
Angel Arch 84
Druid Arch 92
The Thumb 107
Green Mask Panel 109
A narrow section of Buckskin Gulch 120
Wavy patterns on the walls of Buckskin Gulch 122
Buckskin Gulch, approaching the confluence with Paria Canyon 125
View of the South Rim of the Grand Canyon from
    Bright Angel Canyon 140
Ribbon Falls, Grand Canyon National Park 143
A view of Granite Gorge from the Tonto Trail 160
On the Tonto Trail 165
The Colorado River from the Tonto Trail 166
Truchas Lake 181
View north along Trailrider's Wall 184
Pecos Wilderness closed because of fire in 2011 189
Hoodoos in Middle Fork Canyon, below Jordan Hot Springs 197
Rock pinnacle below Jordan Hot Springs 199
Dramatic-looking pinnacle in Middle Fork Canyon
    below the Meadows 200

Maps

I.1	Trip Locator	2
1.1	Highline Trail Location	4
1.2	Highline Trail (West)	14
1.3	Highline Trail (East)	15
2.1	Under-the-Rim Location	22
2.2	Under-the-Rim (North)	31
2.3	Under-the-Rim (South)	32
3.1	Zion Park Traverse Location	36
3.2	Zion Park Traverse (West)	48
3.3	Zion Park Traverse (East)	49
4.1	Coyote Gulch and the Escalante River Country Location	54
4.2	Coyote Gulch and the Escalante River Country (West)	65
4.3	Coyote Gulch and the Escalante River Country (East)	66
5.1	Salt Creek Canyon and Chesler Park Traverse Location	72
5.2	Salt Creek Canyon and Chesler Park Traverse (North)	88
5.3	Salt Creek Canyon and Chesler Park Traverse (South)	89
6.1	Grand Gulch and Bullet Canyon Traverse Location	98
6.2	Grand Gulch and Bullet Canyon Traverse	106
7.1	Buckskin Gulch and Paria River Canyon Location	112
7.2	Buckskin Gulch and Paria River Canyon (West)	123
7.3	Buckskin Gulch and Paria River Canyon (East)	124
8.1	North Rim to South Rim: North Kaibab and Bright Angel Trails Location	130
8.2	North Rim to South Rim: North Kaibab and Bright Angel Trails (North)	144
8.3	North Rim to South Rim: North Kaibab and Bright Angel Trails (South)	145
9.1	Tonto Trail: Grandview to Hermits Rest Location	150
9.2	Tonto Trail: Grandview to Hermits Rest (East)	162
9.3	Tonto Trail: Grandview to Hermits Rest (Middle)	163
9.4	Tonto Trail: Grandview to Hermits Rest (West)	164
10.1	Pecos Skyline Trail Location	172
10.2	Pecos Skyline Trail (West)	182
10.3	Pecos Skyline Trail (East)	183
11.1	Gila River Canyons Loop Location	190
11.2	Gila River Canyons (West)	202
11.3	Gila River Canyons (East)	203

Trail Profiles

Highline Trail   6
Under-the-Rim Trail   23
Zion Park Traverse   38
Coyote Gulch and Escalante River Country   56
Salt Creek Canyon and Chesler Park Traverse   74
Grand Gulch and Bullet Canyon Traverse   99
Buckskin Gulch and Paria River Canyon   114
North Rim to South Rim: North Kaibab and Bright Angel Trails   132
Tonto Trail: Grandview to Hermits Rest   152
Pecos Skyline Trail   174
Gila River Canyons Loop   192

Acknowledgments

Thanks for my projects ever seeing the light of day mainly go to my wife, Robin, without whom nothing would ever come to fruition. I would also like to acknowledge the now retired Joanne O'Hare and Kathleen Szawiola at the University of Nevada Press for their help in launching the Best Backpacking Trips series. A big thank you goes to the current staff at UN Press for all their assistance. Keith Catlin, Tic Long, Andy Montessoro, and Dal and Candy Hunter joined me for the trips I contributed to this volume, and their presence on the trail was much appreciated.

—Mike

As with any book of this scope, many people contributed directly and indirectly to the completion of the work—from the tireless efforts of dozens of farsighted conservationists, who helped set aside the lands I now joyfully explore today, to modern hikers I've met on the trail and who anonymously offered suggestions and trip recommendations.

As usual, a few people deserve specific attention and appreciation. I would like to take note, for example, of David Eisbernd, my hiking partner on the trip down Buckskin Gulch and the Paria River. Showing remarkable restraint, he put up with my twisted humor and somehow managed to stop himself from strangling me in the middle of the night after I had accidentally dropped his expensive digital camera in quicksand earlier that day. Chris Paris, the condor project director of the Peregrine Fund, was gracious enough to read my essay on California condors and ensure that it was up to date and that the numbers and history were accurate. Jan Stock, at Bryce Canyon National Park, read and corrected my essay about the meaning of her magnificent park and provided a helpful photo of Mary and Ebenezer Bryce. I also want to give a warm (pun intended) thank you to the anonymous and very helpful woman just outside the fire-ravaged Pecos Wilderness in New Mexico. She saw this tired hiker trying to get back to his car and exit the area before wildfires trapped him and his vehicle. She gave me a lift, opened the gate that had been locked behind my car to keep others from entering the now-closed wilderness, and generally saved me a whole lot of time and trouble. I wish I knew her name so that I could thank her properly.

Finally, and most importantly, I want to thank my wife, Becky Lovejoy, for, well, for everything. You make it possible for me to pursue my hiking passions and just generally make life worth living.

—Doug

Introduction

Best Backpacking Trips in Utah, Arizona, and New Mexico is our second book following a guide to similar excursions in California and Nevada. The idea for a destination backpacking book for the great trips of the West was birthed one summer when my best friend, Tic, found himself the victim/beneficiary of a job loss due to the corporate raiding of Rupert Murdoch's expanding empire. A generous severance package was the positive aspect of being let go after thirty-plus years of service, with a summer free from any obligations toward gainful employment. Along with a couple of other friends, Andy and John, we embarked on a nearly month-long backpacking expedition in the northern Rockies, with the added bonus of intervening forays into civilization to shower, eat, drink, sleep, and relax. After backpacking through the stunning landscapes of the Beartooth Mountains in Montana and the Wind Rivers and Tetons of Wyoming, and upon meeting several groups of fellow backpackers from across the country along the way, the idea of a guide to the classic backpacking trips of the western United States started to evolve.

Backpacking these three trips of a lifetime in one summer was quite an exhilarating experience and a genuine blessing, especially sharing the journey with three good friends. In our fast-paced, workaday world, the opportunity to unplug and decompress in the natural environs of the wilderness for just a week, let alone three, is quite a luxury. For those who appreciate the recuperative tonic of such an opportunity in the great outdoors, we trust this guide will provide the necessary information to plan and execute the best backpacking trips of the western United States. For those who have not taken the plunge into the wonderful world of traipsing through such magnificent country on foot with all the necessary essentials on their backs, we also hope this guide will inspire and encourage them to consider the possibility.

The western states of Arizona, Utah, and New Mexico possess some of the wildest and most scenic backcountry landscapes in the nation. Not only do American backpackers find trips in this region highly desirable, but so do countless international devotees as well. From scenic canyons to alpine summits, and nearly everything in between, this region is a prime area for backpacking trips of a lifetime. The trips begin in Utah with an extended high-altitude romp through the High Uintas, followed by four routes through iconic Southwest desert canyon topography within two national parks, a national monument, a national recreation area, and a primitive area. Spanning the boundary between Utah and Arizona, another canyon trip weaves through the Paria Canyon–Vermilion Cliffs Wilderness. No guide to the Southwest would be complete without routes through Grand Canyon National Park, and we offer two trips with very different perspectives. New Mexico entries include an extended backpack through the high country of the southern Rockies and a loop through beautiful canyon country.

From wherever you live, these guides are designed to help you plan a once-in-a-lifetime backpacking trip to the premier routes in the western states. The majority of trips can be done roughly within a nine-day window, fitting conveniently within a traditional workweek bookended by weekends. This time frame usually includes a day each way for travel to and from the trailheads from most points within the United States.

We begin by helping you identify the top hikes in each of the three states. From there, we cover the aspects of planning a trip, including travel; acquiring gear, lodging, and food; campgrounds near the trailheads; and any local outfitters serving the area, in case you prefer such service. Also highlighted for each trip is a section for any must-see attractions close by that you could easily incorporate into your adventure. We provide information to help you navigate regulations and permits specific to each locale. Along with the customary technical data pertinent to each trip, we highlight any particular concerns or warnings as well. Every attempt has been made to provide an accurate, up-to-date description of each individual hike. Unlike a few guides on the market, we have walked every mile of the trails described herein. We feel confident that you have the complete information you need to plan and carry out any of these trips of a lifetime.

Along with all the previously mentioned details, short historical highlights for most of the areas have been included for your enjoyment in the hope that they will increase your appreciation for the areas themselves and for the people who were instrumental in their discovery or protection.

Lastly, personal vignettes accompany most trips as well. We hope they will inspire and encourage you to, as John Muir so eloquently stated, *"Climb the mountains and get their good tidings. Nature's peace will flow into you as sunshine flows into trees. The winds blow their own freshness into you, and the storms their energy, while cares will drop away from you like the leaves of Autumn."*

Trail Etiquette,
Wilderness Ethics, and Safety

We presume that most people holding this book and contemplating a longer backpacking trip into the magnificent wilds of the American West already have (or should have) considerable experience with lugging around a heavy pack and the associated risks and responsibilities. (If not, *please* pick up a good how-to book on the subject, get some experience with a hiking club in your area, and take several shorter overnight adventures before setting out on any of the trips described herein.) Thus, this obligatory section on how to keep yourself safe and the wilderness unblemished by your visit is short and to the point.

Wilderness ethics in their basic form are very simple and really nothing more than common-sense principles: be light on the land (ideally nobody should even be able to tell you were there) and be courteous to other users. In practice, this means being respectful of other users and following all the "no trace" principles to ensure that the land is undamaged by your presence:

- Always camp in designated sites or on harder surfaces (not meadows) that can accommodate a tent without being damaged.
- Never cut switchbacks.
- Build only small campfires and only in areas permitted by local or seasonal regulations. Always use a backpacking stove for cooking, which is far more efficient than cooking over an open fire.
- Never feed wildlife.
- Never use any type of soap (even biodegradable soap) in any natural water source.
- Pack out *all* of your own litter (even biodegradable egg shells and the like) and pick up any litter you find left behind by others.
- Be quiet, inconspicuous, and respectful both on the trail and in camp, as to not affect the wilderness experience of others.
- Allow horse users the right of way by stepping off the trail on the downhill side.
- Report to land managers any major problems such as trail washouts, trashed-out hunter's camps, illegal ATV damage, and the like.

In other words, be a good wilderness citizen. The land and other trail users will greatly appreciate it.

You also, of course, need to keep your safety in mind. Safety issues specific to particular hikes, such as camp-raiding black bears, lack of water, and extreme heat, are covered in the introductory material or trail descriptions for the individual trips. As for more general safety concerns:

- Never drink water, no matter how clear it looks, without purifying it first. (One of us has had giardia and wouldn't wish the experience on his worst enemy.)
- Fully acclimate yourself before setting off on a long trip in the high elevations of the mountains or elsewhere.
- Be cognizant of the weather and avoid high ridges and mountain peaks during the afternoon, when thunderstorms are common in the mountains.
- Be especially careful when you are hiking in areas with unstable footing—loose boulders, small pebbles, icy patches, and the like. When you are 20 or more miles from your car, even a relatively minor injury can develop into a life-threatening situation.
- Hypothermia is the number one danger to hikers in the American West. So dress in layers, stay dry, eat plenty of high-energy snacks, and know the warning signs to look for so you can avoid this common killer.

Most importantly, exercise plenty of that often rarest of commodities, common sense. In other words, steer clear of anything that a disinterested third party might uncharitably describe as "stupid." If you do that, and have along the necessary gear and experience, you are much more likely to come back safe and sound and have a comfortable and enjoyable trip.

Using This Guide

We intend for this guide to be used primarily by backpackers with at least some experience under their belts, as weeklong excursions are the focus of the trips selected for inclusion. As previously stated, beginning or highly inexperienced backpackers should become proficient at the activity on overnight outings before attempting any of the much more lengthy trips described here. For more information about backpacking, plenty of resources are available. Many cities have local hiking groups, community colleges, or outdoor retailers offering clinics and outings. An excellent book for basic backpacking is *Joy of Backpacking: Your Complete Guide to Attaining Pure Happiness in the Outdoors*, by Brian Beffort. *Mountaineering: The Freedom of the Hills*, published by the Mountaineers, is a technical guide about mountain climbing that contains a great deal of useful information about traveling in the backcountry.

Since backpacking is considered a rigorous physical activity, participants should be in excellent physical shape. Anyone with a lifestyle of lying on a couch all day watching television and eating Twinkies should not expect to be able to suddenly rise up and accomplish even the easiest trip in this guide. The level of enjoyment one experiences on the trail will be directly proportional to one's level of physical fitness. Additionally, some of the trips require advanced skills, such as the ability to navigate cross-country, or the possibility of using an ice axe on steep, snow-covered slopes. Pay close attention to the difficulty ratings and the reason for them when evaluating the suitability of a particular trip.

Following each trip's introduction, the following important information is listed:

Days: We suggest the number of days required to comfortably hike each trip. This number is for the average hiker; some people will want to take more time, and others less. Since all of these trips are located in spectacularly scenic areas, certainly more time could be spent enjoying the scenery. On the other end of the hiking spectrum, ultra-light backpackers in excellent shape could surely accomplish these trips in much less than the recommended time.

Distance: We have made every attempt to record the cumulative distances for each trip accurately, although you may find minor variances from time to time.

Type: This entry lists the nature of each hike. Loop trips start and end at the same trailhead. Shuttle trips start at one trailhead and end at a different trailhead, requiring either two vehicles or being dropped off at the beginning trailhead and picked up at the ending trailhead.

Scenery: As to be expected with trips of a lifetime, all the ones in this guide are highly scenic. On a scale of 1 (lowest) to 10 (highest), we have made a very subjective rating of the trips relative to each other. More than likely, some readers will have a difference of opinion.

Solitude: Similar to the Scenery category, here we list the potential for solitude on each trip. This is a subjective evaluation and may vary from one's own experience. Some people may inadvertently end up on a trip with a high solitude rating at the same time as a group of fifty Boy Scouts.

Technical Difficulty: Another subjective evaluation on a scale of 1 to 10, this entry attempts to evaluate factors such as condition of the trail, degree of navigation required, stream crossings, lack of water sources, sections of cross-country travel, whether an ice axe may be required, and so forth to determine the overall technical difficulty of each route.

Physical Difficulty: Similar to the previous category, we determined how physically demanding each trip might be, taking into account factors such as elevation change, trail grade, altitude, and daily mileage.

Elevation Gain/Loss: The cumulative elevation gain and elevation loss for the entire trip is listed here.

Season: This section indicates the average time of year when the trail is open for travel.

Best: This subheading indicates the optimum time within the open season when conditions are usually at their peak.

Maps: For most trips, the US Geological Survey (USGS) 7.5-minute quadrangles are typically the best maps for backcountry travel, and they are listed here. Other maps, from public or private sources, that may be as helpful, or more so, are also noted here when applicable.

Resources: If available, additional resources that are helpful for background information or trip planning are listed under this heading.

Contacts: Contact information for the appropriate government agencies overseeing the public lands for each trip are noted.

Permits: Necessary permits and how to obtain them appear under this category. National and state parks usually require an entrance fee. Some areas do not require backcountry permits. For areas that do require them, some can be self-issued at trailheads or ranger stations, while others require quite a bit of effort to obtain. We provide all the pertinent information and necessary resources to aid in this quest.

Regulations: Along with permits, many agencies have specific requirements for backcountry travel. As noted in the section on Trail Etiquette, Wilderness Ethics, and Safety, great care and respect should be given to the lands being used. Sometimes this will match the specific regulations listed here, and sometimes these regulations will be exceeded by the standards of minimum impact guidelines.

Nearest Campgrounds: For those parties wishing to camp at a developed campground, either before or after a backpacking trip, campgrounds closest to the trailhead appear under this heading.

Nearest Airports: The closest international airport to the trailhead is noted here, with mileages to the trailheads. Closer municipal airports with commercial service are also listed.

Nearest Outdoor Retailers: In case you need to purchase or rent backpacking equipment, the closest outdoor retailers appear here, with mileages from trailheads.

Outfitters: For groups desiring a guide on their backcountry adventure, contact information for appropriately licensed outfitters appears under this heading. A wide range of services is oftentimes available, from simply dropping supplies at a prearranged destination to hauling gear and patrons and providing all meals.

Transportation Logistics: This category is for any specific concerns regarding transportation to and from the trailheads, including lengthy car shuttles, car rentals, public transportation options, and road conditions.

Backcountry Logistics: Symbols highlight any potentially significant concerns you may need to prepare for on each trip. (A = altitude, B = bears, FF = flash floods, H = possibility of extreme heat, H20 = waterless sections of trail, L = lightning, N = navigation possibly required, PI = poison ivy, Q = quicksand, R = rattlesnakes, Sn = possible snow-covered slopes, St = stream crossings,

Su = sun, Tc = ticks, W = inclement weather, XC = cross-country sections.) Any additional concerns for safe backcountry travel are noted in this section. If applicable, special conditions are noted.

Amenities and Attractions: Since the focus of this guide is on vacation backpacking trips, we have included this section, which highlights things of note in some of the communities closest to the trailheads. Lodging, dining, special attractions, and activities are highlighted for those interested in the addition of a more civilized touch to their backcountry adventure.

Directions to Trailhead: Accurate directions are given to all trailheads.

Trip Description: The main part of each backpacking trip is the trail description, which should be accurate and up to date.

Possible Itinerary: Following each description is a possible itinerary with corresponding mileages and elevation figures. These itineraries are meant to be suggestions only. Undoubtedly, other plans may be equal to or better than these suggestions. Feel free to follow our suggested itineraries if they fit your needs.

Alternates: If appropriate, an alternate route may be suggested, in case, for whatever reason, plans do not work out for a specific trip.

Green Tips: The backcountry of the West is a very special resource, more than worthy of our care and consideration. For those who want to give something back, we have listed an organization involved in efforts to preserve and protect an area.

Legend

— — — — — —	Featured Route		
– – – – – –	Secondary Trail	$	Fee Entrance Station
• • • • • • • • • • • • •	Beach Route	⌂	Ranger Station
··············	Cross-country Route	?	Visitor or Information Center
⚠	Primitive Campsite	⛺	Picnic Area
◭	Developed Campsite	1,140'	Elevation
T	Trailhead	◄ 2.3 ►	Distance Between Points
P	Parking	■	Point of Interest
▲	Mountain	ᕼ	Spring

THE TRIPS

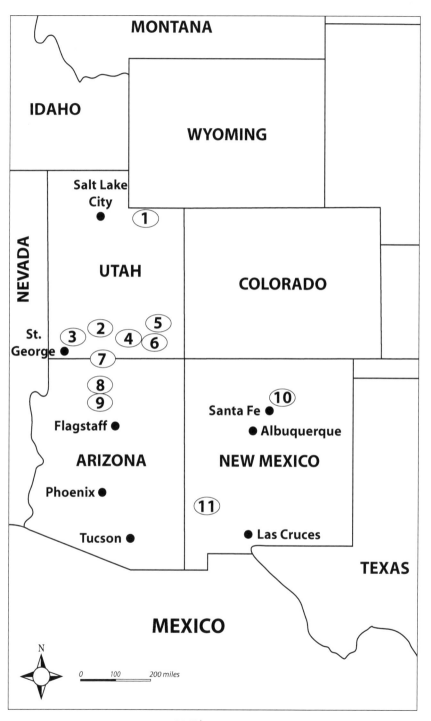

MONTANA

IDAHO

WYOMING

Salt Lake
City
●

(1)

NEVADA

UTAH

COLORADO

(5)
(2)
St.
(3)   (4)   (6)
George ●
(7)

(8)
(9)   (10)
Santa Fe ●
Flagstaff ●
                     ● Albuquerque

ARIZONA   NEW MEXICO

Phoenix ●
                (11)

Tucson ●   ● Las Cruces

                              TEXAS

MEXICO

N

0   100   200 miles

I.1 Trip Locator

PART I

UTAH

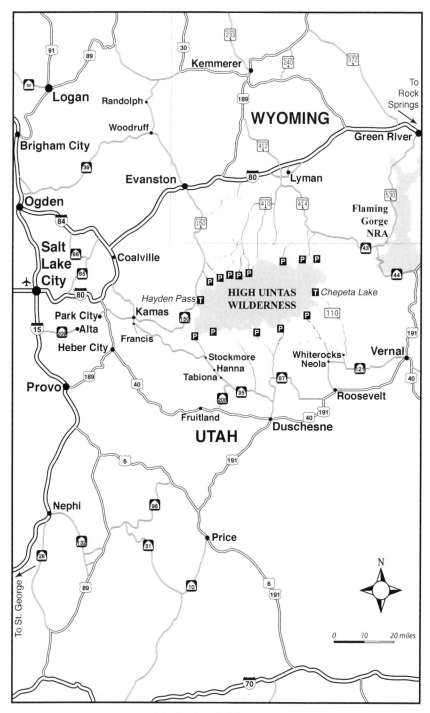

1.1 Highline Trail Location

Rocky Mountains
High Uintas Wilderness
Ashley National Forest and Uinta-Wasatch-Cache National Forest

───────────── **TRIP 1** ─────────────

Highline Trail

The wilderness holds answers to questions
man has not yet learned to ask.

—NANCY NEWHALL

THE UINTA MOUNTAINS span a distance of more than 150 miles, with a narrow, high-elevation spine of 60 miles from Leidy Peak to Hayden Peak, forming the High Uintas. While most western mountain ranges trend north to south, the Uintas form the most significant east-west range in the continental United States; the High Uintas are also the largest alpine area in the intermountain west. Blanketing the range is the 456,705-acre High Uintas Wilderness, where 545 miles of trail typically provide access through glacier-carved canyons filled with lush forests to basins below the crest that hold beautiful alpine lakes. In contrast, the Highline Trail closely follows the crest of the range, through the wilderness and across a series of high passes, from one stunningly gorgeous basin to the next.

The route described here follows a 65-mile section of the Highline Trail from Chepeta Lake, just outside the eastern wilderness boundary, to Hayden Pass, just outside the western boundary. In between, the route crosses seven high-elevation passes—North Pole, Anderson, Tungsten, Porcupine, Red Knob, Dead Horse, and Rocky Sea—and visits several stunning basins, including Painter, Garfield, and Naturalist. During the journey the elevation ranges from 9,800 feet to 12,700 feet, with a side trip opportunity to scale 13,528-foot Kings Peak, Utah's highest summit. Sweeping views are nearly constant companions, not only from the high passes but also from the generally open

5

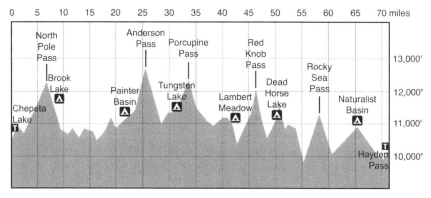

Highline Trail

terrain customary at alpine and subalpine elevations. The Highline Trail also visits several attractive lakes, fine places to pitch a tent or drop a line.

The remote east side of the wilderness is uncrowded and lonely, offering large doses of serenity and solitude. You'll likely see more people near Kings Peak, as peakbaggers routinely leave the Henrys Fork trailhead for an attempt to summit the state's highest mountain. Beyond Kings Peak, the traffic subsides again until you near Naturalist Basin, a popular destination less than a two-hour drive from the metropolitan area of Salt Lake City and a three-hour hike from the Mirror Lake or Hayden Pass trailheads.

The Highline Trail offers incredible mountain scenery in an uncrowded wilderness. Upon completion of the journey, you'll understand why the Highline Trail is Utah's premier long-distance mountain trail.

Days: 5–9

Distance: 72 miles

Type: Shuttle

Scenery: 7

Solitude: 8

Technical Difficulty: 8

Physical Difficulty: 8

Elevation Gain/Loss: +12,350'/−10,985'

Season: Early July to early October

Best: Late July to mid-August

Maps: USGS—Chepeta Lake, Fox Lake, Kings Peak, Mount Powell, Garfield Basin, Mount Lovenia, Oweep Creek, Explorer Peak, Red Knob, Hayden Peak USFS—High Uintas Wilderness

Resources: *Utah Thirteeners*, by David Rose

Contacts:

- Ashley National Forest Supervisor Office
  355 North Vernal Ave., Vernal, UT 84078
  435-789-1181   www.fs.usda.gov/ashley
- Roosevelt Ranger District
  650 W. Highway 40, PO Box 127, Roosevelt, UT 84066
  435-722-5018
- Duchesne Ranger District
  85 West Main, PO Box 981, Duchesne, UT 84021
  435-738-2482
- Uinta-Wasatch-Cache National Forest
  857 W. South Jordan Pkwy., South Jordan, UT 84095
  801-999-2103   www.fs.usda.gov/uwcnf
- Kamas Ranger District
  50 E. Center St., Kamas, UT 84036
  435-783-4338

Permits: Not required, except for a recreation fee for parking at the Hayden Pass trailhead. Recreation passes can be purchased at the Slate Creek Fee Station, along the Mirror Lake Scenic Byway on the way to the ending trailhead, during regular daylight hours, as well as from ranger stations and retail outlets in Kamas and Evanston. Interagency passes are also accepted.

Regulations: Maximum group size is fourteen. No campfires in Naturalist Basin.

Nearest Campgrounds:

- Pole Creek Lake—11 miles from start
- Butterfly—0.2 miles from end; Mirror Lake—4 miles from end

Nearest Airports: Salt Lake City International Airport (SLC)—193 miles

Nearest Outdoor Retailers:

- Dick's Sporting Goods—8 miles from SLC
  The Gateway
  41 S. Rio Grande, Salt Lake City, UT 84101
  801-456-0200
- Patagonia Outlet—10 miles from SLC
  2292 Highland Dr., Salt Lake City, UT 84106
  801-466-2226

- Kirkham's Outdoor Products—11 miles from SLC
  3125 S. State St., Salt Lake City, UT 84115
  800-453-7756
- Recreation Outlet—11 miles from SLC
  3160 S. State St., Salt Lake City, UT 84115
  801-484-4800
- REI—15 miles from SLC
  3285 E. 3300 S., Salt Lake City, UT 84109
  801-486-2100

Outfitters: None

Transportation Logistics: No public transportation reaches either trailhead for the Highline Trail. State Highway 150 (Mirror Lake Scenic Byway) sees considerable traffic during the summer months as the primary access to the popular Mirror Lake Recreation Area and the Hayden Pass trailhead, but the road to the Chepeta Lake trailhead on the east side of the Uintas is quite remote. Plan on a five-hour drive between the two trailheads, with several miles of dirt road on the final approach to Chepeta Lake.

Backcountry Logistics: (A, L, N, Sn, W, XC) The Highline Trail lives up to its name by traversing the High Uintas at elevations between 9,800 and 12,700 feet, so you must effectively acclimatize to these elevations. Snow on the high passes may be a factor in early season. Thunderstorms are a distinct possibility throughout the summer, and much of the terrain in the High Uintas is open and without cover—not the preferred place to avoid a lightning strike.

Unfortunately, much of the trail in the Ashley National Forest is in very poor condition. The first mile or so from Chepeta Lake was supposedly rerouted in the mid-nineties, but nowadays a sizable stretch of discernible tread is nonexistent—without blazes and a keen sense of direction, you may be tempted to quit the trip almost before you begin. Beyond this initial stretch, the trail becomes easier to follow, but just barely. Cairns, some quite large, will help guide you through numerous sections of indistinct tread. Except for some fresh sawdust where a couple of downed trees were cut below Dead Horse Lake, the trail in the eastern portion of the High Uintas seemingly hasn't seen any maintenance in at least the last decade or so. For all practical purposes, much of the eastern segment of the Highline Trail should be considered a cross-country route, not a bona fide trail.

The condition of the trail on some of the high passes, Porcupine Pass in particular, is potentially hazardous. Inadequate drainage has resulted in numerous washouts. The boot-beaten route that has developed in place of the trail provides tenuous footing across a high-angle slope that's ripe for tragedy. Extreme caution should be exercised at all times.

Poor construction and routing of the trail has resulted in significant drainage problems in early season. Much of the trail across meadows can be quite wet and boggy through July. August is perhaps the best time to avoid these soggy conditions, although wildflower season may be waning by then.

The poor condition of the trail, coupled with the near-constant need for route finding, makes the Highline Trail a trip exclusively for experienced backpackers.

Amenities and Attractions: Roosevelt is the jumping-off spot for the eastern side of the High Uintas. The town has a modest assortment of gas stations, fast-food restaurants, motels, and grocery stores, but nothing much of distinction. A half-hour east, the larger community of **Vernal** offers much better food and lodging alternatives.

The small town of **Kamas** lies at the gateway to the west end of the High Uintas and the Mirror Lake Scenic Byway. Despite the small size, Kamas offers famished backpackers a few opportunities for enjoying a meal after several days of consuming nothing but trail food. At the top of the list is **Summit Inn Pizza and Ice Cream** (80 S. Main), recently voted as having the state's best pizza. If you're craving greens, order one of their tasty made-to-order salads while waiting for your pie to cook. The only potential downside to this little culinary paradise is the lack of beer to wash down the pizza, thanks to Utah's strict alcohol laws. The traditional mom-and-pop burger, fries, and shake can be had at **Dick's Uinta Drive Inn** (235 Center St.), which is a popular spot for out-of-town visitors and locals alike. Grocery items can be secured at **Food Town** (145 W. 200 S.).

For overnight accommodations near the western trailhead, you'll have to travel about 15 miles southwest of Kamas to **Heber City**. A much larger town, Heber City offers a fair selection of motels, gas stations, grocery stores, drug stores, and restaurants. If you're looking to beef up before heading out on the trail, tackle the prime rib dinner at the nonfranchise **Claim Jumper** (1267 S. Main St.). This western steakhouse originally occupied a space in the Park City Hotel but relocated to Heber City after a fire in 1973.

Directions to Trailhead: From the town of Kamas (ranger station), follow State Route 150 (Mirror Lake Scenic Byway) for about 35 miles to the well-marked Highline trailhead at Hayden Pass, making sure to pick up your parking pass at the Slate Creek Fee Station along the way. The parking lot fills up quickly on weekends. Facilities include running water and a vault toilet. This will be your ending trailhead.

After dropping a vehicle at Hayden Pass, return to Kamas and turn south onto State Route 32 for 2 miles to the community of Francis and a junction with State Route 35. Turn left and proceed eastbound on SR 35 for about 60 miles to a junction with State Route 87. Turn right and head south on SR 87 for approximately 6 miles to the town of Duchesne (ranger station) and a junction with US 40. Turn left and follow Main Street through town, continuing on US 40 for 28 miles to Roosevelt. In Roosevelt, turn left onto State Route 121 and proceed northbound 10 miles to Neola. Remaining on SR 121, turn right and proceed east for 5 miles to a junction with Whiterocks Highway. Turn left here and follow the highway past the tiny community of Whiterocks and continue, as the road becomes Farm Creek Road.

About 22 miles from Whiterocks, the pavement ends where you make a left turn near the Elkhorn Guard Station, signed POLE CREEK LAKE, ELKHORN LOOP ROAD, CHEPETA LAKE, UINTA CANYON. Now on Forest Road 117, proceed on dirt surface for approximately 14 miles to a junction where Road 117 heads west to Pole Creek Lake. Bear right at this junction, now on Forest Road 110, and continue another 11 miles generally north to the signed Chepeta trailhead, just before Chepeta Lake. The ample parking lot has a vault toilet.

Trip Description: The first mile of the Highline Trail from Chepeta Lake will more than likely be the most frustrating part of your journey, as there doesn't appear to be any distinct tread to follow. A sign marked NORTH POLE PASS with an arrow will at least point you in the right direction. From there, look for blazes on trees on a winding route through a light forest of Douglas firs, lodge-pole pines, and Engelmann spruces. Downed logs across the "trail" may make route finding even more of a challenge. A sign at the trailhead proclaims that the trail was rerouted in the mid-nineties to avoid some boggy meadows, but the extremely poor condition of the tread suggests the reroute was the last time any maintenance was performed on this stretch of trail. Heading generally west should eventually lead out of the forest and across meadows, where large cairns mark the route, to the small and shallow pond referred to as Lower Reader Lake (also known as Sharlee Lake), 2 miles from the trailhead. Campsites in the trees on the south shore will tempt late-starting backpackers or parties that have used up extra time searching for the correct route.

The trail heads away from Lower Reader Lake through stands of forest, alternating with open meadows, for a half mile to a crossing of Reader Creek

Human-sized cairn on the Highline Trail

and a junction with a route to Upper Reader Lake. Continue across meadows and through small pockets of forest to a junction with a very faint trail heading southeast to Whiterocks Road. Eventually the grade increases on the way to the top of a ridge sprinkled with alpine flowers, where the trail turns northwest to pass above Taylor Lake (campsites). A series of switchbacks is followed by an arcing ascent, marked by cairns to North Pole Pass (12,240'±) at the boundary of the High Uintas Wilderness.

With a stunning vista ahead, the rocky trail winds down steeply into the Shale Creek drainage, eventually reaching more hospitable terrain near Brook Lake. Head through a stand of conifers, cross a stream, and then pass above the north side of Fox Lake. Although cairns are present, the route is easily lost before reaching more defined tread near the northwest shore. A pretty lake at first glance, at least during the early summer, you'll undoubtedly notice the dam at the west end of Fox Lake. Later in the season, the water level drops considerably, which diminishes the scenic value a tad. Reach a junction near an old cabin at the far end of the lake, where a trail branches south to Crescent Lake and then heads over Fox Queant Pass, and another trail heads north to Divide Lake and Divide Pass. Located only 8.5 miles from the West Fork Whiterocks trailhead, Fox Lake receives plenty of traffic from organized groups and horse packers. If you need a campsite and prefer more solitude, Brook Lake might be a better choice.

Beyond Fox Lake, the Highline Trail follows the outlet for a half mile to a boulder hop over a tributary, proceeds across an open meadow, and then crosses a lightly forested rise, before dropping to a pair of signed junctions; the first junction is with nonexistent tread heading southwest toward a

Along the Highline Trail

connection with the Uinta River Trail, and the second junction, about a mile farther, is with more distinct tread traveling northwest to Davis Lakes.

Away from the second junction, the trail passes through alternating sections of open meadow and forest before dropping down to a picturesque vale, bisected by a Uinta River tributary. In this vale is a junction with a connector heading south to the Uinta River Trail.

A moderate climb leads out of the vale and proceeds through forest to the top of a rise. Drop off the rise to the crossing of a small stream and continue through the trees to a junction with a short lateral heading north to forest-rimmed Kidney Lakes. Good campsites can be found around the two larger Kidney Lakes, as well as at Rainbow, Wilderness, and Davis Lakes.

A mile past the Kidney Lakes junction, switchbacks take you down to the crossing of a multibraided stream, aided by some well-placed logs and boulders. A short climb from there leads to a junction with faint tread heading southeast. Beyond the junction, you pass along the edge of a meadow on the way to Gilbert Creek, which may require a ford in early season. Over the next couple of miles, the trail climbs, stiffly at times, across boggy meadows and through stands of conifers to a broad, forested rise. Stroll across the top of the rise and then begin a nearly mile-long descent into the lower reaches of Painter Basin, the first in a series of sweepingly scenic basins through which the Highline Trail passes.

After reaching the floor of Painter Basin, the Highline Trail starts up the canyon, crosses a refreshing-looking brook, and proceeds to a junction, where the Uinta River Trail 044 heads east, and Trail 043 heads south toward Trail

Rider Pass. Good campsites can be found in small groves of trees in the lower part of the basin.

Break out of the trees for good and continue up the canyon, through subalpine vegetation, for about a mile to another junction, where Trail 068 veers northwest toward Gunsight Pass, and the Highline Trail heads west toward Anderson Pass. Another 0.75 mile of gentle stroll through the upper end of picturesque Painter Basin brings you to the start of 2 miles of steeper climbing on the way to Anderson Pass. An initial climb leads to a small flat, bisected by a gurgling brook and bordered by low rock hills, where you could establish a camp with a stunning view of the basin. Beyond this brief respite, the stiff ascent resumes, taking you higher and higher into the alpine zone. Reach the 12,700-foot pass amid a sea of rock and take in the superb view of Painter Basin behind and down the canyon of Yellowstone Creek ahead.

From Anderson Pass, the trail makes a long, descending traverse across the north side of the ridge before switchbacking across rocky terrain toward the floor of the upper basin. After 3 miles of descent, you cross Yellowstone Creek and then start climbing again toward Tungsten Pass. Midway through the ascent is a junction with the Yellowstone Creek Trail on the left and Trail 054 to Smiths Fork Pass on the right. Continue the uphill journey, passing a tarn and some small ponds before the final push to the (11,440'±) pass, by far the easiest pass on the Highline Trail.

Drop shortly away from Tungsten Pass to the upper part of Garfield Basin, a windswept plain of alpine tundra with two sizable lakes, Tungsten and North Star. Despite the open and exposed terrain and only fair campsites, these two lakes offer the only reasonable settings along the Highline Trail at which to spend the night between Anderson and Porcupine Passes. With the luxury of extra time, descending farther down Garfield Basin on Trail 059

Side Trip to Kings Peak: At 13,528 feet, Kings Peak is the highest peak in Utah. Relatively short access from Henrys Fork trailhead to the north means that you're apt to see other humans bound for the summit, especially if you happen to arrive here on a weekend. The route is rated class 2 and therefore not difficult for peakbaggers with rudimentary climbing skills. From Anderson Pass, simply follow use trails along the ridge toward the summit. Higher up on the mountain, the route veers slightly away from the ridge and scrambles over some boulders to an area just below the summit. It then heads directly toward the top. Not unexpectedly, the view is spectacular.

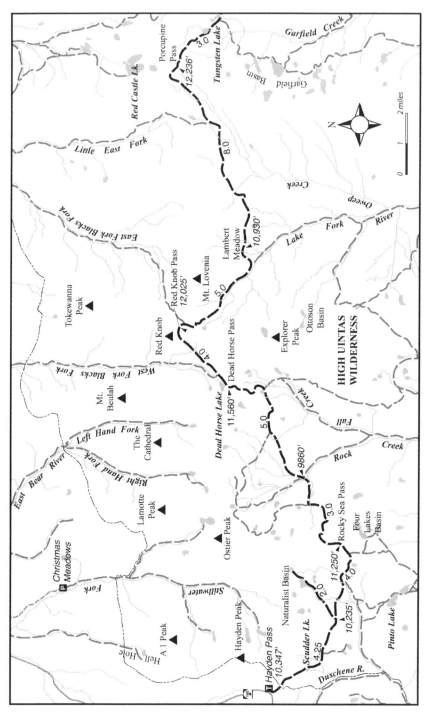

1.2 Highline Trail (West)

Garfield Creek

Red Castle Lk.

Porcupine Pass 12,236'

3.0

Tungsten Lake

Garfield Basin

Little East Fork

8.0

Oweep Creek

East Fork Blacks Fork

Lambert Meadow

10,930'

Lake Fork River

N

Tokewanna Peak

Red Knob Pass 12,025'

Mt. Lovenia

5.0

Red Knob

4.0

Dead Horse Pass

Explorer Peak

Ottoson Basin

HIGH UINTAS WILDERNESS

West Fork Blacks Fork

Mt. Beulah

Left Hand Fork

The Cathedral

Dead Horse Lake 11,560'

5.0

Fall Creek

Rock Creek

East Bear River

Right Hand Fork

Lamotte Peak

Ostier Peak

9860'

Rocky Sea Pass 11,250'

3.0

Four Lakes Basin

Christmas Meadows

Fork

Stillwater

Naturalist Basin

2.0

4.0

10,235'

Hayden Peak

Scudder Lk.

Pinto Lake

A 1 Peak

Hell Hole

Hayden Pass 10,347'

4.25

Duschene R.

0 1 2 miles

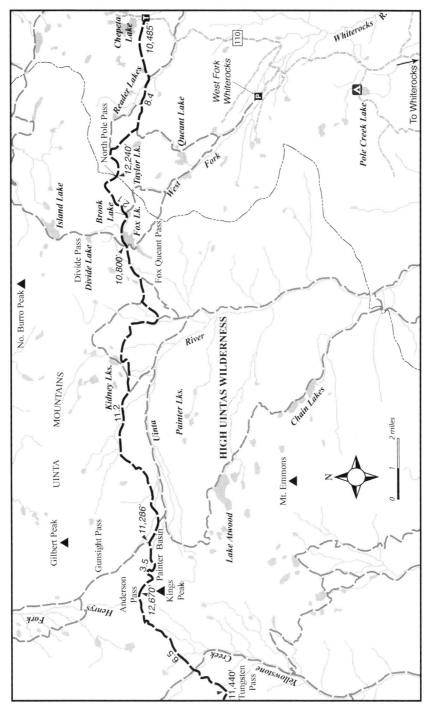

1.3 Highline Trail (East)

to the lower lakes will provide more hospitable surroundings, especially if a thunderstorm is threatening.

Traverse the gentle terrain of upper Garfield Basin for a mile before a more moderate ascent heads toward Porcupine Pass. At the head of the basin, steeper switchbacks zigzag across the canyon headwall, eventually leading to the 12,236-foot pass. At the pass, you have another sweeping view down the upper canyon of Oweep Creek.

On extremely poor tread, follow a descending traverse across the canyon headwall, exercising caution in areas where the trail has been washed out. Eventually surer footing is gained as the trail curves southwest and drops toward the floor of Oweep Creek canyon. With the treacherous descent from Porcupine Pass behind you, the route follows a series of cairns through open terrain, down a picturesque valley sandwiched between the Uinta crest on the right and a row of rugged cliffs to the left. The only detriment to the otherwise idyllic setting is the potential of encountering large herds of sheep, as the valley is a traditional grazing area. About 2.75 miles from Porcupine Pass is a junction with Trail 103, heading north to Squaw Pass.

Continue the pleasant descent down the valley through alpine tundra, crossing the main branch of Oweep Creek, 0.75 mile past the junction. The tread is easily lost in the thick vegetation bordering the creek, but the trail becomes distinct again well above the north bank. A tributary is crossed about a mile farther, beyond which conifers become more pronounced. Mildly rising tread over the next 1.5 miles is followed by a short climb and then a mile-long traverse around the nose of a ridge before a moderate descent leads to Lambert Meadow.

Away from Lambert Meadow, the trail dives down the northeast side of Lake Fork River canyon, through thick forest for 0.75 mile to a junction with Trail 061, heading southeast to the Moon Lake trailhead.

Turn right at the junction and proceed upstream on a steady climb through the forest, crossing the river a few times before breaking out of the trees in the upper part of the canyon. Once again, cairns will help guide you across the alpine tundra where the tread disappears.

Steeper trail at the head of the canyon zigzags up the rocky slope to Red Knob Pass (12,050′±) and another superb view—perhaps the most alpine-looking vista from the Highline Trail.

After taking in the inspirational view, avoid the temptation to head directly down from where the trail meets the crest, which frequently leads Highline Trail hikers onto some difficult terrain (don't follow Trail 102 down to East Fork Blacks Fork either). Instead, follow the rocky ridge southwest for a while to where a distinct path begins a diagonal descent toward the saddle

Side Trip to Crater Lake: Backpackers not in a hurry to get over Red Knob Pass can follow a straightforward cross-country route to picturesque Crater Lake. Leave the Highline Trail at approximately 11,100 feet and head south-southwest across the open tundra for about 2.5 miles, head around a minor ridge, and then make a short climb up to Crater Lake. The lake is cupped into a spectacular but stark basin at the base of Explorer Peak and often has floating icebergs into early August.

between Red Knob and Peak 12,248. The trail passes immediately below the saddle and arcs around the head of the basin before descending southwest toward the verdant upper canyon of West Fork Blacks Fork.

Reaching the floor of the canyon, you cross a seasonal stream and then begin a moderate climb through subalpine firs toward the main stem of the creek. Once along the creek, zigzag more steeply up the drainage to beautiful Dead Horse Lake, nestled directly below the Uinta crest. Fair campsites can be found near the trail or above the north shore.

From Dead Horse Lake, the trail climbs stiffly up the north-facing, rock-strewn wall of the canyon via switchbacks to Dead Horse Pass. Snow may obscure portions of the trail in early season, which may require a bit of route finding to stay on course. After a 600-foot climb, you stand on top of the 11,550-foot pass and have one last glimpse of the stunning scenery of West Fork Blacks Fork canyon before embarking on a descent into the upper reaches of Fall Creek.

Descent from Red Knob Pass

Drop away from Dead Horse Pass, across the south-facing slope of the east half of the heart-shaped basin at the head of the Rock Creek drainage, through open terrain. After 1.5 miles, the grade eases at the floor of the upper basin near Ledge Lake, where a trail heads southeast toward Phinney Lake. Head west on a gently graded section of the Highline Trail through open forest and meadows, passing below the ridge forming the upper-middle part of the heart. At 3 miles from the pass, you reach a junction with Trail 122, which provides access to the lakes of upper Rock Creek.

Another mile of nearly level tread leads to the edge of Rock Creek canyon, where a steep mile-long descent down the forested west-facing wall drops you alongside the tumbling stream and continues steeply down past some pretty cascades to a four-way junction. Even though the elevation here is around 9,850 feet, which is the low point of the route, after previously traveling through the alpine and subalpine zones, you may find Rock Creek canyon dry and hot.

Now you're faced with regaining all the lost elevation on the way down Rock Creek. Fortunately, the ascent is not quite as steep as the descent, with the trail winding moderately up the canyon of a tributary stream. After a mile, you reach a junction with a trail heading north to the upper Rock Creek lakes.

The Highline Trail bends south from the junction and continues climbing into a mostly open, tarn-dotted basin below Rocky Sea Pass, where groves of Engelmann spruce shade some campsites. From the far side of the basin, the trail climbs steeply up the east wall of the heart to the pass. The sweeping westward view from Rocky Sea Pass includes Naturalist Basin backdropped by Mount Aggasiz and the High Uinta crest.

Drop away from the pass, through open rocky terrain, on a steady mile-long descent to a junction with the trail to Four Lakes Basin. From the pass, you are now on lands administered by Wasatch National Forest, and you may notice a marked improvement in the overall condition of the trail. Overnighters will find scenic campsites in the basin, with Dean Lake offering perhaps the best chance for solitude.

For the next several miles, the Highline Trail offers little in the way of the stunning scenery you've grown accustomed to over the previous days, as the path heads generally east through a mostly viewless forest of lodgepole pines and Engelmann spruces. A steady descent leads through the trees to a junction with the East Fork Pinto Lake Trail just prior to a ford of the East Fork Duchesne River, 2.5 miles from Rocky Sea Pass.

From the ford, almost a mile of gently rising tread is followed by an almost imperceptible descent to the next junction. Here, the route into popular

Naturalist Basin turns northeast. Despite the heavy traffic, especially on weekends, the highly scenic basin should not be missed. At only about 6.5 miles from the trailhead, the lovely area offers a fitting final night's campsite before the conclusion of your journey along the Highline Trail. (If you decide to bypass this beautiful basin, knock off 4 miles from the total distance.)

Away from the junction, a little over a mile of gently graded trail continues through the trees to a junction with a trail on the left to Packard Lake, a popular day hike from the Mirror Lake and Highline trailheads. The trail drops shortly from the junction to a crossing of a stream and then bends north around a hill to uninspiring Scudder Lake. Beyond the lake, the trail drops to a meadow before starting the final 1.5-mile climb to the Highline trailhead, crossing the wilderness boundary along the way. Midway through the climb, you reach a junction with the trail from Mirror Lake and proceed ahead for a spell to where the trail makes a winding ascent up to the ending trailhead parking lot.

Possible Itinerary

Day	Camps and Side Trips	Distance (mi.)	Elevation (ft.)
1	Chepeta Lake TH to Brook Lake	9.4	+1,935/–1,455
2	Painter Basin	12.5	+1,345/–1,280
3	Tungsten Lake	10.0	+2,150/–320
4	Lambert Meadow	10.5	+1,200/–1,615
5	Dead Horse Lake	8.0	+2,135/–2,190
6	Naturalist Basin	15.0	+3,025/–3,265
7	Out to Hayden Pass TH	6.5	+560/–860

Green Tips: Wilderness, UT—www.wildernessutah.com.

Guided by Old Friends

After daylong drives from Reno and San Diego, our party of three met in Heber City and enjoyed a hearty steak dinner for our last night in civilization. The next day involved leaving Andy's truck at the ending trailhead near Hayden Pass and then making the long drive to the starting trailhead at Chepeta Lake. By the time we finished the last-minute adjustments to our packs and actually set foot on the trail, it was well into the afternoon. Immediately, an unexpected difficulty arose with the nearly complete lack of any discernible tread on the ground. This was supposedly the premier long-distance trail in Utah, and the absence of a well-defined path was a bit puzzling. A sign at the trailhead informed us that the trail had been rerouted for environmental concerns in the mid-1990s, but by all appearances, no maintenance had been performed in the two decades since. In fact, there was no recent evidence of anyone even having walked this way. Our progress was frustratingly slow, as we had to backtrack repeatedly, negotiate our way around downed timber, and scour the landscape for any hint of the location of the actual trail. The only helpful clues were very occasional tree blazes. As more time passed without any defined tread, our minds turned to the unpleasant notion that perhaps the entire 70-plus-mile route would be in the same condition. Even though we all were thinking the same thought, no one dared to utter anything out loud, as if doing so would somehow initiate a self-fulfilling prophecy. With every frustrating step, our countenances became more and more surly. Having come all this way, the prospect of abandoning the trip was highly unpalatable but, with each unguided step, a more and more likely scenario.

One less tree blaze might have tipped the scales toward quitting, but we pressed onward, eventually leaving the trees behind at the fringe of a large meadow. Lacking the prospect of encountering any of the infrequent blazes that had guided us previously, we surveyed the clearing ahead and found no indication of the correct route. Without any marker to the contrary, we simply headed west, figuring some sort of landmark would eventually appear from which we could gain our bearings. Some time later, we gazed upon the first of many human-sized cairns that we would see in the numerous meadows and treeless basins to come. Having usually seen much smaller cairns in other areas of the West, commonly made up of only a handful of smaller rocks, these five-foot piles of neatly stacked stones provided an unusual but much appreciated apparition. With our late start and slow progress, the sun was now sinking low on the horizon, which hastened our need to find a suitable place to spend the night. Fortunately, we had successfully navigated to the Reader Lakes, where a conveniently located campsite beckoned.

After a cloudy and chilly night with some light rain, the next day dawned bright and sunny, which undoubtedly aided our otherwise glum dispositions. As we got under way, our spirits were also buoyed by the continued presence of defined trail, which we had picked up just before reaching the lakes. Although the trail would disappear from time to time in the days ahead, locating the correct route would never be as difficult as on the first day, and the conditions seemed to improve the farther west we traveled. Where defined tread was absent for considerable stretches, the human-sized cairns guided us onward like welcome old friends. Without them, we may have ultimately aborted the trip and missed some of the intermountain West's most stunning topography.

— Mike

Paunsaugunt Plateau
Bryce Canyon National Park

─────────── **TRIP 2** ───────────

Under-the-Rim Trail

You can perhaps imagine my surprise at the indescribable beauty
that greeted us, and it was sundown before I could be dragged
from the canyon view. You may be sure that I went back the next
morning to see the canyon once more, and to plan in my mind
how this attraction could be made accessible to the public.

—J. W. HUMPHREY, UPON FIRST SEEING BRYCE CANYON IN 1915

EVEN THOUGH the backcountry offers plenty of outstanding scenery, the
narrow confines of Bryce Canyon National Park, as well as the famously
crowded roads and day hiking trails, keep this preserve off the radar screen
of most backpackers. But the park does feature one stunning long route,
the aptly named Under-the-Rim Trail, which every lover of overnight hiking
should consider. Despite the fine scenery, the trail is lightly used, in part
because even better scenery, with more of the park's famous and remarkably
colorful hoodoos, can be enjoyed from road viewpoints or on day hikes in
the crowded but gorgeous Bryce Amphitheater. Nonetheless, backpacking is
arguably the best (and is certainly the least crowded) way to appreciate the
park's beauty. With such light use, the Park Service only irregularly maintains
the trail, so expect deadfall along parts of the route.

Days: 2–4
Distance: 22.9 miles
Type: Shuttle
Scenery: 8

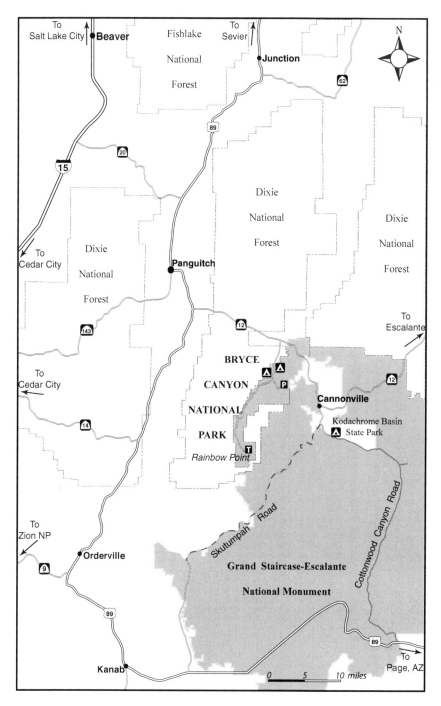

2.1 Under-the Rim-Location

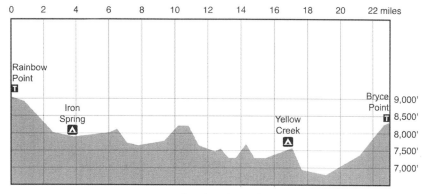

Under-the-Rim Trail

Solitude:	5
Technical Difficulty:	4
Physical Difficulty:	5
Elevation Gain/Loss:	+4,700'/−5,500'
Season:	Mid-April to early November
	Best: May and June, September and October
Maps:	Trails Illustrated—*Bryce Canyon National Park*
Contacts:	Bryce Canyon National Park
	PO Box 640201, Bryce, UT 84764
	435-834-5322

Permits: Backcountry permits are required. Without advance reservations, all permits are on a first-come, first-served basis, available at the visitor center. Cost for a permit is $5 for a party of one or two people, $10 for parties of three to six, and $15 for larger groups of between seven and fifteen people. The visitor center opens at 8:00 AM. Since the trail is generally lightly used, if you show up early, securing a permit should be fairly easy.

Regulations: Camping is allowed only at designated sites, and fires are strictly prohibited. Campsites are limited to six persons per site, except the Yellow Creek group site, which is limited to fifteen. Hikers are required to follow all the usual no-trace principles.

Nearest Campgrounds: Bryce Canyon National Park has two large full-service car campgrounds, North Campground and Sunset Campground. Sunset is open only in the summer months. Several good campgrounds are located nearby on Forest Service land.

Nearest Airports:
- St. George Municipal Airport (SGU) — 155 miles
- McCarran International Airport, Las Vegas (LAS) — 270 miles
- Salt Lake City International Airport (SLC) — 275 miles

Nearest Outdoor Retailers: Although some food and a few supplies are available at **Ruby's Inn General Store** (26 S. Main; 866-866-6616), just outside the park, the nearest full-service outdoor retailer is in St. George.
- Big 5 Sporting Goods
  245 North Red Cliffs Drive, Suite 1, St. George, UT 84790
  435-688-1211

Outfitters: None (although companies do take visitors on day hikes and horseback rides in the much more popular Bryce Amphitheater area, north of the recommended backpack).

Transportation Logistics: If you do not have a car, reaching Bryce Canyon National Park by bus is possible. Greyhound and other major companies do not reach the park, but Bundu Bus operates a "hop on, hop off" service that provides relatively easy and convenient access. This system permits you to purchase a pass for a specified period, which allows you to get on and off any buses traveling from either Las Vegas or Salt Lake City to various smaller towns and national parks in the Southwest, including Bryce. During the busy season, you will need a reservation to get on the bus (having a general "hop on, hop off" pass does not guarantee you a spot on a bus), but if you follow a prearranged schedule, this should be easy to set up in advance. For prices (not cheap) and details, go to bundubus.com.

Although you can drive into the park with your own vehicle, the easiest way to transport yourself and your gear to and from the trailheads is to use the park's convenient, free shuttle bus system. Just leave your car at the shuttle parking lot outside the park, ride the longer shuttle to the southern starting point, hike the trail, then take a local shuttle bus from the northern trailhead back to your car.

To reach the southern trailhead (the trip's recommended starting point) at Rainbow Point, you need to make a reservation (up to twenty-four hours in advance) for a one-way trip on the twice-daily shuttle.

Tip: Since obtaining a backcountry permit is easier than getting a reserved space on the shuttle to Rainbow Point, your best plan is to get the shuttle reservation first, and then go to the visitor center for your backcountry permit.

A dozen or more local shuttle buses, which are constantly leaving and arriving at the shuttle parking lot in Bryce Canyon City, regularly service the northern part of the park, including Bryce Point at the ending trailhead. Along their route, these local buses stop at all major attractions and trailheads in the northern section of the park. Reservations are not required for this local shuttle, which runs every ten to thirty minutes, depending on the season (May to October) and the time of day.

Although you can do this trip in either direction, south to north is generally better, as the shuttle bus logistics are much easier and there is a net elevation loss of 800 feet (though with a great deal of up and down in between).

Backcountry Logistics: (H, H2O, N, R, Su) Lack of water is an issue for much of this hike, with only four generally reliable sources en route. By late summer, most designated campsites are without water.

After the spring snowmelt, and for a day or two after summer thunderstorms, the ground turns into sloppy and sticky goo, which can be difficult and tiring to negotiate. In addition, small floods frequently wash out short sections of the trail, which create minor navigational difficulties.

In midsummer, the lower elevations along the trail can be very hot, although you will still be much more comfortable here than hiking in the lower-elevation deserts to the east, or the canyons of Zion or Grand Canyon national parks to the south.

Amenities and Attractions: In Bryce Canyon City, just outside the park, you will find a variety of tourist-oriented businesses, including hotels and small restaurants. Except for the very good **Ruby's Inn General Store** (26 S. Main, 866-866-6616), few of these establishments are particularly noteworthy.

A few nearby natural attractions deserve mention, though often overlooked by visitors only interested in the more famous national parks. **Red Canyon**, on national forest land just a few miles west of Bryce along Highway 12, offers gorgeous and colorful hoodoo scenery well worth a stop. For more privacy, explore some of the similarly scenic canyons hidden off the main highway to the north. **Casto Canyon** is especially fine and offers a superior mountain bike ride. Southeast of Bryce, check out **Kodachrome Basin State Park**, with excellent trails, comfortable campground, and striking desert scenery. If your car can handle bad roads, be sure to drive another 9.5 miles east of Kodachrome Basin on the rough Cottonwood Canyon Road to impressive **Grosvenor Arch**. A final recommendation, especially for those who appreciate slot canyons, is the hike through **Willis Creek Canyon**, a few miles down the rough but usually passable Skutumpah Road, southwest from Cannonville.

Directions to Trailhead: Throughout southern Utah, signs to Bryce Canyon National Park (and most other major attractions) are everywhere, so finding the park from any major road or city coming from virtually any direction is quite simple. From St. George, the easiest route is to drive 51 miles north on Interstate 15, leave the freeway at Exit 59 for Cedar City, and then proceed east on Highway 14 for 41 very scenic miles to a junction with US 89. Turn north, drive 21 miles, then turn east on Highway 12 and proceed 13 miles to a prominent junction with State Highway 63, where large signs direct travelers toward the park. Turn south and drive 1.5 miles into the bustling tourist community of Bryce Canyon City to the signed shuttle bus parking lot on the left (east). To reach the visitor center, where you must go to pick up a back-country permit, continue south on Highway 63 another 2.5 miles, then turn right into the visitor center parking lot, immediately after you pass through the park's entrance station.

If driving your own car to the trailheads, then continue south from the visitor center for 1.7 miles to a well-signed junction. To leave a car at Bryce Point (the recommended exit point), turn left (southeast) and drive about 1.9 miles to the large and busy road-end parking lot.

Tip: Be sure to take 10 minutes to make the short walk north to Bryce Point viewpoint, one of the most spectacular vistas in the park.

To reach Rainbow Point (the recommended starting point), return to the main road, turn south, and drive about 14 miles to the road-end turnaround and parking lot.

Bryce Canyon: What's in a Name? When you consider that Ebenezer and Mary Bryce would eventually have one of our country's most beautiful and renowned national parks named after them, you would think they would seem happier about life. Based solely on the handful of photos of the dour-looking couple that exist today, however, there doesn't appear to be much for them to smile about.

Perhaps Ebenezer was just tired of the same old Scrooge and "bah humbug" jokes. Or maybe they were miffed that their name was nearly not used for this place at all or that, from a geologic perspective anyway, the name has never been particularly accurate.

Ebenezer and Mary Bryce (Courtesy National Park Service)

Geologically, Bryce Canyon is technically not a "canyon" at all, since it was carved not by flowing water but by chemical erosion from the small amounts of acid in rainwater and by a process known as *frost wedging*, where water in the cracks of rocks freezes, expands, and eventually pushes the rocks apart and destroys them. Nor does Bryce have the characteristic two sides of a typical canyon. Bryce is better described as a series of cliffs and intricately carved amphitheaters exposing the eastern side of the large Paunsaugunt Plateau. One can only suppose that the incorrect name is a result of a rather lax understanding of geologic terms by the early pioneers, or that the name Bryce Erosion-Carved Plateau Edge just didn't have the same appeal.

How this "non-canyon" came to bear the current family name is a little more complicated. The Bryces were Mormon pioneers who, in 1875, moved with their family to the recently established (and soon to be abandoned) settlement of Clifton, near the confluence of the Paria River and Henrieville Creek. Not long after their arrival, Ebenezer and Mary relocated themselves to the town of *New* Clifton, located in Henderson Valley, just a few miles east of what would become the national park. While at his new home, the hardworking Ebenezer assisted in the development of an irrigation ditch, bringing water from Paria Creek seven miles to the new settlement. More significantly, he also built a road up toward the pink cliffs above his home, in an effort to make the timber in that region more accessible to the pioneers. The upper terminus of the road was in a spectacular amphitheater, and in honor of the road's builder, the locals soon began referring to the location as Bryce's Canyon.

In 1880, just five years after he and his family moved into the area, Ebenezer and the rest of the Bryces packed up and headed south to Arizona. Despite their rather abrupt departure, the name Bryce Canyon stuck and continued in common usage, although several attempts were made to select a different moniker for this spectacular location.

Native Americans lived in the region long before Bryce or any other Mormon pioneers made their way into the area. The Paiute Indians were the most recent, starting around AD 1200. Their colorful explanation for the canyon's creation stated that before the Paiute arrived, the Legend People had lived there, and because of some unknown "bad" thing these people had done, Coyote had turned them all into rocks. The hoodoos and pinnacles seen today are these people standing in rows or sitting down, and holding onto one another. Their faces are still painted as they were before their transformation. The Paiute called this place Angka-ku-wass-a-wits (red painted faces). Although more historically accurate, this original name has apparently never been considered a likely candidate to replace Ebenezer's.

In March 1919, the federal government became involved when the Utah legislature passed a bill urging Congress to designate the area a national monument. The name they suggested was the wonderfully illustrative Temple of the Gods National Monument. Perhaps in a bow to separation of church and state, nothing became of this suggestion.

The desire to protect this area under some name continued. Thanks to the tireless efforts of a local Forest Service supervisor named J. W. Humphrey, who visited and was awed by the canyon in 1915, along with some Union Pacific Railroad executives, who saw a huge profit potential in bringing tourists into the region, Congress was repeatedly encouraged to establish some level of protection for the canyon's natural splendor. Finally, on June 8, 1923, President Warren G. Harding set aside Bryce Canyon National Monument. But unlike the Paiute's Legend People, that name was far from set in stone. On June 7, 1924, Congress passed a bill to establish Utah National Park once all the land inside the new monument had been acquired. Once the land was purchased, the name was restored, and Bryce Canyon National Park became official on February 25, 1928. Today, old Ebenezer should rest easy, as his name is now firmly established and no one seems to be out there clamoring for an alternative.

Trip Description: The trail starts from the southeast end of the Rainbow Point parking area, near a sign for the Bristlecone Loop Nature Trail. Follow this wide path for 130 yards to where the route divides. Bear left, proceed gently downhill for 0.1 mile, and then turn left onto the signed Under-the-Rim Trail. This path continues downhill another 0.15 mile to a junction with the Riggs Spring Loop, which is another backpacking option in the park that can be done either instead of the Under-the-Rim Trail or as an addition.

For the Under-the-Rim Trail, veer left and switchback steadily downhill, past excellent viewpoints of the incredibly colorful and hoodoo-filled hillside below Rainbow Point. At about 0.7 mile is a particularly striking view, where the trail passes along the top of an eroding ridge of bright reddish soils. More downhill (a lot more) takes you past superb viewpoints, not only of the nearby cliffs and hoodoos of Bryce Canyon, but to the east across the vast Grand Staircase–Escalante National Monument and over to distant Navajo Mountain. As you descend, note how the dominant vegetation gradually shifts from high-elevation white firs and limber pines to lower-elevation quaking aspens, ponderosa pines, Douglas firs, and bigtooth maples. Manzanitas and Gambel oaks are the most prevalent groundcover shrubs at the lower elevations.

After steadily losing 1,300 feet, the sometimes sandy and always circuitous trail ceases descending and travels up and down in partial forest, never far from the base of the colorful cliffs, spires, and hoodoos for which this park is famous. Frequent small gullies cross the route, and though these are normally dry, summer thunderstorms often cause small floods that wash out short sections of the trail. Fortunately, navigating across these washouts is generally easy—simply look for cairns on the other side of the gully.

At 3.9 miles you pass the campsite at Iron Spring. Just 100 yards after the camp turnoff is the signed side trail to the spring itself, set amid lush riparian vegetation. A first night's camp here is an attractive option, as the spring is one of the few reliable water sources on the trail, even though doing so makes for a rather short day's hike. Unfortunately, the water from Iron Spring has a noticeable metallic taste that filtering is unable to remove. You may want to add some flavoring to make the water more palatable.

Continuing north from Iron Spring, you gain a little more than 100 feet to the top of a minor ridge, where you are rewarded with excellent views of the colorful spires at the head of Ponderosa Canyon. From here you descend about 250 feet in two switchbacks and then traverse across the gully in Ponderosa Canyon. There is sometimes an unreliable trickle of water flowing here, although the area is devoid of campsites. The trail climbs 200 feet to a minor saddle, descends to cross the typically dry gully in North Fork Ponderosa Canyon, and then ascends another 400 feet to a ridgetop junction with the Agua Canyon Connecting Trail, 6.4 miles from the trailhead.

Proceed straight ahead from the junction, descend three rather long switchbacks, and then cross the usually dry creek bed in Agua Canyon. The trail heads gradually downhill, briefly leaving the park along the way, to the normally waterless Natural Bridge campsite on the left. From here, climb nearly 500 feet, initially up a wide gully, then via six sandy and quite tiring switchbacks. The hillside here offers good views of a nearby pinkish orange monolith of serrated pinnacles. At the top of the climb, you walk around the east side of a hoodoo-studded ridge, and then go back downhill into the waterless canyon of Willis Creek.

From Willis Creek you face a long uphill grind. Fortunately, most of the climb is quite gradual, but on the negative side, most of the way is through a recently fire-damaged forest, with almost no shade. At the top of the 500-foot climb, you work your way through patches of unburned forest for about 0.5 mile, and then come to a junction with the Whiteman Connecting Trail. Go straight and just 25 yards later reach the signed Swamp Canyon campsite. There is sometimes a trickle of water in the steep little gulch below this camp, but don't count on it. Just 0.1 mile northeast of this camp is a wonderful viewpoint at Mud Canyon Overlook.

From the Swamp Canyon campsite, you steadily descend along the intermittent little creek in Swamp Canyon. On your left (west), the appropriately named Pink Cliffs provide a wonderfully scenic backdrop. **Warning:** This area is especially prone to washouts from summer thunderstorms. Watch for cairns and navigate carefully.

At 1.6 miles from the junction with the Whiteman Connecting Trail, you reach a junction with Swamp Canyon Connecting Trail. Go right and 50 yards later pass the signed side trail that goes right to normally waterless Right Fork Swamp Canyon campsite. Then go straight and climb about 200 feet, mostly in burned areas, to a nice viewpoint atop a small ridge.

From this viewpoint, you reenter unburned terrain and walk either on the level or gently downhill to a junction with the Sheep Creek Connecting Trail. Go right and just 5 yards later reach a junction with the side trail that goes straight ahead to the Sheep Creek campsite. This campsite almost always has water available a short way downstream (south) of the site.

The Under-the-Rim Trail heads left at the Sheep Creek campsite junction and switchbacks fairly steeply up, past outstanding viewpoints of a nearby colorful castle-type formation. After gaining just over 300 feet, you reach a

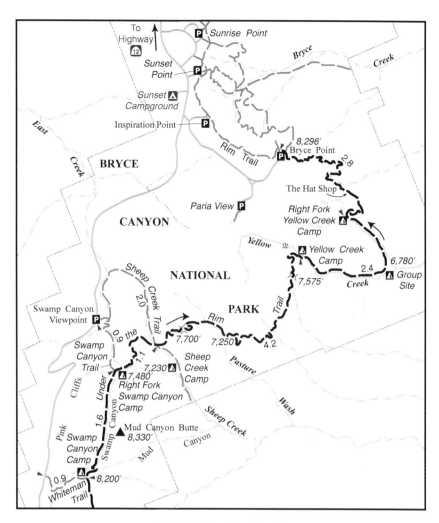

2.2 Under-the-Rim (North)

pass, with excellent views of a row of tremendous pink and orange cliffs to the northeast.

The trail now leads down into the scenic canyon of Pasture Wash. At the bottom you follow the dry wash for a short distance and then make a tiring but well-graded 400-foot ascent to the top of a ridge. From here, there are fine views, especially looking south all the way to Rainbow Point.

You wind downhill from this ridge for 0.4 mile and then make a gradual climb to the top of yet another minor ridge. From here you'll have the first good views of the tremendous cliffs and spires south of Bryce Point. In the valley below is a lush little meadow on Yellow Creek.

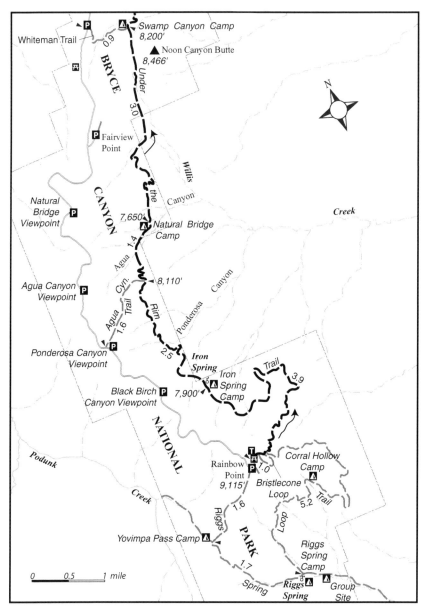

2.3 Under-the-Rim (South)

Several switchbacks take you down from this ridgetop to the lovely Yellow Creek campsite. Not only is water usually available here, but also the scenery is exceptional, making this a choice spot for a second night on the trail.

Below this campsite, the trail goes downstream along small Yellow Creek, which actually does seem to have a slight yellow tint, into a low-elevation

Scene above Right Fork Swamp Canyon

area dominated by hardy limber pines, Gambel oaks, and Rocky Mountain junipers. About 1.2 miles from the Yellow Creek campsite is a signed junction with the short side trail to the Yellow Creek group campsite. You go left and briefly pass through a dry semidesert area with few trees or shade. From here you very gradually ascend the wide canyon of Right Fork Yellow Creek, which in all but the driest years can be relied on for a trickle of water. Go upstream for 0.6 mile to the Right Fork Yellow Creek campsite and then begin a final, tough climb. It's about 1,300 feet up, and the trail is fairly steep, but the scenic rewards are tremendous! The best views are of the colorful cliffs to the north and east.

Scene near Yellow Creek Camp

A major highlight comes about 0.8 mile into the climb at the whimsically titled the Hat Shop. There are no bowlers, bonnets, or baseball caps here; instead, this geologic millinery features dozens of colorful hoodoos and pinnacles, all topped with large caprocks, which have protected the softer pinnacle below from erosion, thus creating these mushroom-shaped "hats." The Hat Shop is a fascinating place and one that few visitors to the park ever see.

Above the Hat Shop, the trail steadily switchbacks uphill for another 2 miles to a junction with a wide and well-used trail just below busy Bryce Point. You turn left and make the final short climb to the parking lot.

The bus stop here has a roofed shelter with benches, where you can wait for your ride back to the shuttle parking lot. The buses pass through at regular intervals, between 10 and 30 minutes, depending on the season and the time of day. The last shuttle bus of the day usually leaves around 7:20 PM, so plan accordingly.

Green Tips: Southern Utah Wilderness Alliance—www.suwa.org

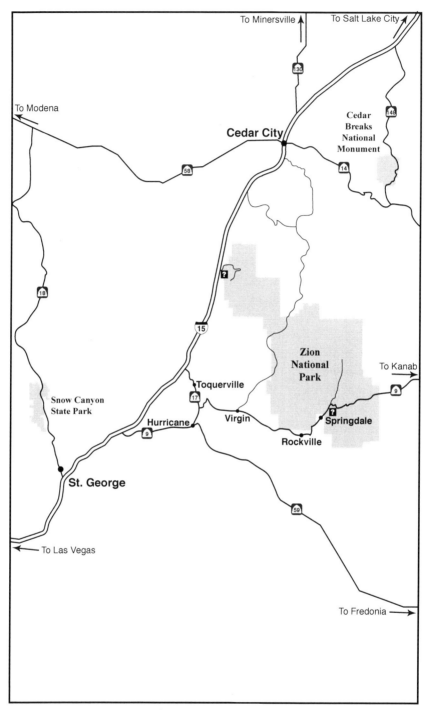

3.1 Zion Park Traverse Location

──────── **TRIP 3** ────────

Zion Park Traverse

> We need the tonic of wildness.... At the same time that we
> are earnest to explore and learn all things, we require that all
> things be mysterious and unexplorable, that land and sea be
> indefinitely wild, unsurveyed and unfathomed by us because
> unfathomable. We can never have enough of nature.
>
> —HENRY DAVID THOREAU

ZION CANYON is one of the true gems of southern Utah and the national park system, where towering sandstone cliffs colorfully stand guard over a stretch of the Virgin River, compelling tourists to crane their necks in attempts to take in the soaring scenery. From spring through autumn, thousands of devotees flock to the canyon each day to take in the amazing sights, jamming the insufficient parking lots near the visitor center in the process. The commercial interests in the neighboring gateway town of Springdale thrive on the steady stream of tourists. Day hikers fan out on a fine network of trails, with an obnoxiously high percentage bound for the harrowing ridgeline ascent of Angels Landing. During the summer months, more ardent adventurers attempt the route along and through the Virgin River via the Narrows.

Fortunately for lovers of wilderness, Zion National Park harbors more than just the overly admired wonders of Zion Canyon. The Kolob Canyons area in the upper part of the park sees a fraction of the people who visit the main canyon, and most of those are left behind once you set foot on the trail. The Zion Park Traverse begins at Lee Pass, in the Kolob Canyons region, and follows the La Verkin Creek Trail through amazing sandstone formations

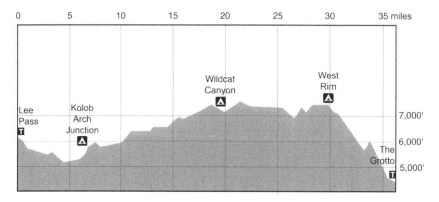

Zion Park Traverse

along Timber Creek before turning upstream along the namesake stream through a deepening canyon to the vicinity of Kolob Arch, one of the largest freestanding arches in North America. From there, after a short, steep climb, the route mildly ascends the bucolic environs of Hop Valley before a steeper climb leads out of the valley toward the vicinity of Kolob Terrace Road. A general traverse then leads across open slopes with wonderful views, alternating with stands of forest on the way toward Wildcat Canyon. Above the canyon, the route follows along the broad crest of Horse Pasture Plateau, where long-range vistas abound. The scenery becomes even more stupendous as you work your way along the West Rim and then embark on the plunging descent into Zion Canyon amid the classic rock formations.

Accomplishing the Zion Park Traverse requires a significant amount of trip planning, particularly in determining and reserving campsites as well as carrying or caching a sufficient amount of water in this often-dry terrain. For those up to the task, however, this route will reward you with some outstanding Southwest scenery.

Days:	4–5
Distance:	36.2 miles (plus 1-mile side trip to Kolob Arch and 2.2-mile side trip to Northgate Peaks)
Type:	Shuttle
Scenery:	9
Solitude:	6
Technical Difficulty:	4
Physical Difficulty:	5
Elevation Gain/Loss:	+5,650'/−7,425'

Season:	April to late October
	Best: Mid-May to early June
Maps:	USGS—Kolob Arch, Kolob Reservoir, The Guardian Angels, Temple of Sinawava
	Trails Illustrated—*Zion National Park*
Resources:	*Joe's Guide to Zion National Park*, available online at www.citrusmilo.com/zionguide/transziontrek.cfm
Contacts:	Zion National Park
	Springdale, UT 84767
	435-772-3256
	435-772-0170 (wilderness information)
	www.nps.gov/zion

Permits: Overnight permits are required. More than half of the permits are available by advance reservation using the park's online reservation system. Reservations can be made beginning on the fifth day of the month, starting at 10:00 AM, three months prior to the day of your departure. Each reservation costs $5 plus an additional amount based on the number of people in your group ($10 for one to two people; $15 for three to seven people; and $20 for eight to twelve people). The remainder may be obtained as walk-in permits up to one day before departure. Both reserved and walk-in permits can be picked up from either the Zion or Kolob visitor center. Camping is limited to designated sites for most of the route of the Zion Park Traverse, including Kolob Canyons and West Rim areas. Some of the campsites can be reserved online, while others are only available with walk-in permits.

Regulations: Maximum group size is twelve. Campfires are not allowed in the backcountry. Toilet paper must be packed out (bags are provided with backcountry permits). Dogs and firearms are not allowed.

Nearest Campgrounds:
- South (4.5 miles from West Rim trailhead)
- Watchman (5.25 miles from West Rim trailhead)

Nearest Airports:
- St. George Municipal Airport (SGU)—50 miles to Lee Pass trailhead
- McCarran International Airport, Las Vegas (LAS)—165 miles to Lee Pass trailhead
- Salt Lake City International Airport (SLC)—280 miles to Lee Pass trailhead

Nearest Outdoor Retailers:

- Canyon Outfitters—6 miles from West Rim trailhead
  849 Zion Park Blvd., Springdale, UT 84767
  435-772-0252
- Zion Outdoor—6 miles from West Rim trailhead
  868 Zion Park Blvd. Springdale, UT 84767
  435-772-0630
- Zion Rock and Mountain Guides—6.5 miles from West Rim trailhead
  1438 Zion Park Blvd., PO Box 623, Springdale, UT 84767
  435-772-3133   www.zionrockguides.com
- The Desert Rat—40 miles from Lee Pass trailhead
  488 W. St. George Blvd., St. George, UT 84770
  435-628-7277

Outfitters:

- Zion Adventure Company
  PO Box 523, 36 Lion Blvd., Springdale, UT 84767
  435-772-1001   www.zionadventures.com
- Zion Rock and Mountain Guides
  1438 Zion Park Blvd., PO Box 623, Springdale, UT 84767
  435-772-3133   www.zionrockguides.com

Transportation Logistics: Without using a shuttle, one hour of driving time separates the Lee Pass and West Rim trailheads. If you plan to cache water at one of the Kolob Terrace Road trailheads, another hour to an hour and a half will be necessary to complete the round-trip from the town of Virgin.

At the conclusion of the trip, you will need to ride the free Zion National Park shuttle bus from the ending trailhead at the Grotto to the overnight parking lot near the visitor center.

Backcountry Logistics: (H2O, L, Su, W) Choosing campsites and water caches will be the most significant challenges to successfully planning the trans-park trek. Most parties reserve a first-night's campsite along La Verkin Creek near the side trail to Kolob Arch. Doing so, however, requires hiking a long distance the next day to reach legal campsites in the Wildcat at-large camping zone. To complicate matters even further, the at-large zone offers little in the way of anything close to a developed campsite. Plan on very primitive conditions when looking for a campsite along the Northgate Peaks Trail or Wildcat Canyon Trail.

During dry periods, reliable water sources are limited beyond La Verkin Creek to a spring about half a mile before the crossing of usually dry Blue Creek, near the head of Wildcat Canyon. Although plenty of water flows through Hop Valley above La Verkin Creek, cattle are allowed to graze in the valley, and the Park Service does not recommend drinking the contaminated water. Without caching water, you should plan on carrying an adequate supply between La Verkin Creek and the spring, and between the spring and the Grotto at the end of the hike. Water can be cached at the Hop Valley trailhead (near Hop Valley Trail and Connector Trail junction), Wildcat Canyon trailhead (1 mile from trail), and West Rim trailhead (0.1 mile from trail). Leave water at the trailheads in collapsible plastic containers, fill up any available bottles or reservoirs, and then carry the collapsed plastic containers with you in your pack. Vault toilets and garbage cans are available at these trailheads. Some groups have been known to overnight at the developed Lava Point Campground.

Amenities and Attractions: Zion has many other trails well suited for day hikes. In the Kolob Canyons area, the 2.5-mile Taylor Creek Trail offers an easy stroll past a couple of historic cabins to the Double Arch Alcove. In the main canyon, the Angels Landing Trail is by far the park's most popular trail, a must-do hike at least once in a lifetime. Plan on getting the earliest start possible, because by midday, the route is teeming with hordes of people, many unfit or ill equipped for the difficulty and exposure on the upper part of the route, where a single-file line of hikers grasp onto a cable while negotiating a sheer face of rock. (Amazingly, there have only been five fatalities over the years.) Other trails in the main canyon include the Emerald Pools, Watchman, Hidden Canyon, and Observation Point trails. The most heralded trail in the park is the all-day or overnight route through and along a section of the Virgin River via the Narrows.

   Springdale has most of the trappings a gateway town outside a national park would usually include, such as motels, cafes, trinket shops, and a large-screen theater. Farther down canyon, the town of **Rockville** has several B&Bs. Many visitors to the park stay a night or two in **St. George**, where a few non-franchise eateries are of note in an otherwise cultural vacuum. In line with the state's strict alcohol rules, check to see if the restaurant where you choose to eat even sells adult beverages. If planning on purchasing any alcohol other than the watery mass-produced beer found at grocery stores, you're forced to find one of the State of Utah's liquor stores, which are not open in the evenings, on Sundays, or on holidays.

You'll likely be ready for something cold to drink and real food at the conclusion of your trip, and the **Zion Park Lodge** has the only alternatives inside the park. The **Castle Dome Café** is a snack bar with outdoor seating, offering salads, pizza, burgers, sandwiches, ice cream, and local microbrews. The **Red Rock Grill and Lounge**, on the second floor of the lodge, offers more upscale dining and a wider selection of adult beverages. The grill has a deck with outdoor seating, which permits disheveled backpackers the opportunity to sit and enjoy a decent meal without driving the other patrons away.

Directions to Trailhead: Whether you have two vehicles or choose to be shuttled to the starting trailhead at Lee Pass by an outfitter, the first leg of your journey will be the hour-long ride from St. George to Zion Canyon. From St. George, drive northbound on Interstate 15 to Exit 16, signed for Hurricane and Zion National Park. Proceed east on State Route 9 through Hurricane to the town of La Verkin. At the junction with State Highway 17, turn right to remain on Highway 9 and continue through Rockville and Springdale to the park entrance. Once inside the park, drive a short distance to the visitor center entrance and turn left, following a sign for parking lot B, which is the overnight parking lot. When you pick up your overnight permit, you will be given a parking permit that must be displayed on your dashboard. Parking is at a premium, so arrive as early as possible to secure a space.

To reach the starting trailhead from Zion Canyon, return to the junction of 9 and 17 in the town of La Verkin. Head north on 17 for 4.2 miles to Interstate 15 and continue north on the freeway. After 12.6 miles, take Exit 40 for Kolob Canyons and turn right into the visitor center. Continue up the Kolob Canyons Road for 3.8 miles to the Lee Pass parking area on the left shoulder.

If you plan on caching water anywhere midroute, you will need to drive up the Kolob Reservoir Road. Follow Highway 9 to the town of Virgin and head north on Kolob Reservoir Road. Follow the road on a sometimes steep climb from the Virgin River to the Lower Kolob Plateau. After 12.8 miles, you'll reach the Hop Valley trailhead. Another 2.8 miles leads to the Wildcat Canyon trailhead. Continue onto the Upper Kolob Plateau, and at 22 miles from Highway 9 is the junction with Lava Point Road. The entrance to the campground is down this road, as is the Lava Point Overlook at the end. To reach the West Rim trailhead, drive almost a mile down the Lava Point Road, turn left, and proceed another 1.5 miles to the trailhead.

Frederick S. Dellenbaugh Born in 1853 in McConnelsville, Ohio, Frederick Dellenbaugh studied fine art for a short time in New York and Europe but actually developed his extraordinary painting skills while in the field. He became accomplished enough to land a position as assistant topographer at the early age of eighteen on John Wesley Powell's second expedition of the Colorado River (1871–1873). Along with Dellenbaugh's paintings of the Colorado, the artist kept a daily journal, a practice he continued on all his extensive travels in the future. During the summer of 1903, Dellenbaugh painted the landscapes of Zion Canyon. His exquisite paintings were exhibited the following year at the St. Louis World's Fair, where onlookers scoffed at the notion of such beautiful landscapes being a reality. That same year he penned an article for *Scribner's Magazine* about the wonders of Zion, in which he stated in part, "Never before has such a naked mountain of rock entered into our minds! Without a shred of disguise its transcendent form rises preeminent. There is almost nothing compared to it. Niagara has the beauty of energy; the Grand Canyon of immensity; the Yellowstone, of singularity; the Yosemite, of altitude; the ocean, of power; this Great Temple, of eternity."

Dellenbaugh's paintings, along with the *Scribner's* article, were instrumental in the eventual park status of Zion Canyon. In 1909, President Taft used an executive order to designate Mukuntuweap National Monument, which Congress upgraded to Zion National Park in 1919.

Frederick Dellenbaugh's extensive travels took him to such places as Alaska, Iceland, Norway, South America, and the West Indies. But he was most known for his paintings, pencil drawings, and photographs of the American West, about which he also penned several books. He eventually retired in upstate New York, passing away in 1935.

Trip Description: Find the start of the trail near the west edge of the parking area. The initial segment of the La Verkin Creek Trail drops away from the parking lot and heads south on red dirt tread, through the open Kolob Canyons topography, with stunning views of the surrounding sandstone terrain, including such features as Beatty Point, Nagunt Mesa, Timber Top Mountain, and Shuntavi Butte. The sometimes steep descent through scrubby pinyon pine and juniper forest eventually delivers you to the stream bed of Timber Creek, which you follow on a mellow romp downstream, crossing the stream

Kolob Canyons View

numerous times on the way. You pass Shuntavi Butte around 2 miles from the trailhead and continue through a scattered forest of junipers and oaks for another mile, to where the trail veers away from Timber Creek, makes a gentle climb over a rise, and then heads east down toward the canyon of La Verkin Creek. New vistas appear of Neagle Ridge, Red Butte, Burnt Mountain, and numerous unnamed sandstone formations. After a fairly lengthy descending traverse, you meet La Verkin Creek, where a use trail heads over to the stream bank near a series of pretty cascades.

After a 4-plus-mile descent from Lee Pass, you now follow a gently rising course upstream, closely along La Verkin Creek, through a steep-sided gorge, soon passing the sites of camps 4–6 in the lower canyon. Gently graded, sometimes sandy tread leads farther up La Verkin Creek to camp 7, near where a spring-fed stream offers the opportunity to gather less silty water than flows through the main creek. As the canyon narrows and the red walls rise up to the sky, ponderosa pines begin to line the trail. Continuing upstream, you soon pass camps 8 and 9 across from each other, hop over a trickling rivulet, pass camp 10, and then reach the Kolob Arch junction, 6.4 miles from the trailhead.

Side Trip to Kolob Arch: From the La Verkin Creek junction, follow initially well-defined tread northward into a narrowing canyon. Farther upstream, the trail deteriorates, the result of repeated washouts in this narrow and steep gorge. If the water level is low, or you don't mind wet feet, walking directly up the stream may be easier than negotiating the path across steep side slopes and over deadfalls. Because of the added difficulties of traveling a less-than-ideal trail, the route seems farther than the half-mile distance from La Verkin Creek.

Eventually, Kolob Arch pops into sight, sitting high up the wall of a side canyon on the left. Dense forest and thick vegetation limit the view, and a national park sign discourages travel farther up the gorge to get a better look. Kolob Arch, one of the world's largest freestanding arches, is tucked closely up against the west wall of the canyon and at first glance may not appear as an arch at all. Upon closer inspection, however, you will see a narrow gap between the arch and the wall. As long as your expectation is not to witness something similar to what you might see in Arches National Park, an unobstructed view of a sandstone arch rising above the immediate slickrock, Kolob Arch is a stunning sight. While heeding the wishes of the Park Service, serious photographers will have to carefully climb above the foliage without trampling the vegetation to get anything but a distant shot of the arch.

From the Kolob Arch junction, the trail continues upstream to a crossing of La Verkin Creek, and then climbs more steeply up the south side of the canyon to a three-way junction with the Hop Valley Trail, 0.3 mile from the Kolob Arch junction. Camps 11 and 12 are both farther upstream, in more remote locations, as few hikers continue up the trail past the junction.

After the easy hiking along Deer and La Verkin Creeks, the stretch of trail climbing the south wall of La Verkin Creek canyon seems quite strenuous in comparison, as the path stiffly zigzags up the slope. Higher up the wall, beautiful views of Gregory Butte, Timber Top Mountain, and the surrounding terrain of the upper canyon offer a fine diversion from the steep ascent. Eventually cresting the lip of the canyon and finding more gently graded tread, you say goodbye to the views as you enter a forest of ponderosa pines and oaks. A brief stretch of climbing is followed by a pronounced descent through the trees, on the way to where the trail meets the stream in the bottom of Hop

Valley, which disappears into the sandy soil farther upstream and then reappears at a spring above La Verkin Creek.

On the way up the gentle and verdant valley, the trail crosses the shallow stream several times. After the first crossing, pass by camps A and B in the upper part of the valley, remembering that the Park Service does not recommend drinking the water in the creek because of the intermittent presence of grazing cattle. Beyond the camps, pass through a gate in a barbed wire fence and continue the easy stroll up the valley, through open vegetation, which allows good views of the canyon walls. After the next stream crossing, avoid the tendency to follow a path up a hillside away from the water—the actual route of this faint section of trail continues alongside the creek, down the floor of the valley. On the way to the upper valley, the trail crosses out of the park and onto sections of private land a couple of times. As the stream bends sharply to the east, you bid farewell to the pastoral surroundings of Hop Valley.

The trail continues south, skirts a boggy meadow, and begins a much steeper climb up the hillside, along the course of an old jeep road, passing a memorial bench on the right along the way. Once again the trail exits the park to cross a section of private land, where you leave the road and follow a section of single-track trail through open terrain. Ahead and slightly to the left is the landmark of Firepit Knoll, which lies directly northeast of your next destination, the Hop Valley trailhead. Pass through another gate in a wire fence and follow gently rising tread across open sagebrush-covered slopes. You eventually exit the signed wilderness, cross a usually dry wash, and then follow the trail through a stand of burned trees on the way to a three-way junction with the Connector Trail, heading east. Ahead a very short distance is the vault toilet and parking area of the Hop Valley trailhead, 6.5 miles from the La Verkin Creek junction. If you plan on caching water, this particular trailhead is closest to the trail.

From the Connector Trail and Hop Valley Trail junction, head east for a short distance to cross Kolob Terrace Road and pick up the resumption of single-track trail on the far side. The sagebrush-covered terrain on this mostly gently graded traverse allows fine views of Jobs Head, Pine Valley Peak, and surrounding cliffs, as the trail moves farther away from the road. After crossing a few minor draws, eventually the route reaches the base of some sandstone slabs, which you must ascend more steeply to the northwest of Pine Valley Peak. At the top of the climb, beautiful views expand across the surrounding ridges and valleys and the more immediate north face of striking Pine Valley Peak. A short, gentle drop leads along the base of the peak and into thicker pine forest, before a stretch of gently rising tread leads to a three-way

Side Trip to Northgate Peaks: Deciding whether to make the 1.1-mile trip to the end of the trail will require some thought. At-large camping is allowed 200 yards away from the trail, which provides the first legal camping since the sites in lower Hop Valley. There are no developed sites, but the terrain is generally flat, so establishing a dry camp is possible. If you camped near the Kolob Arch junction, you've already come nearly 11 miles. Continuing to the at-large zone along the Wildcat Canyon Trail will require almost another 4 miles, bringing the day's total to nearly 15 miles—a long day for many backpackers. Although the 2.2-mile out-and-back route to Northgate Peaks is relatively easy on nearly flat tread, adding another 2-plus miles to your tally might be more than you're willing to hike in a day.

For those up to the task, head south and follow the gently graded Northgate Peaks Trail, through sections of open ponderosa pine forest alternating with grassy meadows. Remain on the main trail ahead at a junction with the Subway Top-Down Route, which descends into Russell Gulch. A fine view from the end of the trail, on top of a volcanic outcrop, includes the two Northgate Peaks immediately to your left and right, the Great West Canyon below, and North Guardian Angel directly south.

junction with the 1.2-mile lateral heading west to the Wildcat Canyon trailhead, 3.8 miles from the Hop Valley trailhead. Continuing ahead, you soon reach the Northgate Peaks Trail junction.

From the Northgate Peaks junction, head northeast through ponderosa pine forest on the steadily rising tread of the Wildcat Canyon Trail, which follows the course of an old, rocky jeep road. About a mile from the junction, the forest opens up, allowing sweeping views into the cleft of Russell Gulch. A short way later, you encounter a sloping meadow, where campsites could be established away from the trail. The ascent continues to a high point near 7,350 feet, followed by a descent past a forested bench, offering the possibility of additional campsites. Continue along the old roadbed on a descending traverse toward Wildcat Canyon. Soon you reach Wildcat Spring, which is marked by a metal sign. Fill up here, as in some years this may be the only reliable water source for the remainder of the trip.

Continue through Wildcat Canyon, with beautiful views of the surrounding terrain along the way. Once you step across the usually dry stream bed of Blue Creek, the trail begins an extended climb, circling around into a tributary

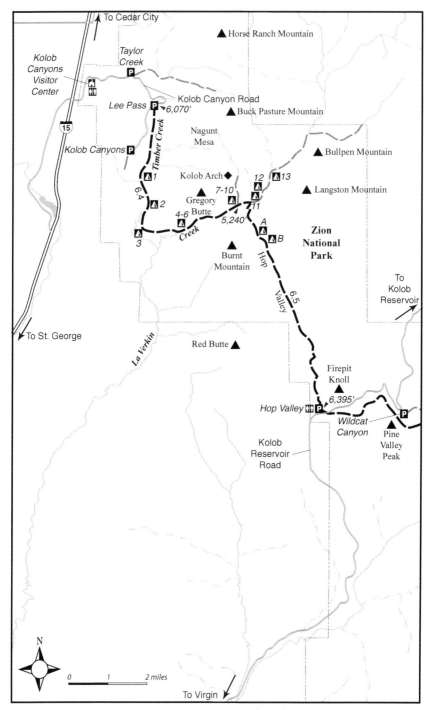

To Cedar City

Horse Ranch Mountain ▲

Kolob
Canyons
Visitor
Center

Taylor
Creek
P

Kolob Canyon Road

Buck Pasture Mountain ▲

Lee Pass P
6,070'

15

Nagunt
Mesa

Bullpen Mountain ▲

Kolob Canyons P

Kolob Arch ◆

12 ▲ 13

Langston Mountain ▲

1

7-10

Timber Creek

2

Gregory
Butte

11

6.4

4-6

5,240'

Zion
National
Park

3

Creek

A

B

Burnt
Mountain

To St. George

Hop

To
Kolob
Reservoir

Valley

6.5

La Verkin

Red Butte ▲

Firepit
Knoll ▲

6,395'

Hop Valley P

Wildcat
Canyon

Pine
Valley
Peak ▲

P

Kolob
Reservoir
Road

N

0   1   2 miles

To Virgin

3.2 Zion Park Traverse (West)

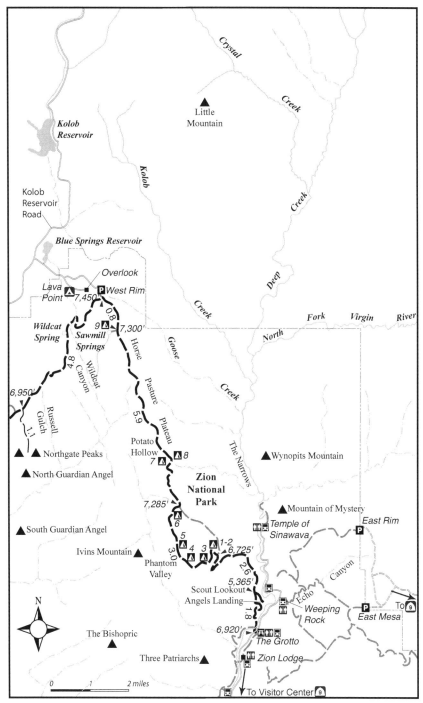

3.3 Zion Park Traverse (East)

Kolob Reservoir

Kolob Reservoir Road

Blue Springs Reservoir

Little Mountain

Crystal

Creek

Kolob

Creek

Deep

Creek

Goose

Creek

North

Fork   *Virgin*   *River*

Overlook

Lava Point

West Rim

7,450'

Wildcat Spring

Sawmill Springs

9

0.8

7,300'

4.8

Wildcat Canyon

Horse Pasture Plateau

6,950'

Russell Gulch

1.1

5.9

Northgate Peaks

North Guardian Angel

South Guardian Angel

Ivins Mountain

The Bishopric

N

Potato Hollow

7

8

Zion National Park

7,285'

6

5

4

3

1-2

6,725'

3.0

Phantom Valley

Scout Lookout

Angels Landing

2.6

5,365'

1.8

6,920'

The Grotto

Zion Lodge

Three Patriarchs

The Narrows

Wynopits Mountain

Mountain of Mystery

Temple of Sinawava

East Rim

Echo Canyon

Weeping Rock

East Mesa

To 9

To Visitor Center 9

0   1   2 miles

canyon, and then ascending to the meadows of Horse Pasture Plateau, where you'll see an old farm implement rusting in the grass. Reach the three-way junction with the West Rim Trail, 4.8 miles from the Northgate Peaks junction. The West Rim trailhead is only 0.1 mile to the north-northwest, and the Lava Point Campground about a mile farther.

Turning southeast, the West Rim Trail follows the crest of Horse Pasture Plateau through scrubby vegetation and widely scattered pines, with excellent and near continuous long-distance views. After 0.7 mile you reach a junction with a lateral on the right, which drops 0.3 mile to camp 9 near Sawmill Spring.

Gently graded tread following near the crest of the ridge continues for the next 3.5 miles, with more wide-ranging views as your constant companions. Charred trees from an extensive 1996 wildfire mar the otherwise fine scenery. Eventually the route drops off the crest and plunges down a gully toward the vicinity of Potato Hollow Spring. Nearing the spring, the trail enters an area of lush vegetation, including stands of aspen. As this is one of the few places with water near the plateau, patient visitors may see a variety of wildlife coming for a drink. Pass by laterals to camps 8 and then 7 before you start to regain all the lost elevation. Ascend steeply at times to a saddle to the east of point 7,370, drop briefly away, and then proceed along a narrow ridge with incredible views of the sandstone country to the south. A short steep climb from the end of this ridge leads back onto Horse Pasture Plateau and a junction with Telephone Canyon Trail, 5.9 miles from the Sawmill Spring junction. Camp 6 is nearby.

Veer to the right at the junction and continue along West Rim Trail, which hugs the west edge of the open plateau, providing stunning scenery along the way. The incredible views continue all the way to the south end of the plateau, where the trail enters stands of ponderosa pines. Amid the trees you pass laterals to camps 5, 4, and 3. Beyond these camps, the trail descends into a gully, followed by a lengthy traverse across a slope peppered with widely scattered junipers and ponderosa pines. The trail descends more steeply, switchbacks, and then drops to a signed four-way junction, 3.1 miles from the previous junction. The lefthand trail is Telephone Canyon Trail, ahead is a short lateral to Cabin Spring, and on the right is the continuation of West Rim Trail, headed to the Grotto Picnic Area in Zion Canyon. Camps 1 and 2, the last legal campsites along the West Rim, are nearby.

From the junction, follow West Rim Trail on a switchbacking descent, which soon follows a conveniently located ledge system down a sheer wall of sandstone. Views along this stretch are quite impressive. After zigzagging

On the descent into Zion Canyon

down to the floor of the canyon, known as Little Siberia, follow dirt tread through thick vegetation made up of ponderosa pines, white firs, bigtooth maples, Gambel oaks, cottonwoods, and willows. After a while, you encounter concrete slabs covering the trail, the first of the manmade improvements along the lower section of the West Rim Trail. Follow the trail as it arcs around the north base of Mount Majestic and then into a narrow gorge, which you cross with the aid of a metal-railed bridge.

From the bridge, a winding ascent leads across sandstone slabs to an open bench, from where you have a fine view of some landmarks of Zion Canyon, including the usual stream of people crawling up Angels Landing Trail. From this vista point, follow footprints on metal signs down the slickrock to the resumption of dirt tread immediately east of Refrigerator Canyon. Reach Scouts Lookout and the junction of the highly popular trail to Angels Landing, 2.9 miles from the Telephone Canyon junction.

From the Angels Landing junction, West Rim Trail plunges toward the canyon floor through usually cool Refrigerator Canyon. Soon you start zigzagging down steep paved sections of trail known as Walters Wiggles. At the bottom of these tight switchbacks, the canyon opens up, and the trail continues a downward course toward the Virgin River. The grade eases in the bottom

Side Trip to Angels Landing: If you've never done the trail to the top of Angels Landing, you're almost obligated to do so before continuing to the ending trailhead at the Grotto. The 0.4-mile spur is short but gains 500 vertical feet in that distance. Those with a fear of heights should avoid the route altogether, as should anyone traveling with small children. Drop your heavy backpacks near the junction and, with the aid of rock steps, guardrails, and metal hand chains, steeply ascend a narrow spine of rock, constantly aware of the tremendous exposure on either side. Depending on the time of day and season, you may experience unwanted logjams at the cables. The best advice is to time your climb either early or late in the day to avoid the largest crush of tourists, some of whom have no business being on this route—the fact that only a handful of people have died here over the years seems somewhat miraculous. The birds-eye vantage from the top of Angels Landing is fantastic, offering an incomparable 360-degree view of Zion Canyon. Once you've taken everything in, return to the junction with the West Rim Trail.

of the canyon, where some side trails offer access to the river for anyone who wishes to soak tired feet. Proceed southbound along the west bank of the river to a footbridge, which leads across the river and over to the Grotto Picnic Area and shuttle bus stop 6 (restrooms).

Depending on your immediate destination, board the bus and head down canyon. The Zion Lodge is the place to stop for a cold beverage or a meal. Otherwise, continue to the visitor center and the overnight parking lot to retrieve your vehicle.

Possible Itinerary

Day	Camps and Side Trips	Distance (mi.)	Elevation (ft.)
1	Lee Pass TH to Kolob Arch junction	6.4	+325/–1,150
	Side trip to Kolob Arch	1.0	+150/–150
2	Wildcat Canyon	12.6	+2,750/–600
	Side trip to Northgate Peaks	2.2	+200/–200
3	West Rim camps	10.6	+1,600/–1,500
4	Out to the Grotto Picnic Area	6.6	+975/–4,175

Green Tips: Southern Utah Wilderness Alliance—www.suwa.org

✳ Unseasonably Idyllic ————————————————————

Anyone who lives in the Southwest for any length of time becomes acutely aware of the region's propensity for drought cycles, despite the best efforts of the Bureau of Reclamation and the Corps of Engineers to make us believe that the desert should be constantly in bloom and golf courses perpetually green. While some residents keep a watchful eye on the weather and the annual water supply, perhaps only a small percentage appreciates one of the limited benefits of a dry winter—straightforward access to recreational lands.

Such was the case when Dave and I loaded up the car and headed east for a long New Year's weekend in the desert Southwest. Very little moisture had fallen so far that year, and the temperatures were forecast to be unseasonably warm for the next several days. While snowbirds headed for warm havens like Palm Springs, and many outdoor lovers set their sights on places like Death Valley or Joshua Tree national parks, we had a different plan in mind. After a multihour drive, we reached a pocket of what would have usually been snow-dusted terrain in southern Utah. With sunny skies above our heads and bare ground beneath our feet, we hoisted our packs onto our backs and headed out on the trail. Not surprisingly, we had the upper reaches of Zion National Park completely to ourselves. After a several-mile hike, we reached our destination and set up camp for the next couple of days. That night we celebrated New Year's Eve by donning all our clothing and sitting out on a cloudless evening to watch the stars, joyfully nursing cups of hot chocolate laced with peppermint schnapps.

The next morning dawned bright and beautiful, but the air was quite chilly until the sun's rays effectively warmed the high desert air. After a leisurely breakfast, we went on a short day hike to a beautiful sandstone arch. By midday the air temperature was ideal, and we were still without the company of fellow humans— the upper part of the park had become our own personal domain. Below the arch was a smooth sandstone slab, well suited for a relaxing lunch break. Fully sated after eating and with no place to rush off to, we were overcome by the desire for a nap. Although not devotees of the practice, we shed all our clothes and lay down on the slab to bask in the warm sun. We were all alone, sunbathing on New Year's Day at 5,500 feet in the middle of Zion National Park and a stunning landscape. Surely, it doesn't get any better than this.

— Mike

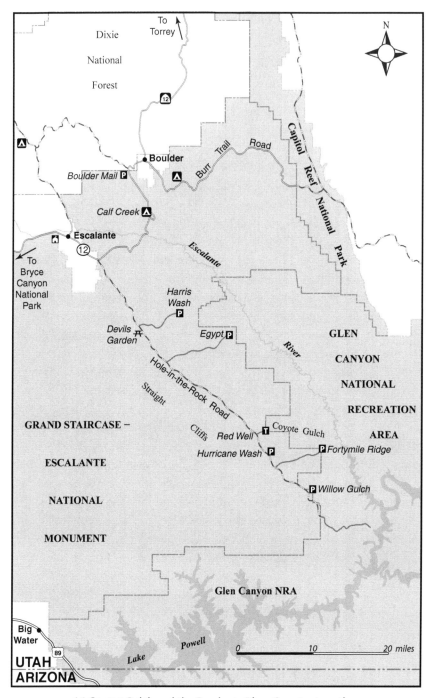

4.1 Coyote Gulch and the Escalante River Country Location

**Grand Staircase–Escalante National Monument
and Glen Canyon National Recreation Area**

——————————— **TRIP 4** ———————————

Coyote Gulch and
the Escalante River Country

As to when I revisit civilization, it will not be soon.
I have not tired of the wilderness....
It is enough that I am surrounded with beauty.

—Everett Ruess (young artist, poet, and writer who
disappeared in the Escalante region in 1934)

THE ESCALANTE RIVER COUNTRY is a desert-canyon lover's dream. Dozens of dramatically scenic canyons snake through this area's colorful layers of sandstone, taking the hiker to lush springs, past near-idyllic campsites, around or beneath arches and natural bridges, and through generally outstanding scenery. A backpacker could spend a lifetime in this landscape, happily exploring the hundreds of cliff-walled gulches and washes, discovering rarely seen arches, crawling through narrow slot canyons, and generally enjoying dramatic desert scenery. Since only one or two of the canyons are heavily traveled (in particular Coyote Gulch), crowds are generally not an issue.

What *are* issues, however, are the extreme summer heat, possibility of flash floods, lack of potable water, and sometimes terrible roads to these remote locations. You can mitigate these downsides with some careful planning. Since most of the heat and flash floods occur between mid-June and mid-September, you should plan your visit for the spring or fall. In fact, the Escalante River country (and southern Utah in general) offers perhaps the

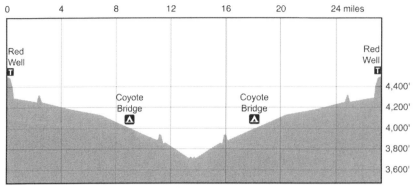

Coyote Gulch and the Escalante River Country

finest shoulder season hiking in the United States. The water difficulties can be handled by carefully choosing which canyons to hike. A few canyons, such as Coyote Gulch, have perennial creeks, where finding water is not a problem. The main canyon of the Escalante River, of course, has a major (at least by desert standards) stream flowing all year. To deal with the roads, visit during the drier seasons of spring and fall and drive or rent a car with good ground clearance. Four-wheel drive is sometimes helpful though not usually required to reach the more popular canyon hikes when the roads are dry.

Although there are countless possible options for backpacking in this area, hikers have voted with their feet for Coyote Gulch as the supreme desert canyon in the region. This turns out to be a reasonable decision, as the magnificently scenic route down this gorgeous 600-foot-deep defile offers a wonderful sampling of Escalante country's best attributes—arches, natural bridges, several small waterfalls, permanent water, towering cliffs, and extremely colorful landscapes. All by itself, this relatively short backpacking trip is well worth a trip to this remote area. If you have the time, however, the Escalante country is worthy of several more hikes. A sampling of the best of the Escalante River country's countless great day-hiking possibilities are mentioned in the Attractions and Amenities section below. For additional backpacking options, see the Alternatives section at the end of the trail description.

Days: 3–4

Distance: 27.4 miles round-trip (15.9 miles as a shuttle trip)

Type: Loop or shuttle

Scenery: 9

Solitude: 4

Technical Difficulty:	5
Physical Difficulty:	5
Elevation Gain/Loss:	+1,400'/−1,400' (round-trip)
Season:	March to November **Best:** April and May, mid-September through October
Maps:	Trails Illustrated—*Canyons of the Escalante*
Resources:	*The Undaunted: The Miracle of the Hole in the Rock Pioneers*, by Gerald N. Lund; *Hole in the Rock*, by David E. Miller; *Hiking Grand Staircase—Escalante and the Glen Canyon Region*, by Ron Adkison
Contacts:	Escalante Interagency Visitor Center 755 W. Main, Escalante, UT 84726 435-826-5499

Permits: Overnight permits are required. As of 2014, they are unlimited, free, and available at self-service stations at all developed trailheads.

Regulations: Dogs are prohibited in Coyote Gulch. Groups are limited to a maximum of twelve persons. Human waste bags are strongly encouraged, especially in Coyote Gulch, but they were not required as of 2013. You *are* required to pack out all toilet paper. Fires are prohibited in the canyon of the Escalante River and below the rim in any of the tributary canyons, including Coyote Gulch.

Nearest Campgrounds: Calf Creek Campground—14.5 miles northeast of Escalante. There are endless opportunities for dispersed camping on the vast areas of national monument land on the way to the trailhead (free permits are required).

Nearest Airports:
- St. George Municipal Airport (SGU)—210 miles
- Salt Lake City International Airport (SLC)—301 miles
- McCarran International Airport, Las Vegas (LAS)—337 miles

Nearest Outdoor Retailers:
- Escalante Outfitters—38 miles
  310 W. Main St., PO Box 575, Escalante, UT 84726
  435-826-4266
  (Although their supplies are limited, this is still a useful place for a last-minute stop and is your best bet in the small town of Escalante.)

Outfitters:

- Escalante Canyon Outfitters
  2520 S. Lower Deer Creek Rd., PO Box 1330, Boulder, UT 84716
  www.ecohike.com
- Escalante Outfitters
  310 W. Main St., PO Box 575, Escalante, UT 84726
  435-826-4266

Transportation Logistics: Although most people use their own vehicles, licensed outfitters can shuttle people to trailheads in the region. Companies change frequently—contact the Escalante Interagency Visitor Center for a list of currently licensed outfitters and guides.

When the surface is dry, Hole-in-the-Rock Road, at least as far as the trailheads for Coyote Gulch, is generally a good, graded dirt and gravel road well suited for passenger cars. The road is noticeably rougher, however, once you cross into Kane County, 16 miles from the Highway 12 turnoff. Unfortunately, after significant rains, the Hole-in-the-Rock Road can be very slippery and subject to washouts, which can make travel difficult or impossible without four-wheel drive. The side road to Red Well trailhead and Fortymile Ridge Road both receive less maintenance than Hole-in-the-Rock Road and can be very rough. When they are dry, these roads are usually drivable in most passenger cars with decent ground clearance. With any appreciable precipitation, four-wheel drive will be necessary, especially for the last 1.8 miles of Fortymile Ridge Road. Contact the Escalante Interagency Visitor Center about current conditions.

Backcountry Logistics: (FF, H, Q, R, St, Su) There is a perennial stream in Coyote Gulch, which you must repeatedly cross or walk in for many miles on the way through the canyon. Expect wet feet and wear old boots, wading sandals, or shoes that you don't mind getting wet. An additional pair of dry lightweight camp shoes would be a blessing.

If you plan to go beyond Coyote Gulch and hike in the Escalante River Canyon, that stream ranges from knee to waist deep, and crossings will be cold and uncomfortable, especially in the spring. When the water is thigh deep or higher, these crossings may be dangerous. The typically drier days of autumn offer a better time to hike the main canyon, which includes many crossings of the Escalante River.

There is a danger from flash floods, especially (but not exclusively) during the summer thunderstorm season. Never camp at low places near the stream and watch the weather carefully while you hike. Coyote Gulch is open enough that hikers can *usually* escape to higher ground and avoid being washed away by a flood. The high water may last for some time, and even after the water recedes, the resulting mud and deep quicksand may make travel impossible. In addition, even if you *can* get back to your car, you may find that driving out is now impossible due to road damage. Carry enough food, water, and other supplies to last for at least a few extra days.

Even without a flood, quicksand is fairly common in the canyons, although rather rare in Coyote Gulch. Test the ground with a hiking staff before walking across any suspect areas.

Coyote Gulch is always popular, but even more so during Easter week and over Memorial Day weekend, when solitude seekers should go elsewhere.

Additional hazards include rodents, ravens, and ringtails raiding backpackers' food supplies at popular campsites. Rattlesnakes and scorpions are present, the latter requiring you to watch your step, especially at night. **Tip:** Don't forget to shake out your boots before putting them on in the morning.

Amenities and Attractions: The small town of **Escalante** is a bit shy in amenities but does have acceptable motels, basic outdoor supplies, and decent food. In addition to a couple of fast-food eateries, slightly better than average, homestyle meals can be had at **Circle D Restaurant** (425 W. Main, 435-826-4125) and **Cowboy Blues Restaurant** (a local favorite at 530 W. Main, 435-826-4577).

Don't pass up a quick visit to the **Escalante Interagency Visitor Center**, prominently located on the south side of Highway 12 at the west end of town. Here you can purchase maps and get answers to questions about destinations and road conditions. The visitor center also has several worthwhile displays.

Although manmade amenities are in short supply, the natural attractions in this area could fill volumes. A comprehensive listing of all the nearby desert wonders is beyond the scope of this book, but a few are so outstanding and so easily seen that they should not be missed. The most famous and deservedly popular local day hike is to **Calf Creek Falls**. This tall and stunningly beautiful waterfall is at the end of an easy and very scenic 3.1-mile trail starting at Calf Creek Campground, 14.5 miles northeast of Escalante.

Along Hole-in-the-Rock Road on the way to Coyote Gulch, be sure to take about an hour to explore the photogenic wonderland of colorful rock formations and miniature arches in **Devils Garden Outstanding Natural Area**. Somewhat more time (at least three or four hours) is needed to hike down to and explore **Peek-a-boo and Spooky Canyons**, two *extremely* narrow and twisting slot canyons that require some experience, significant athleticism, and a *very* skinny frame to explore. Both are about 0.5 mile long and generally less than 100 feet deep but range from 2 feet to only 8 *inches* (or possibly even less) wide. You will be forced to take your pack off, scramble around, and squeeze through some ridiculously tight spots, but it's great fun! The trailhead is accessed from Dry Fork Road, which is often very rough and may require four-wheel drive. Further south along Hole-in-the-Rock Road, about 7.9 miles beyond the Hurricane Wash trailhead, is an unsigned turnoff for the short but often rough road to the trailhead for **Willow Gulch**. From here you have access to a nontechnical 2-mile one-way hike to impressive **Broken Bow Arch**.

Directions to Trailhead: First, make your way to the isolated town of Escalante, which is located along scenic State Highway 12 in south-central Utah, about 40 miles east of Bryce Canyon National Park, and about 65 miles southwest of the west entrance to Capitol Reef National Park. From the east end of town, drive 5 miles southeast on Highway 12, then turn right (south-southeast) onto signed Hole-in-the-Rock Road. From here, carefully watching your odometer is important, since turnoffs may not be signed.

Follow this well-graded gravel and dirt road for 31.4 miles to the turnoff for Road 254, where a small sign reads RED WELL 1.5. There are several possible entry and exit points for Coyote Gulch, but this road leads to the recommended starting point for an out-and-back trip. Turn left onto this sometimes rough but generally drivable dirt road and proceed 1.1 miles to the road-end trailhead.

Alternate Trailheads: If you prefer to start at the somewhat more popular Hurricane Wash trailhead, then continue straight on Hole-in-the-Rock Road from the Red Well turnoff and drive 3.2 miles, 34.6 miles from Highway 12, to the parking pullout and signed trailhead immediately before the crossing of shallow Hurricane Wash.

Two other popular trailheads for reaching Coyote Gulch are off Fortymile Ridge Road. With two vehicles, the best plan starts from the end of this road, hikes down to the mouth of Coyote Gulch, and then walks up the canyon to Red Well. To reach Fortymile Ridge, continue driving Hole-in-the-Rock Road another 2.3 miles south from the Hurricane Wash trailhead, then turn left onto signed Fortymile Ridge Road. Follow this sandy and badly washboarded route for 4.4 miles to a turnoff for a short spur road that goes left (uphill) to the Fortymile Tank trailhead parking area, near a large livestock-watering tank. The 2-mile, mostly cross-country route heading north from here is a shortcut to the dramatic central part of Coyote Gulch. This route is not for everyone, however, as it concludes with an extremely steep and demanding (but generally reasonable) scramble down slickrock to the canyon floor immediately upstream from Jacob Hamblin Arch.

Shuttle Trailhead: To reach the final possible trailhead (and the recommended starting point if you have two cars), continue driving east on Fortymile Ridge Road another 0.8 mile to a sign warning that deep sand is ahead and that four-wheel drive is recommended. (Even more important than four-wheel drive is good ground clearance and experience driving on desert sands.) Many people park here and walk the final section of road, which is a good plan when driving an ordinary passenger car. The road continues another 1.8 miles to the trailhead. **Note:** If you attempt to drive this final distance, remember that when driving through sand, it is crucial to maintain your speed and momentum (going 25 mph is *much* better than going 5 mph), because without these, getting stuck in the sand is quite easy.

John Wesley Powell, the One-Armed Wonder Okay, so the common complaint these days is that we are all too busy, right? Our fast-paced world forces us to be constantly on the go, with the result that we can never actually get anything *done*. Well, folks, pull up your bootstraps, quit complaining, and read a bit about the amazing life of John Wesley Powell.

In the American Southwest, Powell is remembered as the iron-willed leader of a remarkable scientific and exploration expedition. In 1869, Powell and nine companions used four rather flimsy wooden dory boats (basically overgrown rowboats) to trace the unexplored course of the Green and Colorado Rivers from Green River, Wyoming, to the mouth of the Virgin River in Nevada, almost 930 miles downstream. It was an incredibly difficult and dangerous adventure, involving enormous rapids, no chance to resupply, complete solitude, and charting a course that no human being had ever attempted. The party nearly drowned countless times and almost starved to death. Three of the original members died, possibly in an Indian ambush after leaving the main expedition in Arizona's Grand Canyon, convinced the party was doomed to perish in the raging rapids or from a shortage of food. Despite this lack of confidence, Powell's emaciated party eventually succeeded when they emerged from the Grand Canyon and reached a tiny Mormon settlement. During the course of his dramatic adventure, Powell discovered and named numerous canyons, side streams, palisades, and other features. By simply completing the journey, Powell disproved the opinions of most experts, who believed the trip was impossible because of waterfalls and other obstacles. He also added significantly to the map of America, made some important scientific discoveries, and came to some brilliant conclusions about the geology of the Colorado Plateau—conclusions that no trained geologist had ever even considered.

This singular accomplishment would have been more than enough to ensure Powell a prominent place in the annals of American history. But John Wesley was a restless and energetic man with a great deal more to his story.

John Wesley was born in 1834 in rural western New York, the son of a poor traveling preacher. Powell's family instilled wanderlust in their son as they moved westward to Ohio, Wisconsin, and finally Illinois. His education was necessarily sporadic, and although he did some study at both Wheaton and Oberlin Colleges, he never obtained a degree. With a restless nature and a keen interest in geology and other aspects of natural history, young John Wesley spent his early twenties on a series of grand outdoor adventures. These adventures included a four-month walk across the state of Wisconsin; rowing the entire Mississippi River from St. Anthony, Minnesota, to the Gulf of Mexico; paddling down the Ohio River from Pittsburgh to St. Louis; and rowing down the Illinois River and up the Mississippi and Des Moines Rivers into central Iowa. In between, he was a schoolteacher and was elected to the Illinois Natural History Society, serving as its secretary.

At the age of twenty-seven, Powell followed his abolitionist sympathies and enlisted in the Union army near the start of the Civil War. With typical energetic zeal, he entered the war as a private, was elected a sergeant major by his peers, was commissioned as a second lieutenant, recruited his own artillery company and served as its captain, eventually made the rank of major, and finished the war as a lieutenant colonel (although he continued to be called "major" for the rest of his life). Early in the war he was severely wounded at the battle of Shiloh, where he lost most of his right arm, a wound that would cause him pain for the rest of his life. Despite this disability, Powell fought in at least eight more major battles.

After the war, our one-armed wonder was a professor of geology and natural history at Illinois Wesleyan University and regularly lectured at

Illinois State Normal University. He helped found the Illinois Museum of Natural History, serving as the curator. Powell also led a party of students and scientists on an exploration of the state of Colorado, climbed Pikes Peak, and explored the upper reaches of the Colorado River. Traveling throughout the High Plains, he took special care in recording the lives and languages of various tribes of Native Americans. All of this was accomplished in just the five short years between the end of the Civil War and the start of his much-heralded expedition down the Colorado River.

Never one to let moss grow between his toes, no matter how well earned a little rest might have been, Powell used his knowledge and fame from his river trip to continue leading a ridiculously busy life. In 1871–1872 he retraced his Colorado River excursion in a second, almost equally dangerous adventure. He also founded a regular gathering of intellectuals, called the Cosmos Club, who met at Powell's home in Illinois; lobbied for and helped start the United States Geological Survey and served as full-time director for thirteen years; founded the Smithsonian Institution's Bureau of American Indian Ethnology and served as director for twenty-three years; did pioneering work in the classification of American Indian languages that is still considered valuable today; was the first to recognize and describe the geologic forces of erosion and slow uplift that led to the creation of the Grand Canyon; was responsible for the research and ideas behind the current irrigation policy in the American West as well as the founding of the Bureau of Reclamation; lectured extensively on geology and American Indian policies; provided invaluable assistance to and helped coordinate the scientific studies and work of other men and institutions too numerous to mention; was a gifted wordsmith who wrote and published two best-selling books, which are still considered classics in travel and natural history writing; eventually received honorary degrees from Harvard and Heidelberg Universities; and had a long and apparently happy marriage, which included raising one daughter. I don't know about you, but I'm exhausted just contemplating all Powell has done.

The Escalante River country, particularly Glen Canyon along the Colorado River, was one of the areas Powell was among the first to explore and name. In his typically colorful and awe-inspired prose, Powell wrote of this canyon, "wonderful features—carved walls, royal arches, glens, alcove gulches, mounds and monuments. From which of these features shall we select a name? We decide to call it Glen Canyon." Sadly, the magnificent depths of Glen Canyon are now inundated by a huge reservoir, which ironically carries Powell's name. But today's hiker can still explore the Escalante River and its side canyons to get a wonderful taste of the dramatic scenery that so impressed Powell. Perhaps now you can also appreciate some of the accomplishments of the remarkable one-armed man who is most closely associated with this extraordinary region.

Trip Description: Note—This trail description assumes that you have only one vehicle and are starting from Red Well.

Follow a path heading east across bright red sandy soils on an old road along the top of a rounded sagebrush- and grass-covered ridge. At just shy of 0.2 mile, pass a sign noting your entry into Glen Canyon National Recreation Area. Soon after, you begin an intermittent descent that ends at 0.5 mile from the trailhead, with a short but steep drop into the very sandy bottom of Coyote Gulch, where usually dry Big Hollow Wash enters from the northwest. Although the walls here are low, rounded, and rather uninteresting, the scenery will improve dramatically farther down Coyote Gulch. Typically, there is no water in the gulch at this point, but that too will soon change.

At just under 1 mile, you reach the first cluster of large Fremont cottonwoods, indicating that water is not far below the surface. The canyon already starts to narrow, with low but increasingly colorful walls and nice views looking west, back up the canyon to the Straight Cliffs.

About 0.2 mile below the first cottonwoods, the canyon makes the first of many wide curves and meanders, a pattern that will become monotonously familiar as you keep hiking. Seeping springs provide the canyon's first water, initially just a trickle, but the creek soon grows into a fairly respectable stream. There are plenty of potential campsites in the next mile or two on cottonwood-covered benches just above the little creek. Another pattern you'll soon grow accustomed to is the need to repeatedly cross the creek. Initially, hopping over the flow is straightforward, but eventually you'll be forced to wade, which results in many miles of hiking with wet feet. Adding to the creek's volume in the spring is the flow from often-misnamed Dry Fork Coyote Gulch, the wide mouth of which you pass at around 1.9 miles.

About 2.6 miles from the trailhead, the creek plunges over a small waterfall into a narrow little slot canyon, forcing hikers to detour via a desert ridge to the north (left). After a little over 0.1 mile, the route returns to creek level and soon passes the first large streamside rock, which has been undercut by the water. Ferns cluster around a seeping spring at the base of the rock. Nearly all springs in the canyon feature this appealing look of verdant greenery. In a preview of things to come, the nearly vertical canyon walls are

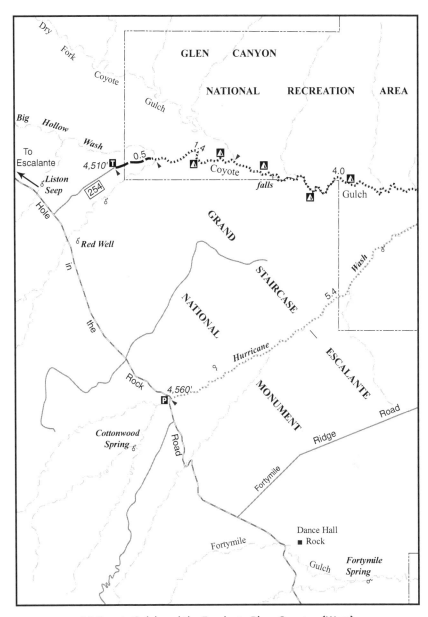

4.2 Coyote Gulch and the Escalante River Country (West)

already impressive, with those on the south (right) side of the canyon rising 150 feet or more in salmon and orange splendor.

At about 3.4 miles, you pass through a gate with a sign reminding hikers that dogs are not allowed in Coyote Gulch. The next couple of miles feature many creek crossings and excellent canyon scenery. Inviting campsites are

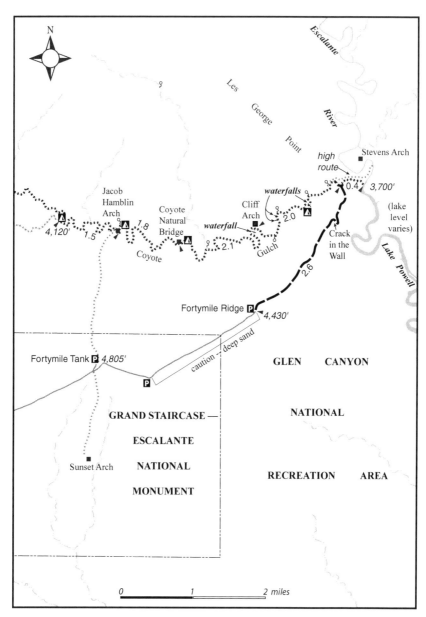

4.3 Coyote Gulch and the Escalante River Country (East)

numerous on sandy benches, with shade from the canyon walls and both cottonwood and boxelder trees. The canyon continues to get deeper and more spectacular the farther you go downstream.

At 5.9 miles, large Hurricane Wash angles in from the right (southwest), and the relative peace and solitude you enjoyed in the upper canyon ends, as many visitors enter the canyon via this route, evidenced by several well-established camps near this junction.

From this point on, the scenery is dominated by towering (and sometimes overhanging) amphitheaters, which grace almost every turn in the creek, and by sheer cliffs rising 300 feet or more. All of the rock is extremely colorful, with reddish orange being the dominant hue, streaked, as always, with black "desert varnish." The scenery is almost enough to distract you from the fact that walking in the creek is generally your only option now. Resign yourself to wet feet, along with a sore neck from craning up at the canyon walls.

About 1.5 miles below Hurricane Wash, an enormous fin of sandstone juts out from the north wall, forcing a wide meander in the canyon. The fin has a huge opening, creating the massive formation known as Jacob Hamblin Arch. Well-used campsites are plentiful here. The best water is from several reliably flowing springs located a little below the arch. To accommodate the high number of campers, a composting toilet was installed on the right (south) side of the canyon, about 150 yards below Jacob Hamblin Arch.

A little over 1 mile past Jacob Hamblin Arch, the creek slides over a short cascade, which sounds more impressive from a distance than it looks up close. You then wade through a little narrows and, about 0.5 mile later, follow the creek directly under Coyote Natural Bridge. The opening beneath this impressive feature is at least 25 feet high, and the photo opportunities of your hiking partners walking beneath the bridge are excellent. Just below the natural bridge, the canyon widens a bit, allowing room for several more excellent campsites.

The overwhelming canyon scenery and colorful sandstone walls remain a welcome constant as you continue downstream. About 2 miles from Coyote Natural Bridge is a boulder jam and the first of the canyon's four waterfalls. Bypass this boulder jam via a steep scramble route heading up and over a rocky area on the left (north) side of the canyon. **Tip:** After working your way around this obstacle and dropping back down to creek level at the base of the 15-foot falls, be sure to look up to the left for a good view of Cliff Arch, which juts out from the north canyon wall.

About 0.5 mile past the first waterfall, you must scramble along the canyon's right (south) wall to bypass the next two waterfalls. These two falls are only about 100 yards apart, and as you hike past them, you'll enjoy good looks down onto these short but attractive waterfalls. **Warning:** Getting back down to creek level after you pass these falls is a bit tricky, involving a steep slide down slickrock and some moderately challenging scrambling. This short section may be uncomfortable for hikers with a fear of heights.

Hikers at Coyote Natural Bridge

Just below the two waterfalls, you pass a couple of showering springs, and then walk another 0.2 mile to a building with a composting toilet visible well above the creek on the left (north). This toilet sits on the opposite side of the canyon from an excellent campsite under an overhanging ledge. Immediately below this camp is the canyon's fourth and final waterfall, a sliding cascade that tumbles down a slickrock slope. You circumvent this feature with an easy scramble down the right side of the waterfall. Below here, the canyon twists and narrows for the next 0.4 mile, allowing you no choice but to spend almost the entire distance wading in the creek. The scenery is very impressive in this lower section of the canyon, as the walls tower more than 600 feet above the floor.

Once the canyon straightens out and widens a bit, you pass a pair of small springs near the start of the easy-to-miss and rarely used "high route" to the Escalante River. Stick with the main canyon, which just past the springs heads around a final short bend to the north (left) before depositing you at the start of a large boulder jam. Conveniently, a trail bypasses this obstacle on the right. After less than 0.1 mile, this bypass trail intersects the usually unsigned path that comes down a sandy slope from Fortymile Ridge (see description below).

To continue to the mouth of Coyote Gulch, keep left at the junction and soon come to a potentially difficult slickrock traverse with a fair amount of exposure. At the end of this traverse, you must descend a short but rather scary pole "ladder" to go over a small overhang and return to the creek. Anyone who is afraid of heights should not attempt this section. The final 0.2 mile is a simple wade down the creek to the Escalante River.

Most of the time, the Escalante River at the mouth of Coyote Gulch is a flowing stream between thigh and waist deep. Hikers heading up the canyon for additional destinations simply turn left (upstream) and start the long but scenic trek up the river. On those rare occasions when Lake Powell is completely full, however, the mouth of Coyote Gulch may be under the reservoir's water. During these periods, hikers wanting to go up the Escalante River must backtrack up Coyote Gulch to a point just below the two springs that you passed after the narrow, twisting section below the fourth waterfall. Here you should look for cairns marking a high route that follows a sloping ledge on the north wall of Coyote Gulch. After almost 1.2 poorly marked miles, you drop down a small ravine to reach the Escalante River, not far below enormous Stevens Arch.

Access route via Fortymile Ridge: If you are doing a one-way car-shuttle hike and started your trip from the end of Fortymile Ridge Road, then you will reach the mouth of Coyote Gulch via a different path. From that trailhead, an obvious trail goes initially downhill, heading northeast across deep and tiring sand for about 1 mile. The trail then leaves the sand and follows cairns across a wonderland of potholes and desert slickrock for 0.8 mile to the lip of the Escalante River Canyon. From here, there are absolutely spectacular views looking north to the lower reaches of Coyote Gulch, the twisting Escalante River Canyon, and huge Stevens Arch (the largest span in the Escalante region).

View from above Crack in the Wall

To reach the bottom of Coyote Gulch, make your way a short distance to the right along the lip of the drop-off to the last cairn. From here, look directly beneath you and to the left to find a feature called Crack in the Wall. This is a ridiculously narrow (as little as 1 foot wide) slot that nature has carved into the top of the canyon wall. Hikers must crawl or walk down this slot for almost 75 yards, usually pulling their packs behind them or holding them overhead, because there just isn't room for both hiker and pack at the same time. At a point about 50 yards down the crack, you must negotiate a steep and sliding 20-foot drop-off, where many hikers prefer to lower their packs with ropes before going down themselves. Finally, you emerge at the top of a long, partially vegetated slope of deep sand. From there, walking down the slope is a simple matter, losing almost 600 feet on the way to a small saddle between two enormous sandstone towers. The final section of trail is down a second, shorter sand slide to the previously mentioned junction with the path coming down Coyote Gulch.

Note: Climbing up the sand slope from the bottom of Coyote Gulch is extremely tiring. In addition, getting down Crack in the Wall is both easier and somewhat safer than trying to go up, so for both of those reasons, hikers who choose to do this trip as a one-way trip should start at Fortymile Ridge and end at Red Well, not the other way around.

Possible Itinerary

Day	Camps and Side Trips	Distance (mi.)	Elevation (ft.)
1	Red Well TH to Coyote Bridge	9.2	+100/–600
2	Day hike to mouth of Coyote Gulch	9.0	+700/–700
3	Out to Red Well TH	9.2	+600/–100

Alternates: Since all the other backpacking possibilities in this magnificent region are less heavily traveled than Coyote Gulch (usually much less heavily traveled), your chances for solitude on any of the following trips are excellent.

A few of the better backpacking options, which are less technically demanding and have more or less decent road access, include the following: *Harris Wash*—a 20.5-mile round-trip out-and-back hike down a beautiful canyon with a permanent creek for water. From the end of the wash, you have relatively easy access to a side trip up equally beautiful (but dry) Silver Falls Canyon on the other side of Escalante River. *Egypt Loop*—a 20-mile loop hike, starting from the Egypt trailhead, that goes down the steep defile of Fence Canyon, then follows the main Escalante River downstream for 5.6 miles, before going up Twentyfive Mile Wash to a cross-country return over open desert to the trailhead. *Coyote Gulch–Harris Wash Traverse*—a magnificent 71-mile car-shuttle adventure connecting Coyote Gulch and Harris Wash with a rarely hiked 46-mile section of the dramatic main canyon of Escalante River. This trip, recommended only for experienced backpackers, involves some bushwhacking and countless knee- to waist-deep river crossings. *Boulder Mail Trail*—a fascinating and wildly scenic 16-mile one-way hike that follows a historical route once used to deliver mail and supplies across the slickrock and canyon country between the towns of Escalante and Boulder. A car shuttle is required (nearly all on paved roads) and good route-finding skills are a must, but the scenery is terrific.

With a copy of the Trails Illustrated *Canyons of the Escalante* map, you can easily find dozens of additional places well worth exploring. No matter how much time you spend amid these canyons, I guarantee it will be worth the extra vacation days.

Green Tips: Southern Utah Wilderness Alliance—www.suwa.org

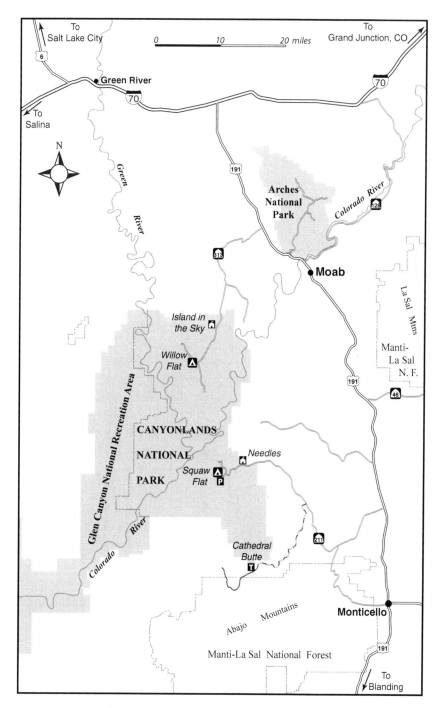

5.1 Salt Creek Canyon and Chesler Park Traverse Location

Canyonlands National Park

Salt Creek Canyon
and Chesler Park Traverse

The most weird, wonderful, magical place on earth—
there is nothing else like it anywhere.

—Edward Abbey, describing Canyonlands

As stated by the great environmentalist and author Edward Abbey, Canyonlands National Park is a unique and fascinating place. The park truly is a wonderland of rock. The area teems with remarkably colorful rock formations, spectacular arches, dozens of old Anasazi ruins and rock art sites, dramatically beautiful canyons, and views that seemingly extend forever. Even if you are a backpacker with thousands of miles on your well-worn boots, you likely will find very little in your previous experience that compares with the remarkably scenic and fascinating landscape found within the park.

Even so, backpacking in Canyonlands is not for everyone. The biggest obstacles are the heat, which can be debilitating in summer, and water, or more accurately, the lack thereof. Except in Salt Creek Canyon, where water is usually available, you may have to carry all the water you will need on your back (a minimum of a gallon per day in this dry climate). Quite possibly, depending on the time of year and recent precipitation, you may need to purify and carry as much as a *three-day supply* of water when you leave Salt Creek Canyon. Consequently, your pack will be awfully heavy—something to keep in mind, especially since many of the trails are steep and technically demanding, traversing slickrock while fully exposed to the searing desert sun.

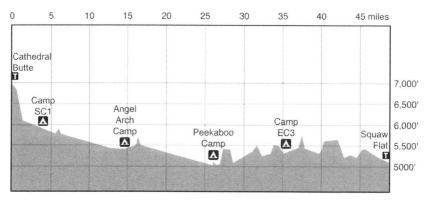

Salt Creek Canyon and Chesler Park Traverse

Such warnings are not meant as discouragement. Experienced backpackers will have a blast hiking over the slickrock, climbing up and down little ladders, crawling through slot canyons, squeezing through holes in the rock, and generally enjoying the sometimes challenging but always scenic topography. By timing a trip for spring or fall (the so-called shoulder seasons), most of the heat can be avoided. Especially in the spring, water may also be easier to locate, thus keeping backpacks at a more reasonable weight. So be prepared for the rigors of the desert, but also be prepared for its many wonders: dramatic sandstone scenery, fascinating geology, Native American history, impressive arches, nights *full* of stars, and so much more—an experience not soon forgotten.

Days:	4–7
Distance:	48.9 miles (including all recommended side trips)
Type:	Shuttle (shuttle service available)
Scenery:	8
Solitude:	4
Technical Difficulty:	8
Physical Difficulty:	7
Elevation Gain/Loss:	+3,900'/–5,700' (including side trips)
Season:	March to November
	Best: Late March to early June, September through October
Maps:	Trails Illustrated—*Canyonlands National Park*
Resources:	*Desert Solitaire*, by Edward Abbey; *Canyonlands National Park, Favorite Jeep Roads and Hiking Trails*, by David Day

Contacts:

- Canyonlands National Park
  2282 SW Resource Blvd., Moab, UT 84532
  435-259-4351 (backcountry information)
  435-719-2313 (general visitor information)
  www.nps.gov/cany

Permits: Overnight permits are required and limited in number. Permits are available either on a first-come, first-served basis up to twenty-four hours in advance of your trip, or by advance reservation (fee). The reservation fee is nonrefundable and as of 2013 was $30. During the popular spring and fall seasons, getting a reservation is highly recommended.

Regulations: For the area of the recommended trip, backcountry camping is restricted to specific designated sites, except for the Salt/Horse at-large back-packing zone (in lower Salt Creek Canyon), where you can camp anywhere as long as you follow the general park guidelines on no-trace camping.

Pets are not permitted on trails or anywhere in the park's backcountry. Never step off trail onto the fragile cryptobiotic desert soils, which are full of life and very easily damaged.

Entering, defacing, or in any way damaging any Native American ruins, rock art sites, old cowboy camps, or other archaeological and historical sites in the park is strictly prohibited.

Nearest Campgrounds:

- Squaw Flat Campground—at the exit trailhead

Nearest Airports:

- Grand Junction Regional Airport (GJT)—175 miles

Nearest Outdoor Retailers:

- REI—174 miles
  644 North Ave., Grand Junction, CO 81501
  970-254-8970
- Canyonlands Outdoor Sports—58 miles
  446 S. Main St., Moab, UT 84532
  435-259-5699
- Pagan Mountaineering—58 miles
  59 S. Main St., Ste. 2, Moab, UT 84532
  435-259-1117

Outfitters: Consult the park's website for more information: www.nps.gov/cany.

Transportation Logistics: No public transportation leads to these trailheads, so you'll need at least one car. There are numerous shuttle companies in Moab, but most cater to rafters and mountain bikers and won't drive the rough road to the starting trailhead near Cathedral Butte. Coyote Shuttle does provide this service (435-260-2097). As of 2014, the cost was $250 for up to four people, with a charge of $25 for each additional member of your group.

The road to the northern trailhead is paved, but the southern trailhead requires travel on a fairly rough gravel and dirt road, which may require four-wheel drive after heavy rain or snow.

Backcountry Logistics: (B, H, H2O, L, R, Su) The most difficult part of hiking in Canyonlands is the potentially dangerous effects of the sun and heat. Summer high temperatures average around 100°F, and the sun can be relentless. With good reason, most backpackers avoid the park from about mid-June through early September. Even in the more comfortable spring and fall seasons, the temperatures can sometimes be quite oppressive, and water may be scarce, especially in the fall. Always wear a hat, use SPF 15 or greater sunscreen, and wear long-sleeve shirts to protect against the sun's rays. Carry, and drink, *a lot* more water than you think you will need, and certainly a lot more than you usually drink when hiking in wetter environments. A minimum of one gallon per person per day is the usual standard. Fortunately, water is usually available year-round in Salt Creek Canyon, although it must be treated before drinking. Water is *not* available in Chesler Park, however, and the all-important liquid is only intermittently found in Lost, Squaw, and Elephant Canyons. Usually you can find water in at least some of these canyons in the spring, but not in the fall. Even in the spring, most campsites do not have water nearby. Carry all you will need, including enough to make a dry camp.

The trails between Peekaboo Camp and Chesler Park traverse steep and sloping slickrock, including a few rather scary ladders and some tricky scrambling. When wet slickrock really lives up to its name, particular caution is required to safely traverse the often-slippery surface. For experienced hikers, this can all be great fun. Novice hikers and anyone especially afraid of heights, however, should not attempt these trails.

Although snakebites are relatively rare in Canyonlands, rattlesnakes are present. Hikers are advised to watch their step and check the area carefully before sitting down to rest. Also avoid walking around at night without wearing your boots.

Even though Salt Creek Canyon is desert country, which is not usually considered good habitat for black bears, the animals have recently made their way down into the canyon from the nearby Abajo Mountains. The bears may be found here at any time of year but are especially common in the fall, when attracted to the tasty fruit of the prickly pear cactus. The bruins are a potential threat to your food supply, so backpackers in Salt Creek Canyon should either use the bear boxes provided at certain designated campsites or hang food at night from a tree limb at least 7 feet off the ground.

Amenities and Attractions: In the last few decades, Moab, Utah, has transformed itself from a tiny and rather sleepy little mining and ranching community into a bustling tourist-oriented town catering to "adventure sports" enthusiasts. The place is overrun with people who come to visit the nearby national parks, rock climb, take river trips, hike, enjoy jeep tours, and, most of all, mountain bike. Catering to all these adventure-oriented people is a wide array of motels, fast-food joints, bike shops, and gift stores. As with most tourist towns, the prices charged for these amenities tend to put off many of the bare-bones backpacker types.

If you prefer natural attractions, then hightail out of crowded Moab and head for the many superb outdoor attractions nearby. Don't miss **Arches National Park**, with its numerous excellent day hikes to a dozen or more photogenic arches. Unfortunately, the park has little to offer backpackers. **Dead Horse Point State Park** is another not-to-be-missed spot, with an amazing view of the twisting Colorado River Canyon and surrounding deserts. While there, be sure to continue farther south on paved roads into the Island in the Sky district of Canyonlands National Park, where the top attraction is the dramatic and accurately named **Grand View Point**. Wonderful hiking trails, mountain bike routes, and jeep roads head off from there to myriad destinations in all directions.

For an outstandingly scenic drive that also takes you past some excellent rock-climbing and hiking locations, take State Highway 128 north and east from Moab along the Colorado River. The drive also allows you to visit the impressive **Fisher Towers**.

To escape the desert heat, drive up into the nearby **La Sal** or **Abajo Mountains**, where some of the summits reach over 12,000 feet. Both ranges offer shady forests, attractive meadows, and some very pleasant hiking trails.

Directions to Trailhead: From Moab, drive 39.5 miles south on US 191 to a junction with State Highway 211. Turn right (west), following signs to Canyonlands National Park, and proceed 20.8 miles to a junction with gravel Beef Basin Road. This road is signed BEEF BASIN & ELK MOUNTAIN, and there is a BLM parking area at the turnoff.

To pick up your permit and leave a car at the recommended ending point, go straight at the junction, still on the paved highway, and drive 14.2 miles to the entrance station for Canyonlands National Park. After another 0.3 mile, you will reach the Needles Visitor Center, where you can stop to pick up your (preferably reserved) backcountry permit. From the visitor center turnoff, continue driving for 0.6 mile, go straight at a junction, and then drive 2.1 miles to a second junction. Turn left, following signs to CAMPGROUND, proceed 0.3 mile, and then turn left once again, this time heading toward Squaw Flat Campground A. Proceed 0.8 mile through the campground and park on the left at the well-signed trailhead.

To reach the recommended starting point for the hike, return to the junction with Beef Basin Road and turn west. After only 0.5 mile the gravel road fords Indian Creek: simple enough when the water is low, but impossible when recent rains flood the creek. Beyond Indian Creek the road gets progressively rougher, with ruts and some rocks. The road is usually fine for most cars with decent clearance when dry, but four-wheel drive may be required after significant rainfall. Go straight ahead, past an unsigned road going left, 9.5 miles from Highway 211, and then continue another 8.2 miles to the unsigned but obvious parking area on the right for the Cathedral Butte trailhead. There are usually other cars here, but even if not, the trailhead is easy to recognize, with a location shortly past prominent Cathedral Butte and right on the lip of the obvious drop-off for Salt Creek Canyon. There are excellent views of the canyon and Cathedral Butte from the trailhead.

The Timeless Landscape of Canyonlands National Park As Einstein famously stated, time is relative. And although he was not speaking specifically about Canyonlands, he might as well have been, as this is a landscape both unimaginably old and remarkably young at the same time.

Canyonlands National Park has been described as a wilderness of exposed and naked rock—which sounds vaguely naughty. Those exposed rocks vividly display a geologic record going back several hundred million years. To trained geologists, the rocks show dramatic evidence of different periods when the landscape was covered with ocean, tropical rain-forest, or parched inland desert. They can see where ancient sand dunes and layer upon layer of sediment laid down by long-gone lakes and seas have solidified into the sandstones and shales that dominate the land-scape of today. They can calmly describe the processes by which uplifts and faulting have contorted the land and how water, ice, and even wind have slowly eroded away the rock into canyons, needles, joints, grabens, arches, and myriad other features.

But most of us lack the geologist's training and dispassionate scientific viewpoint, so when we look at the oddly contorted pinnacles and arches and the bizarrely colored rocks that are the legacy of those millions of years of buildup and erosion, we see an unreal Dr. Seuss–like terrain. Such was the case for the first explorers of the area, who left maps full of fanciful place names like the Dollhouse, Paul Bunyan's Potty, Druid Arch, Monster Tower, Chocolate Drops, Cleopatra's Chair, and Zeus Rock.

What makes this timeless land seem so young is that those "early" explorers were here so recently. After all, this is a place where major and prominent features, such as Druid Arch and the Maze, were not discovered, or at least named, until the 1950s or 1960s. The vast Colorado Plateau was the last significant part of the lower forty-eight United States to be explored by European Americans. Even as recently as the 1950s, when efforts began to protect this landscape, only a few lonely cowboys and intrepid miners had set foot on much of the land. But despite the area's remoteness, the efforts to protect this unique landscape came just in the nick of time.

As with so many of the now-iconic national parks in our country, the preservation efforts at Canyonlands were led by just a handful of important individuals who saw beauty and value in wilderness that others envisioned as only a place to settle, a pasture for cattle, a source of profitable minerals, a site for a dam, or simply a dry wasteland. At Canyonlands, the two visionaries who deserve the lion's share of the credit for the park's creation are Bates Wilson and Stewart Udall.

From 1949 to 1972 Bates Wilson served as superintendent of Arches National Monument (now a national park), which is only about 16 miles as the golden eagle flies northeast of the current boundaries of Canyonlands National Park. His first view of Canyonlands came from an airplane in the spring of 1949, shortly after he arrived in Utah, and his infatuation with the region took hold shortly thereafter. He explored much of the area with his family and friends. He spearheaded efforts to have the region's abundant archaeological sites cataloged and researched, and he lobbied the Park Service to do an official investigation of the area as a potential national park. Most significantly, he led government officials and others on tours of the region, featuring lengthy talks over campfires and hearty dinners.

Stewart Udall, who eventually earned something close to legendary status in conservation circles, served as secretary of the interior from 1961 to 1969. Like Wilson, Udall had initially seen Canyonlands from the air, as he flew to a conference of park superintendents at Grand Canyon National Park in early 1961. At that time, the Bureau of Reclamation had plans for building a huge dam just downstream from the confluence of the Green and Colorado Rivers. In addition, this was during the cold war, and Canyonlands was near the center of the uranium boom, which peaked in the 1950s. Miners built a web of jeep roads across the landscape as they searched for the suddenly important mineral. But where others envisioned a dam or a mine, Udall saw the makings of a new national park. At the conference he met Bates Wilson and spoke with him about the Canyonlands area. Then in July 1961 Udall joined Wilson on one of his tours of Canyonlands.

Initially, Wilson and others had pushed for a much smaller park, encompassing some 32,000 acres around the spectacular Needles region. But park planners and Secretary Udall saw things on a bigger scale, and they soon advocated for a huge 1 million-acre park. After much heated debate and input from other interested parties, Congress eventually created Canyonlands National Park on September 12, 1964. Including additions made in 1971, Canyonland's size is now 337,598 acres, the largest park in Utah.

Time is fickle, so we cannot know what this place we call Canyonlands National Park will look like in another thousand years, let alone hundreds of thousands, or hundreds of millions—unimaginably long time frames to us, but nothing to the rocks. At least for the time being, thanks to the efforts of men like Bates Wilson and Stewart Udall, this land will remain relatively untouched and protected from the short-term but sometimes devastating effects of our modern society.

Trip Description: The trail begins next to a large signboard on the west side of the parking area.

The climate at this elevation is cooler and a little wetter than you will experience for most of the trip, amid relatively dense woodland of Rocky Mountain junipers and pinyon pines. After less than 100 yards, the trail begins a long descent into the drier and warmer regions of the park, with a steep and winding downhill on very rocky tread. After about 0.5 mile, the grade levels off on a rolling benchland for 0.2 mile, before the descent resumes on steep and rocky tread. This time the steepness lasts for only about 0.2 mile before you drop at a much gentler grade beside a usually dry gully. At the bottom, where the gully meets the main stem of East Fork Salt Creek (usually waterless at this point), is an unsigned and easy-to-miss junction with a rarely used trail on the left.

Remaining on the main trail, walk down the sandy streambed of East Fork Salt Creek. After about 100 yards, the trail climbs out of the gully near a sign marking your entry into Canyonlands National Park. Heading north-northwest, the route is now remarkably level across a treeless expanse covered with grasses, tumbleweeds, prickly pear cacti, and sagebrush in the wide upper reaches of Salt Creek Canyon. Coyote and deer tracks mark the presence of wildlife in the area. The scenery features almost continuously fine views of the rounded, distant, and colorful canyon walls.

A little over a mile after you enter the park, you go back down into the sandy gully for a short distance, then return to the brush-covered benchland for 0.2 mile before reaching the southern edge of a large marsh. During our last reconnaissance, the trail effectively disappeared here amid a tangle of reeds, willows, grasses, and other marsh vegetation. The best course was to go around the marsh on either the right or left side, either direction involving about 0.4 mile of difficult bushwhacking through sage and other tough shrubs until the official tread reappeared near the canyon walls on the northeast side of the marsh. Recently, the Park Service was considering rerouting the trail to go around the marsh, so conditions may be considerably different (and, we hope, better).

Emerge from the marsh at a pretty little sliding waterfall fed by the springs in the marsh. Below this point, Salt Creek usually flows all year. About 0.15 mile past the waterfall is historic Kirk's Cabin, an old cowboy cabin that was built more than one hundred years ago, complete with a chimney and most of the roof. The remains of an old wagon are also nearby.

About 100 yards past Kirk's Cabin, a short side trail on the right leads to Camps SC1 and SC2. The main trail continues straight ahead, soon passing through a dilapidated fence. About 0.4 mile later, you come within 100 yards of the canyon's first Anasazi ruins on the right. Watch carefully, as the ruins are easily missed; they are definitely worth checking out if only for the contrast with Kirk's Cabin. At more than a century old, the cabin is holding up quite impressively. But the condition of the Anasazi ruins are nearly as good after well over *seven hundred* years. If you look to the west from the area of the ruins, you'll see huge Kirk's Arch standing majestically on the skyline. The large rocky span is more than a mile away, and there is no reasonable way to get close, but even from this distance, the sight is impressive.

Just beyond the ruins, you go around a rock formation and then come to the wide opening of Big Pocket on your right. With extra time, exploring this scenic side canyon can be fun, as you may find at least three more small ruins tucked away in isolated alcoves in the canyon walls.

North of Big Pocket, the main canyon of Salt Creek grows progressively narrow, but for the next several miles, it remains fairly wide. This middle section is arguably the most scenic part of the canyon and certainly the most interesting, with the highest concentration of Anasazi ruins and rock art to admire. On the downside, the wide and flat floor of the canyon is carpeted with tough sagebrush bushes and sticker-covered tumbleweeds, which must be hiked through or pushed aside. Wear long pants to avoid giving your legs a real beating.

Shortly after you pass the north wall of the Big Pocket side canyon, the trail takes you a little to the right (east) of a prominent balancing rock. Immediately past this rock look for an unsigned boot trail heading left (west).

Back on the main trail, about 0.4 mile north of the Big Ruins turnoff, look to your right for the beautifully shaped span of Wedding Ring Arch, which sits on the canyon wall about 160 yards east of the trail. A little after the trail

Side Trip to Big Ruins: The 0.4-mile route to the left leads to a view of Big Ruins, the largest and most impressive Anasazi site in Salt Creek Canyon. The faint but reasonably good trail to this viewpoint is well worth the time for marveling at the more than twenty stone buildings tucked precariously into a ledge high on a cliff face. Morning is the best time to view these east-facing ruins, when they're in the sun. There is no safe (or legal) way to get close to the ruins, which are at least 150 feet up a sheer cliff without ladders, so bring binoculars and take your photos from a respectful distance.

passes to the north of this arch, an unsigned 0.1-mile side trail leads back to a good photo spot beneath this lovely landmark.

As you hike north from Wedding Ring Arch, Fisheye Arch comes into view high on the east (right) skyline. Although the trail remains a good distance away, the arch is still a prominent landmark visible from several points along the way. At a fairly sharp right turn in the trail, about twenty minutes north of Wedding Ring Arch and almost directly west of Fisheye Arch, look for a little alcove 120 yards west (left) of the trail, where there is a small, ground-level Anasazi ruin. A short spur trail leads to this site, which is well worth a quick detour to investigate. If hiking in the fall, you may find small ripe squash here, hardy ancestors of the plants that Native Americans cultivated more than seven hundred years ago. (That's over seven centuries of surviving droughts, foraging animals, trampling humans, and floods, among countless other hazards. So how come my garden vegetables die so easily?)

About 0.7 mile north of these ruins, the trail once again approaches the eastern wall of the canyon. Here you will see a small cave a little above the trail on the right. In this cave there is another small ruin. More importantly, this cave contains a large pictograph, about 6 feet tall, depicting an armless fellow gaudily painted in red, white, and blue, thus leading to his being named the All American Man. The Park Service forbids entry into the cave, a tricky climb to reach anyway, which makes the rock art difficult to photograph without a telephoto lens.

Not quite 0.1 mile past the All American Man, the trail makes a short but very steep climb through a narrow notch in a fin of sandstone projecting from the east wall of the canyon. The view from the little pass at the top of the climb is worth the effort, with especially good vistas to the north of numerous colorful rock walls that surround the gradually narrowing canyon. After descending from the little pass, the trail crosses flat terrain for 0.7 mile before coming very close to another fascinating site. About 30 yards to your right, in a small ground-level alcove, are several old Anasazi ruins and the conspicuous pictograph given the appropriately descriptive name of the Four Faces. The style of this well-preserved pictograph suggests that it was painted not by the Anasazi (who built the ruins), but by the later Fremont people.

Soon after you depart from the Four Faces site, you cross Salt Creek and walk another 0.2 mile to the junction with the signed spur trail to Camp SC3. The camp is quite comfortable and a fine place for a night in the wilderness, even though it's located a long way from the nearest water. About 0.5 mile beyond this camp is the hike's next major landmark, Upper Jump, a beautiful

Angel Arch

little stair-step waterfall on Salt Creek tumbling about 25 feet down into a deep pool. The dramatic scenery includes colorful canyon walls and towering pinnacles, which helps to make this an ideal lunch stop.

Beyond Upper Jump, the canyon becomes much narrower and wetter, with tall canyon walls and thick riparian vegetation of willows, cottonwoods, and reeds crowding the area alongside the creek. Unfortunately, there are also lots of tamarisks, a nonnative invasive species that the Park Service is having a difficult time controlling. The narrowness of the canyon forces you to make repeated, easy hops over Salt Creek, but only rarely do your feet get wet. The route alternates between the dry benchland covered with juniper trees, tall sagebrush, and rabbitbrush above the creek, and the much denser vegetation you need to fight through near the water. Shrubs and grasses occasionally obscure the correct route, but you can't go too far wrong by simply continuing downstream. The scenery remains excellent throughout, as the route faithfully follows the canyon's wild twists and turns. About 2 miles past Upper Jump, just as you climb out of an extended section down by the creek, look up to the walls ahead to see another large group of Anasazi ruins. The ruins are located about 100 feet up from the trail, on the east wall of the canyon, and include more than a dozen homes and granaries (places where squash, beans, and other food was stored). Scrambling closer to some of the ruins is possible, but, as always, do not enter the ruins or in any way disturb the site.

About 0.5 mile past the ruins is the turnoff to Camp SC4, located on a small bench above the east side of the creek, beneath a stand of tall Fremont cottonwoods. The camp features nice views of the nearby colorful cliffs and pinnacles and has bear boxes. Almost 2.5 miles, and several twists and turns, north of Camp SC4 is the signed junction with Angel Arch Trail, which goes to the right. There are Anasazi ruins in this vicinity (on the north wall of the canyon up to Angel Arch and on the west side of Salt Creek Canyon opposite the trail junction), but these are small and hard to find. If you're looking for a nearby place to spend the night before making the side trip to Angel Arch, then continue straight on the Salt Creek Trail for almost 0.1 mile to large and very comfortable Angel Arch Camp. This camp, and, for that matter, the entire canyon from the Angel Arch Trail junction north to just before Peekaboo Spring, is in the Salt/Horse at-large backpacking zone. Within this zone, you are allowed to camp anywhere (there are no designated campsites) as long as you follow the general no-trace guidelines of camping well away from both the creek and the trail and setting up your tent on sand, rock, or hard soils that have been camped on previously.

Side Trip to Angel Arch: Angel Arch is one of the most spectacular sites in Canyonlands National Park. To visit this natural wonder, turn east at the trail junction and walk up the wide and scenic side canyon, with an intermittent trickle of water and colorful canyon walls. The sometimes indistinct path generally follows an old jeep road, but nature has done such a fine job of reclaiming this human scar that traces of the former road are now hard to find. After 1.5 miles you follow a narrower path that goes up a rocky slope to the right (west), climbing 0.2 mile to a viewpoint below Angel Arch. This absolutely enormous arch (the park's largest), sitting high on the skyline as it catches the morning sun, is truly a sight to behold, so plan to stay awhile to savor this magnificent scene. A rough and difficult scramble route goes up to the base of the arch but is very steep and requires some mildly difficult rock scrambling. Only attempt this route if you are experienced and comfortable with this type of travel.

After returning to Salt Creek, you walk north past Angel Arch Camp and soon return to the pattern of crossing and recrossing the meandering creek. There is plenty of flat ground where you could camp, but only a few places where previous hikers have camped so regularly that the spots are obvious choices for setting up your tent. The tread is often obscure, but cairns assist you with navigation, and the creek and tall canyon walls provide more than enough guidance to ensure that getting lost is next to impossible. Not very long ago, the tread was not at all obscure; until 1998 you could drive a jeep road all the way up Salt Creek Canyon to Angel Arch. After a legal decision forced the closure of the road, the land has rapidly recovered; today only short sections of the trail are recognizable as a former vehicle route. The road closure has also led to a greater abundance of streamside vegetation and a significant increase in the amount of wildlife in the canyon, especially black bears. In addition, the water in Salt Creek has gone from quite silty when the road was open to generally clear.

The landscape remains essentially unchanged for several miles as you walk past numerous picturesque spots, where the creek and a tangle of riparian vegetation provide lovely foregrounds for the towering canyon walls, which are often streaked with dark slashes of "desert varnish." Unlike the middle portions of the canyon, this lower section does not include any easily viewed ruins or rock art sites, but the scenery remains excellent throughout. The first significant landmark is a little over 1 mile below Angel Arch Camp, where you should notice Crescent Arch near the top of the eastern wall of the canyon. Another landmark comes at a sharp turn in the canyon about 6.8 miles below Angel Arch Camp, where you will see an unnamed arch high on the west canyon rim. Another 1.4 miles past the second arch, and partway through a sharp eastward turn in the canyon, look up and to the left to see a hole in the sandstone wall of the canyon about 60 feet above the creek. An obvious foot trail climbs up to this hole, named Peekaboo Window. Hiking up to and then through this feature will save you about 0.4 mile of walking around a particularly long meander in the canyon.

Immediately on the other side of Peekaboo Window is a fascinating pictograph site, complete with an interpretive sign discussing the significance of the art. The most obvious art is of some round shield-like features painted in white. There is also a long, curving line of white splotches painted just above the shields. This art is from the Ancestral Puebloans, dated at up to one thousand years old. Perhaps more interesting is some rather faint reddish artwork of animals, human shapes, handprints, and other figures beneath the white art. These images were painted by the Archaic People and are believed to be between three thousand and five thousand years old.

A trail goes about 120 yards to the right and downhill from the rock art site to Peekaboo Camp, which sits at the end of the sandy and rugged Salt Creek jeep road. Peekaboo Spring is nearby, and there is a restroom building at this site but not much else in the way of amenities.

The trail will soon leave Salt Creek Canyon, so be sure to drink your fill and stock up on water here. Depending on the time of year and any recent precipitation, this may be your last reliable water source for the rest of the trip. If so, you will need to carry almost *three gallons* per person to finish the recommended trip—ugh! In the spring you will probably be able to find water in Lost Canyon and Squaw Canyon, which will make life somewhat easier. Be sure to ask at the ranger station when you pick up your permit for the latest information on water sources.

To continue your trip, take the trail heading left (northwest) from the rock art site and follow this path as it curves to the north on a dry, cactus-studded bench well above Salt Creek. After about 0.3 mile, the character of the trail abruptly changes where the route makes a sharp left turn, going uphill and away from the creek into a little rocky crevasse. This is the start of an extended 2-mile section where virtually the entire distance is over rock. The route requires a bit of athleticism and good balance, but the scenery is terrific.

The trail's initial goal is the colorful slickrock benches and ridges well above Salt Creek Canyon. To reach that target, the trail takes you up a long metal ladder tucked tightly into a very narrow rocky chute. There isn't even

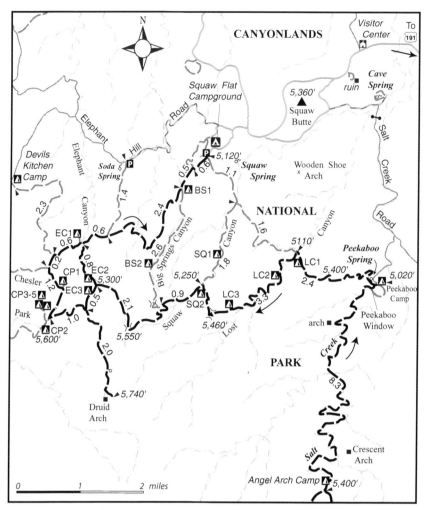

5.2 Salt Creek Canyon and Chesler Park Traverse (North)

enough room to turn around in this chute, so this is no place for hikers with claustrophobia. Once above the ladder, the circuitous trail climbs steeply over the slickrock, as numerous small cairns mark the route. The steep climbing ends on top of a sandstone ridge with terrific views, not only of the colorful cliffs, humps, and ridges of the rock formations close at hand, but also to the east of the distinctive spire of North Sixshooter Peak, about 6 miles away. The snow-covered peaks about 35 miles to the northeast are the La Sal Mountains.

The trail's course now generally stays level, although with many small ups and downs, following the sloping slickrock around a wildly scenic amphitheater, beneath tall cliffs, pinnacles, and hulking peaks of multicolored

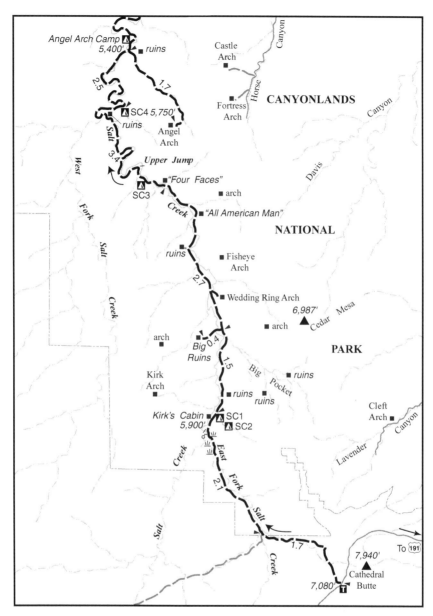

Angel Arch Camp 5,400'
ruins

Castle Arch

CANYON

2.5

1.7

Fortress Arch

CANYONLANDS

Horse

Canyon

SC4 5,750'
ruins

Angel Arch

Salt

West

3.4

Upper Jump

Davis

"Four Faces"

SC3

arch

Creek

"All American Man"

NATIONAL

Fork

Salt

ruins

Fisheye Arch

2.7

Creek

Wedding Ring Arch

6,987'

Cedar

Mesa

arch

arch

Big
Ruins

0.4

PARK

1.5

Kirk
Arch

Big

ruins

Pocket

ruins

Cleft
Arch

Kirk's Cabin
5,900'

SC1

ruins

SC2

Canyon

Lavender

Creek

East

Fork

2.1

Salt

Salt

Creek

1.7

To 191

7,940'

Cathedral
Butte

7,080'

5.3 Salt Creek Canyon and Chesler Park Traverse (South)

sandstone. The route stays high, which allows for continuous views of the surrounding desert and down into the twisting canyons of small seasonal creeks well below. About 0.8 mile from where you first climbed onto the rock, the trail goes out a side ridge, where you must squeeze through a good-sized hole in the sandstone to reach the next trail section. You then contour around a second dramatic stone amphitheater before going over another side ridge and finally (carefully) making your way down the steep slickrock to the desert floor. This wildly scenic and challenging section ends with a short walk on a dirt trail to the signed turnoff to Camp LC1 on your left. Continue straight ahead and walk another 0.1 mile to a junction in the sandy bottom of Lost Canyon.

Turn left onto the Lost Canyon Trail and follow the bottom of this very sandy and twisting canyon upstream. The canyon is usually dry, but a few pools of water may linger after a heavy rain. During and shortly after large summer thunderstorms, you should beware of flash flooding in this canyon. At 0.8 mile up the canyon is the signed junction with the spur trail that goes right to Camp LC2, a pleasant spot amid huge boulders and a few juniper and pinyon pine trees. This camp is tucked beneath a tall rock formation that provides welcome shade in the late afternoon. **Tip:** In the main stem of Lost Canyon, about 120 yards upstream from the junction with the spur trail to Camp LC2, is often a pool of water at the end of a small creek, which flows for much of the year. Although not to be relied on, especially in the fall, this is a good place to search for water.

For the next mile above Camp LC2, the trail follows what is, for much of the year, a tiny flowing creek, where water is typically available in the spring. The riparian vegetation is thick along this creek, so this is a good place to watch for nesting songbirds. After the creek starts to peter out, you continue on the canyon bottom for about 0.4 mile, and then start to climb before coming to the signed spur trail to Camp LC3, which goes to the right.

The main trail goes straight, climbs a small side canyon for about 0.3 mile, and then ascends a set of crude stone steps, which lead you back up onto the slickrock. Following small cairns, you climb steeply up to a pass with good views to the west of the colorfully striated Needles. From the pass, the trail contours along a rock bench before descending into Squaw Canyon. Once on the valley floor, you soon pass the signed spur trail to Camp SQ2, and then come to a junction immediately after you hop over the gully in Squaw Canyon. For much of the early spring, there is a tiny trickle of water here that flows through a mass of marsh grasses and reeds. **Warning:** The water here cannot be relied on (ask rangers about its availability when you get your permit), but in the spring, this is usually your last chance for easily accessible water on this trip.

You turn left on the trail toward Druid Arch and Elephant Canyon and, for the next 0.3 mile, walk upstream on a bench a little above the intermittent flow of the creek. Squaw Canyon is wider than Lost Canyon, but the extremely colorful sandstone walls are arguably more scenic. In the upper part of the canyon, the trail climbs back up onto the slickrock for 0.6 mile and then comes to a junction with Big Springs Canyon Trail.

Go left here, following signs to Elephant Canyon, and stay on the rock as the trail contours around the head of Squaw Canyon. This is the start of a short but quite challenging section of trail, so go slowly and be careful, especially if the rock is wet and slippery. After about 0.2 mile, the trail squeezes through an extremely narrow little cave, where you may have to remove your pack in order to fit through. Immediately after you make your way out of the 40-yard-long cave, you must hunch over to pass beneath a low overhanging ledge, and then steeply climb over more slickrock before ascending a narrow metal ladder. This leads up to a rocky pass, from which you descend a set of *moqui* holes (small holes that have been carved into the steep rock face to act as hand and footholds) before descending a tall and somewhat exposed wooden ladder. Overall, this 0.5-mile section is quite demanding, both physically and mentally. Most backpackers should be able to handle these obstacles, but they must exercise care and have a fair degree of athleticism. Anyone who is afraid of heights should avoid this route.

The trail now drops into a canyon that is flanked by colorfully banded sandstone walls and spires. The dominant colors are orange red and cream yellow, but others are present as well. The canyon leads down to a junction with the main Elephant Canyon and its popular trail. **Note:** Ask at the ranger station before you leave, but if it has rained recently, there might be a pool of water along the trail about 150 yards before you reach the junction at the bottom of Elephant Canyon. There is usually no water in Elephant Canyon itself.

If you turn right at the junction in Elephant Canyon, you will reach the turnoff to Camp EC2 in about 0.1 mile. Continuing beyond that camp will take you to the exit route for this trip. For now, though, turn left at the junction and walk up the sandy bottom of Elephant Canyon for 0.2 mile to reach Camp EC3. Either this camp or Camp EC2 makes a good base from which to explore the nearby area. A possible itinerary is to spend two nights at one of these camps and use the day in between to explore Druid Arch and dramatically scenic Chesler Park.

The trail continues up Elephant Canyon from Camp EC3 for 0.3 mile to an important junction. The trail to Chesler Park goes to the right, but before going that way, take a couple of hours for the fine side trip to extremely impressive Druid Arch.

Druid Arch

After returning to the Chesler Park junction, go left (west) and make yet another steep, tiring climb over rock. Unique features here include three caves passed along the way that you can enter and explore. At the top of the climb you emerge at Chesler Park, a huge and relatively flat expanse sur-

Side Trip to Druid Arch: To visit Druid Arch, go straight at the junction and make your way up the canyon bottom on a surface that is a mix of deep sand and easier-to-walk-on rock. After about 1.3 miles, you scramble up the left (east) side of the canyon and follow a shelf that allows you to avoid the canyon bottom, which is full of tangled brush and is blocked by a deep pool of water fed by a generally reliable spring. Above this pool is a gentler section of trail, giving you a nice rest before tackling the last 0.3 mile, which is a steep and sometimes tricky scramble up rocks and a little metal ladder. All the effort is worthwhile, however, once you see Druid Arch. Like Angel Arch, Druid is an improbably large arch that sits picturesquely on the skyline. This one, however, is a double arch—a smaller slit arch is on the right of the towering rock formation that forms the main attraction, a truly dramatic scene that should not be missed.

rounded by uniquely colorful columns and pillars that pop up improbably out of the desert sands. The extremely photogenic, almost Dr. Seuss–type landscape is one of the scenic highlights of Canyonlands National Park. The area's popularity should come as no surprise. Day hikers are everywhere.

After hiking about 0.2 mile across Chesler Park, you come to a junction. To explore more of the park, go straight, and 75 yards later you come to the turnoff to Camps CP3, 4, and 5, all bone dry but ridiculously scenic. From there you can explore around the park's perimeter to your heart's content. Adding to the colorful scenery nearby are the snow-covered (in the spring, anyway) Henry Mountains in the distance to the west.

To complete the recommended trip, return to the junction 75 yards west of the turnoff to Camps CP3–5 and turn north, following signs to Elephant Hill. In addition to taking you past still more of Chesler Park's amazingly colorful pillars and rock formations, this path provides access to Camp CP1. After 1.2 miles you come to a junction near the northeast corner of Chesler Park.

Go straight at the junction, still following signs to Elephant Hill, and soon begin the descent of a set of rough stone steps. After losing about 200 feet in 0.2 mile, you come to another junction. Turn right and continue descending for 0.6 mile to a four-way junction at the bottom of Elephant Canyon. The trail to the left goes about 0.1 mile down canyon to Camp EC1. The trail to the right, going up Elephant Canyon, is the return route to Camps EC2 and EC3.

To exit the hike, you go straight at the junction, crossing the gully in Elephant Canyon and immediately beginning a short, stiff climb. The ascent is accomplished via a series of switchbacks, some slickrock scrambling, and a few makeshift stone steps. At the top you go through a short but quite narrow slot canyon before emerging onto a flatter landscape, covered with sagebrush, junipers, and pinyon pines. For scenic variety, the area also features several colorful sandstone rock formations that seem to pop up everywhere in this desert.

You soon go through a second, less narrow chasm and immediately thereafter come to a junction. To the left is the trail to Elephant Hill, which is the most popular trailhead for day hikers heading for Chesler Park. This trailhead is also an alternate exit point for this trip that would save 2.1 miles of hiking (see the map for directions to this location). The recommended route offers better scenery, however, so keep right at the junction and cross more relatively flat and sandy terrain with good views of both nearby sandstone rock formations and distant landmarks such as the La Sal Mountains.

The flat hiking doesn't last long, as after just 0.1 mile you once again find yourself following cairns over slickrock. These cairns guide you into and then back out of yet another gorgeous little canyon, of which there seems to be no end in this aptly named park. Once out of this canyon, you stay high for the next mile or so, following a remarkably level rock bench well above Big Springs Canyon on your right. As you would expect, the views along this section are continuously stunning. Finally, the trail drops down a fairly narrow chute into Big Springs Canyon and, 0.3 mile later, reaches a junction. Camp BS1 is about 75 yards down the trail that goes slightly to the right. The trail that turns sharply right is the trail up Big Springs Canyon.

Possible Itinerary

Day	Camps and Side Trips	Distance (mi.)	Elevation (ft.)
1	Cathedral Butte TH to Camp SC1	3.8	+100/–1,300
2	Angel Arch Camp	10.1	+200/–700
	Side trip to Big Ruins	0.8	+100/–100
	Side trip to Wedding Ring Arch	0.2	—
3	Peekaboo Camp	8.3	+250/–450
	Side trip to Angel Arch	3.4	+350/–350
4	Camp EC3	8.9	+1,300/–900
5	Day hike to Druid Arch and Chesler Park loop	8.3	+1,000/–1,000
6	Out to Squaw Flat TH	5.1	+600/–900

You go straight and make a brief climb to a junction with the trail to Squaw Flat Campground's B Loop. Keep right and cross more slickrock for 0.3 mile, then descend to a dirt path and hike the final 0.2 mile to the recommended ending point at the Squaw Flat Campground A trailhead.

Alternates: For hikers with excellent navigation skills, a high-clearance four-wheel-drive vehicle, a willingness to carry lots of water, and a strong desire to really get away from it all, Canyonlands offers the Maze District. Strictly for well-equipped and highly experienced backpackers, this wildly contorted wonderland has little in the way of designated trails and an extremely confusing landscape, but it does offer some outstanding desert scenery and few crowds, which makes getting a permit quite easy. The district is located on the west side of the Colorado River, with no convenient bridge connection to the main park entrances to the east. Thus, this area can only be reached off rough dirt roads from near the town of Hanksville. Get a good map (you may still get confused), brush up on your GPS skills (even though the devices often don't work in the deeper canyons), and pick your own destination. The more "developed" areas around South Fork Horse Canyon and Chocolate Drops are better for relative novices to desert hiking, while the extremely remote and arch-studded regions around the Fins or Jasper Canyon will test the skills of even the most experienced desert rats.

Green Tips: Southern Utah Wilderness Alliance—www.suwa.org

Edward Abbey Iconoclast, rebel, patriot, anarchist, eco-terrorist—all are terms, among many others, used to describe Ed Abbey. While the accuracy of applying such descriptors could be debated, there is little doubt of his writing talent and his ability to use his prose to inspire others. Living on the cusp of the era of the cult of personality, Abbey achieved a level of notoriety that blurred the line between image and reality.

Cactus Ed was born in rural Pennsylvania in 1927. His mother instilled in him an appreciation of literature and music, while his father influenced his embryonic notions of anarchism, socialism, and atheism. After high school, Abbey journeyed west to the Four Corners region, where his love affair with the deserts of the Southwest began. A two-year stint in the military honed his distrust of large institutions and heightened his opposition to authority. After an honorable discharge, which seems amazing in hindsight, he studied English and philosophy at the University of New Mexico, obtaining a BA in 1951. After marrying the first of his five wives, Abbey spent a year in Edinburgh, Scotland, as a Fulbright scholar. Returning to UNM, he earned a master's degree in 1956 and then went to Stanford for a year on a Wallace Stegner Creative Writing Fellowship.

Like many writers, Abbey struggled to succeed financially early in his career, holding a variety of different jobs to make ends meet. Although two of his early works, *The Brave Cowboy* and *Fire on the Mountain*, were made into a theatrical movie and a made-for-TV movie, respectively, his rise in popularity didn't come until after the publication of his fourth book in 1968, *Desert Solitaire: A Season in the Wilderness*. An autobiographical account based on two seasons as a ranger at Arches National Monument, the book soon became an American nature classic, compared favorably to the works of Henry David Thoreau and Aldo Leopold. Through the desert landscape, Abbey eloquently expressed his philosophies against the evils of civilization and for the protection of wilderness, while bringing the enchanting majesty of the American Southwest landscape to life.

A work of fiction published in 1975, *The Monkey Wrench Gang*, accentuated Abbey's popularity and his growing influence on the fledgling environmental movement of the time. This story of four environmentally influenced misfits resorting to *ecotage* (environmental sabotage) to protest insults to the American Southwest became an instant hit. The book was so influential in the environmental world that the founding of the radical Earth First movement, which would go on to use ecotage tactics, was attributed to Abbey's work, although he never officially associated himself with the group.

Abbey continued to write essays and works of fiction into the 1980s, but *The Monkey Wrench Gang* remained his literary zenith. The legend of Ed Abbey continued to grow, however, and eventually transcended the real man. Even in death (1989) his civil disobedience continued, as, per his wishes, a small group of intimates surreptitiously packed his body in dry ice, drove to an undisclosed location in the desert, and buried him, dousing his grave with whiskey. While the real Ed Abbey remains something of an enigma, understanding his work and the influence it generated is key to understanding the American Southwest in the twentieth century.

Grand Gulch Primitive Area

—————————— **TRIP 6** ——————————

Grand Gulch and
Bullet Canyon Traverse

> I have a hunger for nonhuman spaces, not out of any
> distaste for humanity, but out of a need to experience
> my humanness the more vividly by confronting stretches
> of the earth that my kind has had no part in making.
>
> —Scott Russell Sanders

Arizona's Grand Canyon is probably the backpacker's perfect combination of scenery and geologic history. For the equivalent combination of fine scenery and *human* history, however, you're better off heading for southern Utah's Grand Gulch. This impressive, twisting defile, cut into the sandstone and shale of Cedar Mesa, acts as an outdoor museum of Anasazi culture. Here, dozens of well-preserved ruins and numerous rock art sites are tucked away in a beautiful setting, just waiting for backpackers to explore them. The entire gulch makes for a very long (but worthwhile) hike of more than 100 miles round-trip, but you can explore some of the best of the area on this memorable horseshoe-shaped loop in the upper gulch, with an easy car shuttle or hitchhike in between.

Days: 3–4

Distance: 23.2 miles (including side trip but excluding any road walk or detours to ruins or springs for water)

Type: Shuttle (a relatively short hitchhike is usually feasible)

Scenery: 8

Solitude: 4

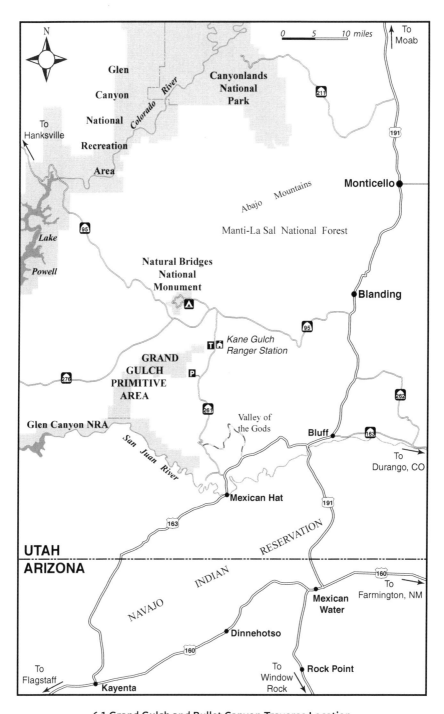

6.1 Grand Gulch and Bullet Canyon Traverse Location

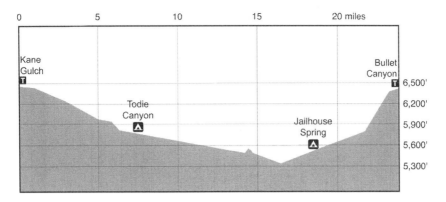

Grand Gulch and Bullet Canyon Traverse

Technical Difficulty: 6

Physical Difficulty: 5

Elevation Gain/Loss: +1,300'/−1,350'

Season: April to November. **Best:** Mid-April through early June, mid-September through October

Maps: Trails Illustrated—*Grand Gulch Plateau*

Resources: *Hiking Grand Staircase–Escalante and the Glen Canyon Region*, by Ron Adkison; *The Delight Makers*, by Adolf F. Bandelier

Contacts:

• Kane Gulch Ranger Station
  Bureau of Land Management
  Monticello Field Office
  435-587-1310

Permits: Overnight permits are required and limited in number. They must be picked up at the Kane Gulch Ranger Station (at the starting trailhead) on the morning of the start date of your trip. The hike is popular, so reservations are strongly advised. You can reserve a permit up to ninety days in advance by calling 435-587-1510. As of 2013, permits for the peak hiking seasons of March 1 to June 15 and September 1 to October 31 cost $8 per person per trip. During the off season, the cost is $5 per person per trip.

Regulations: No fires of any kind are allowed in the canyon, including burning used toilet paper, which should be packed out. No camping is allowed under any of the canyon's alcoves or near any ruins. Camp at least 200 feet from any water source, unless the stream is running and the canyon's narrowness makes such distance impossible (under these circumstances, camp as far away from water as possible). Dogs are not allowed in Grand Gulch. Maximum group size is limited to twelve persons. Most importantly, never destroy, deface, crawl into, or otherwise damage or disturb any of the many ruins and rock art sites in the canyon.

Nearest Campgrounds: Natural Bridges National Monument—10 miles from the Kane Gulch trailhead. There are endless opportunities for dispersed camping on the vast areas of Bureau of Land Management land in the surrounding area.

Nearest Airports:
- Farmington, New Mexico, Four Corners Regional Airport (FMN)— 155 miles
- Albuquerque International Sunport (ABQ)—355 miles

Nearest Outdoor Retailers: None. If you fly into Farmington or Albuquerque, there are some decent sporting goods stores.

Outfitters: No standard trips exist, but custom trips are possible. Check the BLM website for currently licensed outfitters (www.blm.gov/ut/st/en/fo /monticello/recreation/commercial_outfitters.html).

Transportation Logistics: There is no public transportation to these trailheads, so you will need your own vehicle. Fortunately, the road to the starting trailhead is a good paved highway.

If you have only one vehicle, walking the 1.1 miles from the Bullet Canyon trailhead to Highway 261 and then hitching a ride back to Kane Gulch is usually easy and reasonably safe.

Backcountry Logistics: (FF, H, H2O, R, Su) The streams in these canyons have only intermittent flows, depending on recent rainfall and the previous winter's precipitation. A handful of springs provide the only reliable permanent water sources, most of which are in side canyons requiring fairly significant detours to reach. The only fully reliable springs are Todie Spring (7.4 miles), Coyote Spring (13.2 miles), Green Mask Spring (14.4 miles), and Jailhouse Spring (17.8 miles).

There is some danger from flash floods in both Grand Gulch and Bullet Canyon, especially during the summer thunderstorm season. Never camp at low places near the streambed and watch the weather carefully as you hike. While hiking during the day, most of the route is open enough to usually escape any floods, but be careful in narrower sections of these canyons.

Other hazards include rodents, ravens, and ringtails that on rare occasions may try to raid backpackers' food supplies at some of the more popular campsites. There are also a few rattlesnakes and scorpions, so watch where you step, especially at night, and shake out your boots before putting them on in the morning.

Amenities and Attractions: Extremely isolated, the nearest town with anything in the way of amenities is **Monticello** (about 57 miles to the east-northeast), which offers a decent selection of mostly mediocre motels and restaurants.

On the other hand, the natural attractions hereabouts are outstanding and really should not be missed. A day at **Natural Bridges National Monument** is a must. The one-way paved loop road is worth driving, but for hikers, the best plan is to take the 7.9-mile loop past and through all three of the large natural bridges in the preserve. If pressed for time, just make the shorter strolls to **Sipapu** and **Owachomo Bridges**, which are the most spectacular and photogenic spans.

Not far south of Grand Gulch are several excellent destinations easily reached by car. First, drive south on Highway 261 for about 18 miles from the Kane Gulch Ranger Station to where the road turns to gravel and suddenly drops off the edge of a high plateau. From there, follow the sometimes frighteningly narrow and twisted road, which snakes down the view-packed cliff face in a series of tight switchbacks (a remarkable feat of civil engineering), all the way to the bottom of the 1,100-foot cliff. A good paved highway resumes at the bottom of the descent. Once down this dramatic section of road, keep driving south for about another 6.5 miles and then turn west onto Highway 216. This paved route goes 3 miles before ending at **Goosenecks State Park**, where you have a stupendous view of the deeply embedded curving meanders of the San Juan River Canyon.

Finally, your itinerary would not be complete without a drive through the **Valley of the Gods**. This place is similar to the famous (and crowded) Monument Valley on the nearby Navajo reservation, with dramatic towers of red sandstone rising hundreds of feet above the colorful desert floor. A good gravel road snakes through the valley, which is a photographer's paradise. The road to the Valley of the Gods goes west off Highway 261 about 1.5 miles from the bottom of the cliff discussed above.

Directions to Trailhead: Begin your journey by driving to southeast Utah and the prominent junction of State Highways 95 and 261, about 42 miles west of Blanding. Coming from the northwest, this location is 1.9 miles past the junction with the entrance road to Natural Bridges National Monument. Turn south on Highway 261 and drive 4 miles to the Kane Gulch Ranger Station on the left (east) side of the road. This is where you pick up your reserved permit and start the hike.

If you have a second vehicle and are shuttling cars, then leave one at the Bullet Canyon trailhead by continuing south on Highway 261 another 7.3 miles. Turn right (west) on Road 251, following signs to the Bullet Canyon trailhead, and follow this decent dirt road for 1.1 miles to the well-signed trailhead.

A Culture in Ruins To fully appreciate your hike in a scenic and archaeological wonderland like Grand Gulch, it's helpful to have a basic understanding of the people who left so much evidence in this canyon of their remarkable culture. The many ruins and rock art sites found here were the work of the Ancestral Puebloans, or Anasazi, a remarkable group of people who lived in the American Southwest from about AD 200 to AD 1300. While a simple enough statement, there is a great deal of fascinating material and even mystery in the details behind it, so a little more history is in order.

Anasazi is a Navajo word usually translated as "Ancient Ones," although a somewhat more accurate (but less politically correct) version would be roughly "ancestors of my enemies." (This, perhaps, explains the growing use of the term Ancestral Puebloan instead.) Anthropologists believe they descended from tribes of hunter-gatherers who lived in the same geographic area for as long as five thousand years. This earlier group is usually referred to as the Archaic People, and you can still find evidence of their existence in the form of occasional petroglyphs and tools.

Around 100 BC the Archaic People began to farm maize (usually called corn today) and develop the distinctive features of the robust and fascinating Anasazi culture. With a stable food supply, their population rapidly expanded. Archaeologists recognize several different periods within this culture distinguished by differences in the way they built their homes and how they made their baskets, variations in their colorful and skillfully made pottery, changes in their tools, and other factors. Archaic People and their descendant Ancestral Puebloans built large cities in particularly favored locations, and their society had a unique and complex religious tradition. This vibrant culture dominated an enormous part of the American Southwest for almost one thousand years, with a large population and lifestyle closely tied to the climate and geography of this region.

Then in a remarkably short time, starting around AD 1270, they walked away. Yes, I know, that sounds a bit jarring, but from all of the evidence, that is precisely what happened. Countless numbers of once-thriving locations all around the region were simply abandoned. In many places significant quantities of excellent pottery and other presumably quite valuable and useful items were left behind. The best evidence suggests that they migrated to the south and east to the Rio Grande Valley and to the mesas of Arizona, where they eventually became today's Pueblo and Hopi Indians. The rather obvious question is why did they go?

The answer to that question is one that archaeologists have struggled with for decades. Could an outside group have invaded them? Many of the cities and dwellings left behind by the Anasazi were built in caves on the sides of steep canyon walls, which were quite difficult and often dangerous to reach even for normal day-to-day activities. These homes would have been relatively easy to defend against attackers. Only very limited archaeological evidence of any large-scale violence or warfare exists. And besides, if an outside force *had* pushed the Ancestral Puebloans out, why did they, in turn, not stick around and leave evidence of their continuing presence? The largest tribe living in the same general area today is the Navajo, but there is fairly clear evidence that they did not arrive until about AD 1400, some one hundred years after the Anasazi left.

There is similarly no particular evidence of widespread disease suddenly wiping out these people either. Although many millions of Native Americans were tragically wiped out by a whole array of terrible diseases introduced by Europeans, such devastation did not start until around AD 1500.

Finally, the oral traditions of the Hopi and other tribes believed to be descendants of the Anasazi provide no strong evidence of a mass exodus for religious or other reasons.

So what happened? Currently, the best guess is that the Anasazi population had grown so large that the land was becoming depleted and nearing its carrying capacity. Evidence from tree rings indicates that the area was then hit by a protracted and severe drought, which would have made supporting a large human population impossible. So, they just left. If true, this must have been a difficult and tragic forced migration. Strangely, there is almost no evidence that *anyone* stayed behind, even though a smaller population would have been able to survive the drought.

Although the disappearance of the Anasazi people has never been fully explained, what is unquestioned is the remarkable skill of their builders and the magnificence of their art. A hike through Grand Gulch is one of the best ways for the backpacker to appreciate these ancient people, awed by the works their impressive culture left behind. Their society may now be in ruins, but those ruins add so much to the grandeur of this place, infusing a wonderful sense of mystery.

Trip Description: The trailhead is marked with a prominent sign on the west side of the ranger station parking lot. The path immediately crosses Highway 261 and heads west across a sagebrush-covered flat. The trail very soon drops a bit into the wash of Kane Gulch, a low willow-choked defile with an intermittent trickle of water (spring offers the best chance for water here). The well-defined route goes through a metal gate at 0.2 mile, and then continues a gentle descent of the wash for another 0.4 mile to a dramatic spot where the trail passes through a short, narrow cleft between two huge, dark boulders. Past this point, the wash gradually deepens, passing a few groves of quaking aspens and the more abundant Utah junipers, Gambel oaks, and pinyon pines. At a few cooler and wetter spots, there are even a couple of lonely looking Douglas firs in the canyon. The path's surface is a mix of dirt with some sandy areas and slickrock sandstone, where the proper course is marked by small cairns.

At 1.6 miles you keep right to avoid a large pour-off (a steep and usually dry waterfall that drops over the slickrock into an intermittent pool at the base), then keep going into a shallow and increasingly narrow canyon. About 0.3 mile from the pour-off is a nice campsite on a little bench on the left side of the canyon. There may be water from seasonal pools or an unreliable trickle along the canyon bottom.

The scenery soon becomes much more dramatic, with taller and more colorful canyon walls often decorated with the streaks of desert varnish. Near 2.5 miles, the trail follows a rocky ledge well above the wash bottom for a short time, but soon returns to a dirt path near the bottom of the canyon. A second good, most likely dry, campsite comes at 2.9 miles, below a towering rock formation and near a sharp left turn in the canyon.

At 4 miles, you meet often-dry Grand Gulch. Here a trail branches off to the right, soon leading to an excellent campsite on a flat beneath some large cottonwoods. Immediately past this camp is Junction Ruin, which spreads out in a low-level alcove above the creek bed. This ruin is well worth exploring, the first of many you'll encounter over the next couple of days. If the creek in Grand Gulch is dry, water is usually available from Junction Spring, about 0.2 mile up Grand Gulch.

The main route continues down Grand Gulch, which may have pools of water or even a flowing creek, depending on recent precipitation levels. At just 0.2 mile from Junction Ruin is a small unnamed arch about 50 feet up the right canyon wall. A more interesting feature occurs 0.5 mile later, where an unsigned trail branches right and leads 150 yards to an alcove holding several rock art sites and Turkey Pen Ruin, one of the more extensive and interesting ruins in Grand Gulch.

Just 0.2 mile from Turkey Pen Ruin, the narrow opening of bulky Stimper Arch can be seen high on the left canyon wall. Another wide turn in the canyon takes you past the mouth of Fortress Canyon coming in on the right. The main canyon now widens a bit as you frequently walk through large grassy meadows flanked by the tall and impressive canyon walls.

The next major landmark comes at 7.2 miles, where you reach the wide opening of Todie Canyon on the left, with several good campsites. A sketchy trail up Todie Canyon is a rugged but possible exit route for those with less time. All hikers should at least go up the first 0.25 mile of this trail to reach reliable Todie Spring, where you can refill your water bottles. There is a small ruin visible in an alcove high above Todie Spring.

Grand Gulch becomes narrower and more dramatic below Todie Canyon, with soaring walls and tall pinnacles. Enjoy the fine scenery as you cross and recross the usually dry creek bed. Grasses, willows, sagebrush, large cottonwoods, and a few boxelder trees add green to the colorful tableau of yellow, brown, orange, and black on the canyon walls.

You pass a large pour-off 1.6 miles below Todie Canyon (8.8 miles from the trailhead), which usually has a pool of possibly stagnant water at the base named Pour-off Pool. At 9.8 miles you pass a good campsite, where there are usually a few pools of water nearby (don't rely on them—check with the rangers when you pick up your permit). Just 0.2 mile later, a well-used trail branches off to the right, which leads 120 yards to a magnificent alcove holding Split Level Ruin. This ruin is one of the most interesting and well-preserved archaeological sites in Grand Gulch, with several homes, granaries, and kivas. To protect the area from overuse, no camping is allowed in this area.

At a bend in the canyon, 1.6 miles past Split Level Ruin, a trail goes right toward a prominent overhang with a small unnamed ruin. The ruin is worth

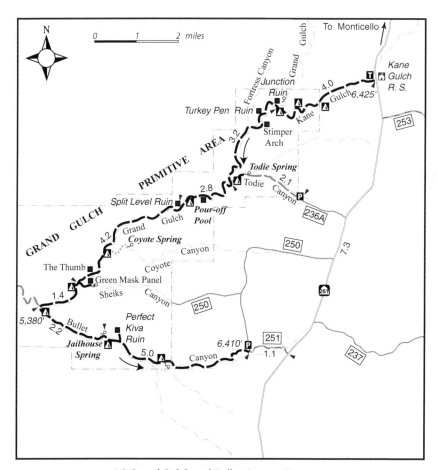

6.2 Grand Gulch and Bullet Canyon Traverse

a look, although much smaller than any of the named sites. If you're thirsty, this section of Grand Gulch tends to have somewhat more pools of water in the streambed left over from storms or spring runoff.

At 12.8 miles you come to a good cottonwood-shaded campsite at the mouth of Coyote Canyon on your left. With no water in Grand Gulch, you can walk about 0.4 mile up Coyote Canyon to Coyote Spring to top off your water bottles. About 0.9 mile below Coyote Canyon, you come to a pour-off that sits just below a large rounded pinnacle on the right side of the canyon. This pinnacle looks remarkably like a massive geologic representative of a hitchhiker's appendage, which not surprisingly is called the Thumb. There is a fair but often waterless campsite at this location. Only 0.5 mile past the Thumb, there is a campsite across from the wide opening of Sheiks Canyon on your left.

The Thumb

After your rewarding side trip up Sheiks Canyon, return to Grand Gulch and keep heading downstream. The next major landmark comes at 15.6 miles (1.4 miles below Sheiks Canyon), where there is an unsigned but obvious junction at the mouth of Bullet Canyon. Although the trail down Grand Gulch continues for another 36 very rewarding miles, Bullet Canyon is the recommended exit route.

Turn left, almost immediately pass several inviting campsites, and then head up fairly wide Bullet Canyon. The scenery is similar to Grand Gulch, but the canyon walls are a bit lower and less imposing. After 0.7 mile, you go left to pass around a dry waterfall, and then meander up canyon for another 1.5 miles. At this point you encounter a number of tall cottonwoods and a mass of rushes, both indicative of permanent water, the small but reliable flow of Jailhouse Spring. Along with good campsites in this vicinity, the rivulet is a welcome spot to refill your water bottles.

Only 0.2 mile past Jailhouse Spring, you'll come to Jailhouse Ruin. The ruins are located on the left (north) side of the canyon about 60 feet up a rock face. Another 0.3 mile past Jailhouse Ruin, a cairn marks a well-used side trail to the left. This 0.2-mile side route leads up to Perfect Kiva Ruin, a partially restored site where the BLM allows visitors somewhat more leeway to crawl around and explore.

From Perfect Kiva Ruin, the trail goes generally east up Bullet Canyon. The tread is often sandy and frequently follows the bottom of the usually dry wash, but the course is easy to follow, and the scenery remains very good. At 1.7 miles from Perfect Kiva Ruin, you come to a campsite where a tiny spring provides a meager flow of good water. The spring is usually reliable but does

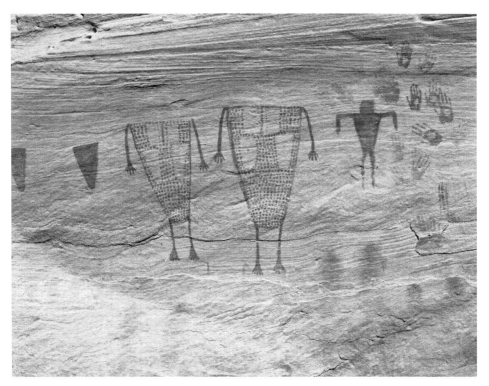

Green Mask Panel

dry up sometimes, so ask ahead. The moisture is reliable enough to support a thick growth of riparian shrubs and rushes. Consequently, the next 0.2 mile of hiking is rather brushy.

About 0.8 mile above this camp and spring, the trail detours to the left to make a short, steep, and rocky 200-foot climb. This ascent takes you to a nearly level rock ledge well above the canyon floor, which offers good views down the twisting chasm of Bullet Canyon. You follow this ledge for about 0.15 mile to where the canyon floor rises to meet you. The next 0.5 mile or so offers some minor challenges as you scramble around boulders, make your way across sloping slickrock, and pass a couple of deep semipermanent pools of stagnant water. The following 0.2 mile is trickier still, as you must crawl up slickrock at a fairly steep angle, occasionally using your hands to pull yourself up. Experienced hikers should have little difficulty, but novices might find this section challenging and even slightly scary. Here you'll also encounter a few fern-choked seeps feeding a usually flowing trickle of water in the upper parts of Bullet Canyon. The canyon itself has now become quite shallow as you near the top.

The now much easier route stays on the floor of the gulch for another 0.5 mile, and then climbs steeply up the left canyon wall, gaining about 150 feet to the top of a pinyon- and juniper-studded mesa. From here, a 0.2-mile nearly level walk leads to the Bullet Canyon trailhead. If you have two cars, the hike is over. With only one car, you'll need to walk the dirt road going east for 1.1 miles to Highway 261, where you can either hike 7.3 miles north to the car or stick out your thumb and pick up a ride.

Possible Itinerary

Day	Camps and Side Trips	Distance (mi.)	Elevation (ft.)
1	Kane Gulch TH to Todie Canyon	7.2	+100/–800
2	Jailhouse Spring	10.6	+300/–400
	Side trip to Green Mask Panel	0.4	+50/–50
3	Out to Bullet Canyon TH	5.0	+850/–100

Alternates: For the truly ambitious, the trip all the way down Grand Gulch to the mouth at the San Juan River is a rigorous but rewarding adventure totaling 103 miles round-trip. If you have less time, consider taking the ruggedly scenic 16.4-mile Owl Creek–Fish Creek Loop, where there are some fine ruins and several impressive arches. This loop is located in the canyon country east of the Kane Gulch Ranger Station.

Green Tips: Southern Utah Wilderness Alliance—www.suwa.org

PART II

UTAH AND ARIZONA

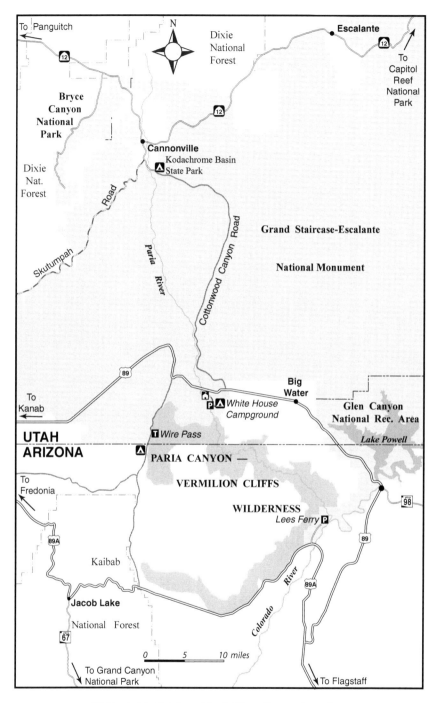

7.1 Buckskin Gulch and Paria River Canyon Location

——————— **TRIP 7** ———————

Buckskin Gulch
and Paria River Canyon

When our cultural and material values are considered on balance,
the ideas of Audubon and Muir have contributed
as much to real happiness as those of Edison and Einstein.

—L. W. LANE

ADEQUATELY DESCRIBING this amazing hike is difficult, because in my tens of thousands of backpacking miles, I have never encountered anything comparable to the slot canyon country found here. The trip is something of an otherworldly experience, as for mile after mile you snake your way through a dark, impossibly deep, and amazingly sheer-sided slot canyon cut into the sandstone of southern Utah. In parts of Buckskin Gulch, the canyon is only 3 or 4 feet wide (but 500 feet deep!), and since the walls often overhang, the gorge frequently feels more like a cave than a canyon. The sun rarely reaches the bottom of the canyon, and if it does, only for a few minutes each day. As a result, the hike is surprisingly cool and shady despite the soaring temperatures in the deserts above. When thunderstorms develop in those vast deserts, even though the clouds may be unseen and as far as 50 miles away, the rains can collect and funnel huge quantities of water through this narrow canyon in dangerous flash floods, from which there is no escape. Debris and logs arching across and lodged dozens of feet above you throughout the canyon are frightening testimonials to the power of these floods. In good weather, however, the scenery is breathtaking, with wavy sandstone walls and

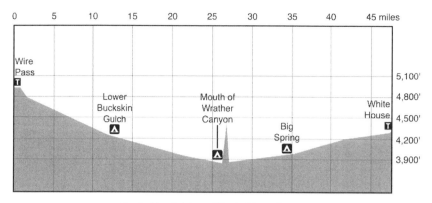

| 0 | 5 | 10 | 15 | 20 | 25 | 30 | 35 | 40 | 45 miles |

Wire Pass 🅣

Lower Buckskin Gulch ⛺

Mouth of Wrather Canyon ⛺

Big Spring ⛺

White House 🅣

5,100'
4,800'
4,500'
4,200'
3,900'

Buckskin Gulch and Paria River Canyon

impossibly steep cliffs. One thing is certain: your neck will get a real workout spending so many hours looking up at the towering canyon walls.

And don't expect that sore neck to get a rest once you reach Paria River Canyon. Although this canyon is wider and sunnier, the walls here are even higher and are much more colorful. There is also more water, in the form of both springs for drinking (water treatment is still required) and a perennially flowing stream. The streambed serves as the trail for most of the way, so for many miles you must either walk in the water or cross the flow so many times that your feet will be wet for many hours each day. Despite this soggy inconvenience, the Paria Canyon features tremendous scenery and idyllic sandy benches well suited for comfortable camping. The combination of Buckskin Gulch and Paria River Canyon makes this arguably the premier slot canyon hike in the world, followed by one of our country's best and most colorful desert canyon hikes—quite a combination in one package!

Days: 2–6

Distance: 47.9 miles (with many longer and shorter options; includes side trip)

Type: Shuttle

Scenery: 10

Solitude: 4

Technical Difficulty: 6

Physical Difficulty: 4

Elevation Gain/Loss: +1,400'/−1,950'

Season: March to November **Best:** April to early June, mid-September through October

Maps: BLM—*Hiker's Guide to Paria Canyon*

Resources: *Hiking Grand Staircase–Escalante and the Glen Canyon Region*, by Ron Adkison

Contacts:

- Vermilion Cliffs National Monument
  Bureau of Land Management
  Arizona Strip Field Office
  345 E. Riverside Dr., St. George, UT 84790-6714
  435-688-3200

Permits: Backcountry permits are required, and the numbers are strictly limited to a total of just twenty people per day from all trailheads. Conveniently, you can make reservations online, up to four months in advance, at www.blm .gov/az/paria. A calendar chart shows how many openings are available on any given day. As of 2013, the permits cost $5 per person (or dog) in your group per day.

Regulations: The use of human waste bags is required in the canyon, available at the Paria Canyon Information Center just off US 89, on the road to the White House trailhead. The center is open from March 15 through November 15 and operates from 8:30 AM to 4:15 PM. Group size is limited to ten people, and campfires are not allowed in the canyon.

Nearest Campgrounds:

- White House Campground—at White House TH
- Stateline Campground—1.3 miles south of Wire Pass TH

Nearest Airports:

- St. George Municipal Airport (SGU)—123 miles
- McCarran International Airport, Las Vegas (LAS)—247 miles

Nearest Outdoor Retailers:

- Big 5 Sporting Goods—123 miles
  245 N. Red Cliffs Dr., Ste. 1, St. George, UT 84790
  435-688-1211

Outfitters:

- Paria Outpost and Outfitters
  PO Box 410075, Big Water, UT 84741
  928-691-1047   www.paria.com

Transportation Logistics: No public transportation options reach the trailhead, so you must have your own vehicle. House Rock Valley Road, which provides access to the recommended starting point at the Wire Pass trailhead, is rocky and can be dangerously slippery when wet. Where this road crosses the normally dry upper reaches of Buckskin Gulch, 4.5 miles from US 89, floods sometimes wash the road out entirely. When the road is dry, most passenger cars should have no problem. Be sure to ask at the information center about the latest road conditions before you go.

Backcountry Logistics: (FF, H, H2O, PI, R, St, Su) There is an *extreme* danger from life-threatening flash floods, especially in Buckskin Gulch and the Paria Narrows, during the summer thunderstorm season. For many miles *there is absolutely no way to escape a flood should one occur.* **Do not**, under any circumstances, take this trip if there is the slightest chance of rain anywhere in the general vicinity.

One rugged boulder jam in lower Buckskin Gulch requires some tricky scrambling to get over, under, or around.

Quicksand and just plain mud are both common. In addition, you should be prepared for hiking with wet feet due to many miles of walking in the Paria River and/or crossing the flow literally hundreds of times.

Lesser hazards include a few areas of poison ivy near the river; rodents and ringtails that have learned to raid backpackers' food supplies at some of the more popular campsites; and a few rattlesnakes and scorpions, requiring that you watch where you step, especially at night, and shake out your boots before putting them on in the morning.

Sources of decent drinking water and good campsites are infrequent. Although the water in the Paria River may look reasonably clear (at least when it isn't muddy from a recent flood), it should be used for drinking only in an emergency, and even then only after lots of treatment (with both chemicals and filtering), primarily because of upstream pollution. Sometimes there will be many miles between springs in the canyon. Since you will have to carry at least a gallon per person per day, and much more when dry camps are a distinct possibility, be prepared to carry a lot of extra weight.

Amenities and Attractions: This area is a *long* way from anything that might be considered an amenity. The nearest restaurants, motels, and grocery stores (don't expect too much) are in Kanab, Utah, or Page, Arizona.

On the other hand, the natural attractions are numerous and enticing. Some top local picks include the hike through the impressive **Cottonwood**

Canyon Narrows, which is accessed by the very rough Cottonwood Canyon Road; the **Toadstools**, a fascinating area of hoodoos and balanced rocks not far east of the White House trailhead; and (if you get lucky with the lottery system and snag a permit), the magnificent and wildly photogenic **Wave** formation, a 3-mile hike from the Wire Pass trailhead.

Although the birds are sometimes seen by lucky hikers in the Paria River Canyon, for a better opportunity to observe wild **California condors**, continue driving south on the rough House Rock Valley Road from the Wire Pass trailhead for about 20 miles to the **Vermilion Cliffs condor viewing site**. Viewing is best in the mid- to late morning, when you have a better than even chance of seeing one or more of these magnificent birds.

Directions to Trailhead: Drive US 89 either 43 miles east from Kanab, Utah, or about 31 miles west from Page, Arizona, to a signed junction near milepost 20.8. Turn south on a good gravel road, following signs for the Paria Canyon Contact Station/Information Center. Proceed 0.1 mile, passing a junction with the road to the White House trailhead along the way, to the information center building. Stop here to pick up the latest weather forecast, information on canyon conditions, and your human waste bags.

To reach the recommended exit point at the White House trailhead, backtrack from the information center toward the highway about 50 yards, turn right (east), and follow a bumpy but decent gravel road for 2.1 miles to the White House Campground and trailhead.

To reach the recommended starting point, drive back to US 89, turn west, and proceed 4.9 miles to a junction near milepost 25.8. Turn left (southwest) on House Rock Valley Road and slowly drive along this rough gravel and dirt road for 8.7 miles to the large Wire Pass trailhead on the west side of the road.

Return of the Condor And then there were none. On Easter Sunday, April 19, 1987, a huge, mostly black-colored vulture, specifically an individual researchers referred to as AC-9, was captured in a remote area of south-central California. For the first time in at least fifteen thousand years (and possibly as long as one hundred thousand years), the skies of the Golden State and all of planet Earth were no longer home to a single wild California condor. Although many feared this condition to be permanent, fortunately the story does not end there.

According to fossil records, condors were once found throughout northern Mexico and the southern and western United States, nesting from Texas to California and along the entire West Coast. The birds fed on the carcasses of huge megafauna, such as giant ground sloths, mastodons, saber-toothed cats, and camels, all of which became extinct in North America during the Pleistocene era, not long after the arrival of the first humans. The condors have been in retreat ever since.

By the time Europeans arrived, condors lived almost exclusively along the West Coast, although their range appears to have expanded briefly back into the Southwest when domestic livestock became a new food source. More recently, the birds survived in a small area of south-central California, their declining numbers continuously affected by hunting, collisions with powerlines, habitat destruction, and inadvertent lead poisoning. In 1967 the condor was listed as an endangered species. A few years before AC-9 was captured, the population had plummeted to a pitiful twenty-two birds, making California condors one of the rarest animals in the world.

Many people are familiar with the decline of the condor. Somewhat less well known is the enormous effort that has occurred since then to save the species. The theory and hope was for the wild birds to be brought into the relative safety of captivity, where they could be carefully bred in order to stabilize and eventually increase their numbers. If successful, they would be released back into the wild. The plan was to establish at least two self-sustaining wild populations and one captive population. Over the decades, many hundreds of scientists, volunteers, zookeepers, veterinarians, government officials, private organizations, and others have been part of the process. Initially the captive breeding efforts were done in the San Diego Wildlife Park and the Los Angeles Zoo, but today the work has expanded to the Oregon Zoo in Portland and the World Center of Birds of Prey near Boise, Idaho. Inevitably, as people gradually learned how to handle, breed, and raise these large and sensitive birds, there were many errors, reversals, unexpected losses, and downright failures along the way. But there have consistently been more happy endings than sad ones, and as of January 2013, there were 400 known condors, with 232 in the wild in five localized populations.

These efforts have not been easy, or inexpensive. At well over $37 million and counting, this is by far the most expensive wildlife recovery effort in history. Those involved remain cautiously optimistic about the success of the condor.

One of the sites chosen for the release of condors back into the wild was the Vermilion Cliffs of the Paria Plateau in far northern Arizona, not far from the Utah border. For backpackers, this remote region offers dramatic scenery and impressive canyons such as Buckskin Gulch and the Paria River Canyon, but for condors the area has everything needed for survival: nesting cliffs, open terrain, few people, and plenty of food. On October 29, 1996, a nascent population of six condors was brought here to acclimate in a holding facility and then be released into the wild on December 12, 1996. Since these birds seemed to thrive, a delighted crowd of onlookers watched the release of another nine young condors into the same area on December 29, 2000. Today, the Arizona and southern Utah wild population includes birds both here and in Grand Canyon National Park, totaling about seventy-five individuals.

A reasonable argument can be made that even though the United States is the richest country in the world, we still do not have infinite resources. The many millions of dollars spent to save the condor could have been used to protect the habitats and save from extinction several dozen other less glamorous and high-profile species. But when you stand on the Vermilion Cliffs and see, perhaps for the first time, a wild California condor using its tremendous 9-foot wingspan to soar on the nearby thermals, not to be thrilled or feel a sense of satisfaction at the reversal of some of the injuries we have inflicted on this planet is difficult. And even if you don't see one during your visit, to hike in a place where the descendants of AC-9 fly free once again is still a special treat.

Trip Description: From the Wire Pass trailhead parking lot you go east, cross the road, and briefly follow a dusty trail into a wide wash with low but colorful rocky hills of reddish sandstone on either side. The desert here has enough moisture to support a few juniper trees, but most of the sparse vegetation consists of sagebrush and rabbitbrush.

The tread soon disappears, and for the next mile your route follows the bottom of the wash, a twisting sand- and gravel-bottomed gully that leads past scenic rock formations of red sandstone. At 0.4 mile, an unsigned path goes right on the way toward a spectacularly photogenic and well-named geologic feature called the Wave, some 2.6 miles away. Access to this amazing area is strictly limited, so don't even think about going there unless you hold one of the few daily permits, which are obtained by the luck of a lottery system. Those who have permits only for Buckskin Gulch and the Paria River Canyon must stick with the wash.

At 1.2 miles, you reach the sudden narrowing at the start of the slot canyon of Wire Pass. The route soon becomes extremely narrow—just 3 feet wide in places—with sheer walls more than 100 feet high. You will have to scramble

A narrow section of Buckskin Gulch

over a few large boulders blocking the route, but the amazing scenery should pull you along. Even on hot days, the canyon feels dark, cool, and shady. After 0.15 mile, the canyon opens up a bit, but soon you're back in the slots, which are even deeper and narrower. At one point, the slot narrows to as little as 2 feet wide, where you may have to take off your pack to get through. At 1.7 miles, the canyon widens out near the intersection with the larger canyon of Buckskin Gulch.

You go right (downstream), where the usually dry canyon soon narrows again. The width varies from 4 feet to more than 40 feet but averages around 10 to 15 feet. As you head downstream, the canyon's depth gradually increases, eventually reaching close to 500 feet near the still-distant confluence with the Paria River. Logs and flood debris are often lodged a disturbing 20 or more feet above you, providing ample evidence of just how dangerous the flash floods in this canyon can be. On the other hand, the magnificent canyon scenery explains why people hike here despite the potential danger. In addition to the canyon's remarkable narrowness and depth, the towering walls display intricate, often wavy patterns of black and red, adding to the unique beauty.

Distances and compass directions soon become very hard to discern as the slot canyon twists and turns in disorienting fashion. Still, even those with the most questionable navigational skills will appreciate that there is only one possible course along the bottom of the canyon, with absolutely no chance of becoming lost. At around 3 miles, you pass a usually reliable spring trickling down the canyon's right wall. This meager flow, along with occasional flash floods, feeds a few deep and surprisingly cold pools, where you may need to wade up to waist deep. Use a walking stick to measure the water depth and check for quicksand before venturing across. The placement of these pools changes with every flood, although the upper part of Buckskin Gulch almost always has more of these obstacles than the lower section. Even though there is practically no elevation change along the way, the deep pools, the abundant rocks, and the soft sand all make for rather tiring hiking.

Though almost no sunlight reaches the canyon floor, hardy plants struggle to make a living here, usually in niches high on the canyon walls and at the handful of wider places in the canyon. Look for boxelders, willows, various sedges, and rushes. Unlike the deep pools and occasional log obstacles that move with each flood, the larger boulder jams are more stable and can generally be relied on as landmarks. The first large and potentially tricky one comes at around 5 miles and is best bypassed on the right.

Wavy patterns on the walls of Buckskin Gulch

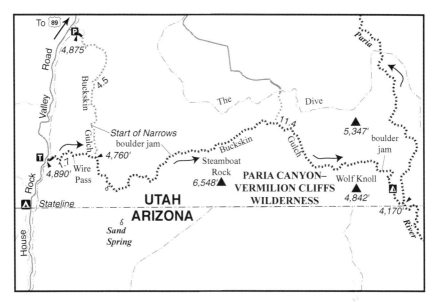

7.2 Buckskin Gulch and Paria River Canyon (West)

The dramatic slot canyon scenery remains more of the glorious same for mile after mile. It's all great fun, although in several of the particularly narrow sections, the dark rock and almost cavelike appearance of the canyon make this hike unsuitable for those with claustrophobia.

Note: Perhaps because of the soft sand or all the stops for picture taking, the miles take longer to hike here than on most trips in other areas. You should plan on averaging, at best, 1.5 miles per hour, rather than the usual hiker's norm of 2 miles per hour.

At around 8 miles, a difficult and easily missed scramble route exits the canyon on the left. Most hikers don't notice this unsigned route, which is the only reasonable exit from the canyon in case of a flood. More miles of slot canyon of varying width follow. At 11.5 miles, you come to a major obstacle, where a boulder jam blocks the route. After first lowering your pack with a rope, scramble about 20 feet down to the bottom. Frighteningly small hand and footholds in the face of a rock on the left side of the canyon are the only aids to your descent. Unless sand and debris have blocked the way, which regularly happens, the safest route is usually to scramble under the largest of the boulders lodged in the middle of the canyon. When available, this squeeze-through opening is aptly referred to as the Rabbit Hole.

About 0.5 mile below the boulder jam, a perennial trickle of water appears on the bottom of the canyon, initially only a foul-looking (and smelling) little

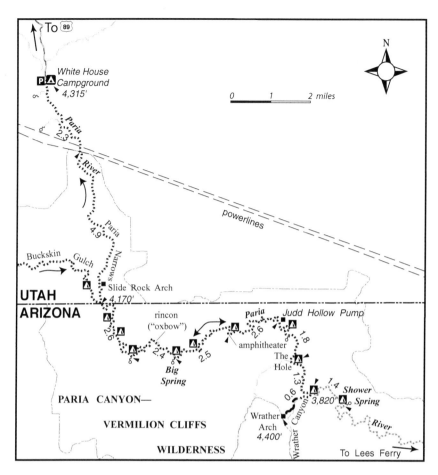

7.3 Buckskin Gulch and Paria River Canyon (East)

creek. In the spring, this little creek has more water and is much more inviting, but in the fall, it's nothing more than a fetid trickle and not a reasonable
source of water. Because of the permanent water, the hiking route is now
rather muddy but is still relatively easy. At 12.5 miles you reach the first good
campsites, on sandy benches under the soaring and colorful canyon walls.
Unfortunately, there is no spring water here, so the smelly creek is your only
source. In fall, hikers should carry enough water for a dry camp. **Note:** When
camping at this very popular and scenic spot, please keep your voice down,
especially at night. The towering canyon walls act as an echo chamber for loud
noises, which would surely bother other campers.

About 0.4 mile below these campsites is the confluence of Paria River
Canyon and Buckskin Gulch, both impressively deep sheer-walled defiles.

Buckskin Gulch, approaching the confluence with Paria Canyon

Depending on the time of year, the previous winter's snowpack, irrigation demands, and recent precipitation, the Paria River's flow ranges from non-existent to that of a reasonably good-sized creek. Unfortunately, the water is typically turbid and laden with nasty chemicals, used for drinking only in an emergency.

The recommended exit point at White House trailhead lies to the left (upstream), which is the route to take if you have only two days for your hike. However, exploring downstream for one to three days before making your exit is well worth the extra time. An excellent goal for a turnaround point is Wrather Arch, 13.8 miles away.

Depending on river flow, those hiking downstream will either have to wade in the stream bed or cross the growing creek dozens (perhaps hundreds) of times. The best plan is to simply resign yourself to wet feet, along with slogging through lots of mud and possibly quicksand near the water. As more than ample compensation, the colorful canyon walls tower as much as 750 feet almost straight up on either side.

Heading downstream, you pass a possible campsite on your right in 0.6 mile, then keep going in countless twists and turns for another 1.2 miles to an even better, but waterless, campsite on a sandy bench on the left. At 2.6 miles below Buckskin Gulch is an excellent campsite under a large tree on a sandy bench. A very tiny but reliably dripping spring on the opposite canyon wall offers drinking water, although you will probably need a lot of time and patience to fill your bottles.

After another 1.2 miles, 17 miles from the Wire Pass trailhead, you reach a *rincon*, an abandoned meander, or oxbow, that the stream's current has cut off by carving through the intervening rock. The river now flows about 15 feet below the course of the old oxbow, providing evidence that this rincon was formed many thousands of years ago. A little less than 1 mile past this impressive landmark is Big Spring, a good-sized and reliable spring pouring from the right (southwest) wall of the canyon, which supports a lush hanging garden of ferns. There are some good, but also popular, campsites across the river from Big Spring. About 0.7 mile below this spring is another excellent campsite, although Big Spring provides the nearest potable water.

The next few miles require lots of wading, but the water is rarely more than shin deep. The scenery up the sheer canyon walls remains continuously amazing, as you follow a series of tight meanders. At 7.5 miles from Buckskin Gulch is a good campsite near a tight bend in the river, beneath a stupendous salmon-colored overhanging amphitheater, 700 feet above. The only drinking water is from a seasonal seep across the river, but the jaw-dropping setting makes a night here quite worthwhile.

A short way past the amphitheater, the canyon grows gradually wider. Even though the canyon is still enclosed by towering and colorful walls, the extra width allows more sunlight to reach the floor, resulting in hotter conditions. The extra light also supports a greater number of plants, such as cottonwoods, boxelders, and willows, adding a new green hue to the surrounding red, gray, orange, and black scenery. You pass through a boulder area with a few deep pools in the river and then come to the rusted remains of the Judd Hollow Pump at 23.2 miles. In 1949 an unsuccessful attempt was made to pump water from the Paria River to cattle troughs on the plateau above. There is a flat campsite next to the pump, but the only water is from the polluted river.

About 0.5 mile past Judd Hollow Pump is a possible campsite and then another near a usually reliable but very hard to locate spring 0.4 mile later. At 24.9 miles you reach the Hole, a deep but short box canyon to the right. There are unreliable seeps here, but reaching them in the depths of the Hole may require skirting some deep quicksand. A possible campsite is on the opposite (left) side of the river.

Downstream from the Hole, your feet won't stay completely dry, but you may not have to wade as much anymore, as brush-covered sandy benches above the river offer the option of extended walks between stream crossings. At 1.3 miles from the Hole, Wrather Canyon opens up to the right. There is a possible camping area opposite the mouth of Wrather Canyon, but camping in Wrather Canyon itself is prohibited.

Once back at the Paria River, you have the option of continuing your downstream exploration or even finishing your trip in that direction, as the lower trailhead at Lees Ferry is 17.8 miles away. Some petroglyphs, a historical ranch site, and good scenery are the prime attractions. After Shower Springs, however, 1.4 miles downriver, springs become rare and unreliable, making potable water hard to find. In addition, the lower Paria Canyon becomes much wider shortly below Wrather Canyon, so the scenery, while still very good, is considerably less dramatic. Therefore, the recommended route turns around at Wrather Canyon and heads back upstream 13.2 miles to the confluence with Buckskin Gulch.

Once back at the confluence, turn right and follow narrow Paria River Canyon. Depending on water levels, the "river" varies from bone dry to a decent-sized creek. To be on the safe side, you should be prepared for wet feet and plenty of wading and stream crossings. The canyon is narrower here than the Paria Canyon below the Buckskin Gulch confluence, but it's not as

Side Trip to Wrather Arch: Having come this far, missing the exciting side trip to Wrather Arch would be a shame. Simply follow a well-used boot path heading up the narrow sandy gully in the bottom of the canyon. After about 0.2 mile, you should come to a tiny flow of clear water trickling down this canyon in all but the driest years. This trickle is a good water source for those camped along the Paria River at the mouth of Wrather Canyon. The rugged boot path follows this tiny creek for a little over 0.2 mile, then very steeply climbs away from the water up the right side of the canyon, across a boulder slope and loose sand, to a viewpoint almost directly beneath massive Wrather Arch. This 200-foot-long monster is one of the largest arches in the Colorado Plateau, appearing large enough to hold a small city in the opening. Unfortunately, the landmark is hard to photograph because of the size and placement of the arch, which comes directly off a sloping cliff face.

much of a slot canyon as that tributary gulch. **Warning:** Quicksand is a major obstacle in this section of Paria Canyon.

After 0.4 mile you reach Slide Rock Arch, a large span created not by slow erosion, but by a huge rock falling from above and lodging into the side of the canyon wall, creating an opening underneath. You encounter another similarly formed but smaller and unnamed arch after another 0.8 mile. As you proceed upstream, through the section aptly called the Paria Narrows, the canyon walls, while still impressive, become gradually shorter.

Instead of coming to an abrupt end, the Paria Narrows gradually open up as striated hills of sandstone rising in rounded mounds (instead of sheer cliffs) on either side of the ever-widening canyon. At 4.9 miles upstream from Buckskin Gulch, you leave the Paria Canyon–Vermilion Cliffs Wilderness, where two sets of powerlines stretch across the now quite wide Paria Canyon. From here, a few more gentle twists and turns, past low cliffs and rounded buttes, for 2.3 miles leads to the obvious path to the right, up to the nearby White House trailhead.

Possible Itinerary

Day	Camps and Side Trips	Distance (mi.)	Elevation (ft.)
1	Wire Pass TH to lower Buckskin Gulch	12.7	+100/–800
2	Mouth of Wrather Canyon	13.6	+100/–450
3	Big Spring	8.2	+300/–50
	Side trip to Wrather Arch	1.2	+600/–600
4	Out to White House TH	12.2	+300/–50

Alternates: As mentioned previously, an obvious and popular option is to continue your trek another 17.8 miles downstream from the Wrather Arch turnoff all the way down to Lees Ferry.

Without a permit for Buckskin Gulch and the Paria River Canyon, a less crowded but still very scenic backpacking alternative is Hackberry Canyon, in the rugged country northwest of the Paria Canyon station.

Green Tips: Southern Utah Wilderness Alliance—www.suwa.org

PART III

ARIZONA

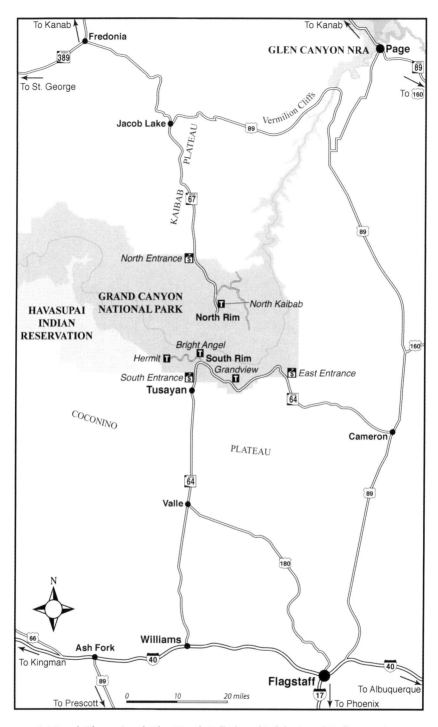

8.1 North Rim to South Rim: North Kaibab and Bright Angel Trails Location

— **TRIP 8** —

North Rim to South Rim:
North Kaibab and Bright Angel Trails

> The wonders of the Grand Canyon cannot be adequately
> represented in symbols of speech, nor by speech itself.
> The resources of the graphic art are taxed beyond
> their powers in attempting to portray its features.
> Language and illustration combined must fail.
>
> —JOHN WESLEY POWELL

DEEMED ONE OF the Seven Natural Wonders of the World, the Grand Canyon is well known to many throughout the world, attracting 5 million visitors annually. Although not as deep as Hells Canyon (7,993 feet) on the Oregon-Idaho border, or Kings Canyon (8,200 feet) in the Sierra Nevada, the overwhelming size and stunningly colorful topography make the Grand Canyon one of the most spectacular gorges on the planet. Beginning at Lees Ferry below Glen Canyon Dam and ending at Grand Walsh Cliff at Lake Mead, the Grand Canyon of the Colorado River runs for 277 miles, attaining a maximum depth of around 6,000 feet. In the heart of Grand Canyon National Park, which encompasses more than 1.2 million acres, a 10-mile gulf separates the more popular South Rim from the 1,100-foot higher North Rim, with the Colorado River coursing through the bottom of the canyon a vertical mile beneath the South Rim. Both sides of this deep canyon expose a rich geologic history, highlighted by a stunningly gorgeous tableau of earthen colors.

For backpackers, a rim-to-rim hike is by far the most highly coveted route through the park, allowing up-close views of the multihued layers of

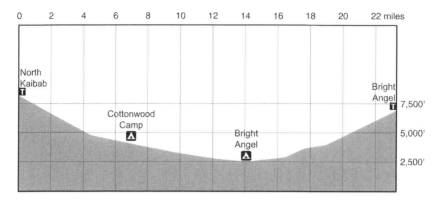

North Rim to South Rim: North Kaibab and Bright Angel Trails

the canyon walls on the way down to the Colorado River and then back up again to the opposite rim. The 23.4-mile journey, usually a three-day affair, is perhaps best done from the North Rim to the South Rim. Heading in this direction allows for a more gradual descent from the North Rim to the river and then a shorter (by 1,000 feet) climb up to a South Rim conclusion. After a 7-mile, initially steep, descent from the North Rim, hikers often spend the first night at Cottonwood Campground, by far the quietest and most relaxed of the three corridor campgrounds en route. After another 7-mile descent, the next night's camp could be set up at Bright Angel Campground near the Colorado River, with Phantom Ranch nearby. Unlike at Cottonwood, backpackers will experience plenty of human activity in this area (although the characteristic hubbub may be overlooked somewhat by the opportunity to sip an ice-cold beer or lemonade from the canteen). Camping at beautiful Indian Garden is another, equally congested overnight alternative, but traveling beyond Bright Angel from Phantom Ranch requires an additional 1.6-mile hike along the river and then a steep 3.1-mile climb up to Indian Garden Campground. Although hiking nearly 12 miles may seem like a long day to some backpackers, this alternative reduces the final day's climb up to the South Rim, from 9.3 to 4.6 miles. Whichever plan is chosen, the last day will be spent scaling the exposed south wall of the canyon, necessitating an early start to avoid climbing during the heat of the day.

Days: 3–4

Distance: 23.4 miles

Type: Shuttle

Scenery: 10

Solitude: 2

Technical Difficulty:	3
Physical Difficulty:	8
Elevation Gain/Loss:	+4,800'/−5,850'
Season:	Mid-May to mid-October **Best:** Mid-May to mid-June and early to mid-October
Maps:	USGS—Bright Angel Point, Phantom Ranch, Grand Canyon; Earthwalk Press: *Grand Canyon National Park Hiking Map and Guide*
Resources:	*Grand Canyon North Kaibab Trail Guide*, by the Grand Canyon Association; *Grand Canyon Bright Angel Trail Guide*, by the Grand Canyon Association; *Beyond the Hundredth Meridian*, by Wallace Stegner

Contacts:

• Grand Canyon National Park
  PO Box 129, Grand Canyon, AZ 86023
  928-638-7864   www.nps.gov/grca

Permits: GCNP charges a $25 entrance fee for private vehicles, good for seven days. The fee is $15 per person for those entering the park on foot, bicycle, motorcycle, or commercial bus. An annual pass is $50. The annual America the Beautiful interagency pass ($80) provides access to all national parks and national recreation areas, including Grand Canyon.

A valid wilderness permit is required for all overnight stays in the Grand Canyon backcountry. Competition for permits is perhaps higher for corridor trails at GCNP than for any other western park. Requests for advance reservations can be submitted by fax on the first day of the month, four months prior to the desired departure day (submitting a fax at one second past midnight on the first day of the appropriate month would not be too soon—provided you don't get a busy signal). The cost of an advance reservation includes a $10 permit charge and a $5 fee per person per night. Check out the park's website for additional information (www.nps.gov/grca). The backcountry office has a phone number (928-638-7875), but the phone traffic is at such a high volume, you shouldn't expect to get through easily. You may get a faster response using e-mail. Good luck!

Those without a permit reservation can show up at the North Rim Backcountry Office well before opening, stand in line, and wait their turn for a crack at any available or canceled reservations. Chances are fair for obtaining a backcountry permit, especially if your group is small and you can hang around for a day or two before departure. If you choose this option, be prepared to camp out, or find lodging (usually outside the park), for up to a few nights. Plenty of day hiking and sightseeing opportunities can fill up your days while you wait.

   If you can't obtain a backcountry permit and don't mind the greater expense of a guided rim-to-rim trip, several commercial enterprises are licensed to perform this service.

Regulations: Camping is exclusively limited to sites at three designated campgrounds between the North and South Rims (Cottonwood, Bright Angel, and Indian Garden). Campfires are not permitted.

Nearest Campgrounds:
   • North Rim Campground—2 miles from start
   • Mather Campground—1 mile from end

Nearest Airports:
   • Grand Canyon Airport (GCN)—7 miles to South Rim
   • Flagstaff Pulliam Airport (FLG)—86 miles to South Rim
   • Phoenix Sky Harbor International Airport (PHX)—231 miles to South Rim
   • St. George Municipal Airport (SGU)—159 miles to North Rim
   • McCarran International Airport, Las Vegas (LAS)—220 miles to North Rim

Nearest Outdoor Retailers: Grand Canyon Village Market (South Rim)

Outfitters: More than twenty licensed outfitters provide guided backpacking trips into the Grand Canyon. Consult the park's website for a current list (www.nps.gov/grca).

Transportation Logistics: The North Rim of the Grand Canyon is in a remote part of northern Arizona, requiring a long car drive from just about anywhere; there are no public transportation options. Rental cars may be picked up at McCarran International in Las Vegas for the four-hour drive to the North Rim. St. George Municipal Airport has service via Delta from Salt Lake City, which would cut the driving time to the North Rim to two and a half hours.

   Due to the park's extreme popularity, many public transportation options have arisen for getting to the South Rim by airplane, bus, or train. The South Rim can be accessed by rental car from airports in Las Vegas, Phoenix, and Tucson. From the Nevada towns of North Las Vegas, Boulder City, and Henderson, three small airlines serve Grand Canyon Airport, where taxi and shuttle service is available to the South Rim (rental cars are not available). A free shuttle bus runs from the gateway town of Tusayan every 15 minutes between mid-May and early September. Once inside the park, three shuttle bus routes provide free access to the major destinations along the South Rim. From the town of Williams, Grand Canyon Railway offers four levels of service on train rides to the South Rim, which take two hours and fifteen minutes, with lodging packages also available. Consult their website at www .thetrain.com for more information.

Although separated by only 23-plus miles of trail, the North Rim and South Rim are 212 road miles and four and a half hours apart from each other by automobile. Between mid-May and mid-October, Transcanyon Shuttle operates a once-a-day van service between the two rims, departing the North Rim at 7 AM, arriving at the South Rim at noon, and departing at 1:30 PM to arrive back at the North Rim by 6:30 PM. In 2014 a one-way ticket cost $85 per person. For reservations or more information, call 928-638-2820, or check out the website at www.trans-canyonshuttle.com.

Backcountry Logistics: (H, H2O, R, Su) Temperatures near the bottom of the Grand Canyon are often extreme, especially during the summer, making spring or fall the best times for a rim-to-rim trip. Many summer visitors are forced to hike the canyon by headlamp during the cooler periods at night, which seems to defeat the purpose of coming all the way to see the canyon in the first place. Access to the North Rim opens on May 15 and closes on October 15, creating a rather narrow window for those hoping to avoid hiking during the hot summer months, which invariably increases competition for the limited number of backcountry permits in spring and fall.

Due to the heat and dryness of this desert climate, potential health hazards include heat exhaustion, heat stroke, and hyponatremia. With thousands of feet of elevation change, weather conditions can vary radically between the rims and the bottom of the canyon, which oftentimes requires backpackers to carry a wide range of clothing to avoid such conditions as hypothermia. During summer the Park Service recommends that hikers not travel during the hottest parts of the day, usually between 10 AM and 4 PM. Drink plenty of fluids to stay hydrated—water is available at regular intervals at rest stops and camps along the 23-mile route. Bright Angel Creek and Garden Creek are perennial streams where water would also be available, although it should be treated or filtered. Also, the Park Service strongly encourages hikers to continually ingest plenty of salty snacks to replenish the body's salts lost through excessive perspiration.

Although potentially wreaking havoc on one's knees, the descent from the North Rim into the canyon will be much less physically taxing than the climb up to the South Rim. Trekking poles are a near necessity. During the ascent out of the canyon, drink fluids, ingest salts, rest often, and go slowly. Medical emergencies are common enough in this section of the Grand Canyon that emergency facilities and helicopter pads to facilitate evacuations have been placed near Cottonwood Campground, the Colorado River, and Indian Garden.

Camping in the inner canyon along this route is limited to three developed campgrounds, Cottonwood, Bright Angel, and Indian Garden. Of the three, demand seems highest for space at Indian Garden, which is arguably the prettiest setting. All the campgrounds have limited shade, picnic tables, running water, and restrooms (flush toilets at Bright Angel). These amenities, along with two hundred guests staying at Phantom Ranch resort, numerous mule-riding tourists, and a plethora of day trippers from the South Rim greatly diminish any sense of a rim-to-rim hike as a wilderness experience, so temper your expectations accordingly.

Hikers should be prepared to encounter plenty of pack trains on the South Rim trails, as they routinely cart tourists and supplies. Step well off the trail to allow them to pass. They tend to kick up quite a bit of dust.

Amenities and Attractions: Located 45 miles north of the North Rim at the junction of Highways 89A and 67, rustic **Jacob Lake Inn** has been serving guests since 1923. Comfortable lodging is available in various facilities, and the dining room serves hearty and pleasing meals for breakfast, lunch, and dinner. The bakery offers a fine assortment of breads, pies, cookies, sweet rolls, and brownies. The inn also has a small store and gas pumps. For more information, consult the website at www.jacoblakeinn.com. Next door is the **North Kaibab Plateau Visitor Center**, where visitors can explore exhibits explaining the interesting ecology of the area, or pick up maps and books about the region. Across the highway in ponderosa pine forest is the fifty-site Jacob Lake Campground, with vault toilets, running water, and the 0.75-mile-long Kai-Vay-Wi hiking and mountain biking trail.

Only 5 miles from the park entrance, **Kaibab Lodge** (www.kaibablodge.com) offers rustic-style lodging in a number of cabins. The main lodge has a restaurant offering casual dining for breakfast and dinner. Across the highway from the lodge is the **Kaibab General Store**, a minimart with gas pumps. Just past Kaibab Lodge is the turnoff into **De Motte Park Campground**, a forested campground with vault toilets and running water, adjacent to an expansive, picturesque meadow. Kaibab Lodge is a convenient distance away if you want to walk over and enjoy a meal rather than cook at your campsite.

Less than 10 percent of the annual visitors to Grand Canyon National Park make the journey to the **North Rim**, which helps lend a decidedly less crowded ambiance to this side of the canyon, as opposed to the overwhelming tourist hubbub usually plaguing the South Rim. The **North Rim Visitor Center** has a small selection of books and maps. National Park–priced lodging is available at the historic **Grand Canyon Lodge**, or in the neighboring cabins (grandcanyonlodgenorth.com). The dining room is a splendid place to secure a meal for breakfast, lunch, or dinner (reservations recommended for dinner), especially if you're seated next to one of the expansive windows with a stunning view of the canyon. The lodge also has a small deli and coffee bar. The quarter-mile-long **Bright Angel Point Trail** begins right outside the lodge, offering a dramatic North Rim view of the Grand Canyon. The **Transept Trail** provides a rim-running, 1.5-mile connection from the lodge to the **North Rim Campground** (for campground reservations, phone 877-444-6777 or visit www.recreation.gov). The **General Store** is adjacent to the campground, with food items, souvenirs, and a small selection of camping supplies, as well as gasoline and an ATM. Laundry and shower facilities are also nearby.

If you have some extra time to spend along the North Rim, make the short drive to the canyon view from **Point Imperial**, or the longer drive to **Cape Royal**, where a 0.3-mile path leads to a spectacular view of the canyon, Angels Window, and of a slice of the Colorado River. The route to Cape Royal offers vista points at **Vista Encantada**, **Point Roosevelt**, and the **Walhalla Overlook**, which also has some Native American ruins across the road. Longer day hikes are available along the Ken Patrick, Uncle Jim, Widforss, and Cape Final trails.

Grand Canyon Village on the South Rim of the canyon has much to offer to the average tourist, but most backpackers starting at the more sedate North Rim will find the activity on the opposite rim to be quite overwhelming, especially after a few days on the trail. The numerous lodging options are typically booked well in advance, and grabbing a bite to eat without reservations usually requires a long wait as well. The nearby **Mather Campground** is often full, but space should be available in the backpackers' area at the completion of a rim-to-rim hike. Free shuttle buses offer a convenient way to access the South Rim's major features, including the campground and trailheads. Except for flaming extroverts, most backpackers will find the congestion in the village to be nearly intolerable.

For those who don't mind rubbing elbows with the masses, the elegant **El Tovar** is the premier place on the South Rim to spend a night, enjoy a meal, or sip a prickly pear margarita on the patio outside the bar. Away from the village, **Desert View Drive** leads to many fine spots, including a glorious vista from **Lipan Point** as well as the **Watchtower**, a circular stone tower designed by Mary Colter on the South Rim's high point. Hikers will have many excellent trails to choose from, many of which are decidedly less crowded than the Bright Angel Trail. The steep **Grandview Trail** to Horseshoe Mesa is a classic 6-mile round-trip hike, while the out-and-back trip to Santa Maria Spring on the **Hermit Trail** is 5 miles long.

Overnighters not fortunate enough to have reservations inside the park will often stay in the gateway town of **Tusayan**, a half-mile-long strip of Highway 64 lined with motels, gas stations, and eateries. The town of **Williams** is a little more than an hour south of the South Rim, and the much larger city of **Flagstaff** is one and half hours southeast.

Directions to Trailhead—Start: Follow ALT 89 to Jacob Lake and then head south on Highway 67 for 30 miles to the North Rim entrance into Grand Canyon National Park. Continue another 11 miles to the Kaibab Trail parking lot, on the left. The access road to the backcountry office (wilderness permits) is a short drive past the trailhead on the right.

End: From Interstate 40, head north from Williams on Highway 64, or northwest from Flagstaff on Highway 180, to the 64/180 junction, and then continue north to the South Rim entrance into Grand Canyon National Park. Follow the South Entrance Road toward Grand Canyon Village and continue on Village Loop Drive to a righthand turn toward the Backcountry Information Center (wilderness permits). The Park Service recommends that overnight backcountry users park their vehicles in Parking Lot E. The Bright Angel trailhead is located a short walk away, just west of Kolb Studio near Bright Angel Lodge.

Clarence Edward Dutton Although John Wesley Powell is the person most associated with the human history of the Grand Canyon, perhaps another man, Clarence Edward Dutton, is more important to our appreciation of its geologic wonder. Born in Connecticut in 1841, Dutton undertook advanced studies at Yale before a long career in the army began shortly after the start of the Civil War. Dutton possessed a keen mind, a remarkable memory, and a voracious appetite for a wide range of interests, with an uncanny ability to both write and speak about a variety of subjects with equal aplomb. Following the war, he cultivated a profound interest in geology while stationed in New York and Washington, DC. His steady ascension in this field was so compelling that in 1875, Powell chose him as a participant for an exploration to the Colorado Plateau. Dutton proved so worthy of Powell's confidence, he continued studying the geology of the region for the next fifteen years, eventually surveying 12,000 acres.

Dutton's importance to the Grand Canyon was due largely to his literary prowess, as the rare person able to meld science and art. His descriptive writing poetically introduced a magnificent landscape to the fledgling American tourist. As the topography was unique when compared with the more mountainous terrain of the West familiar to the general public, Dutton liberally borrowed architectural terms to describe the features of the Colorado Plateau, creating captivating and imaginative prose. His most notable publication stemming from his surveys was *Tertiary History of the Grand Canyon District*, published in 1882, which included the stunning illustrations of Thomas Moran and William Henry Holmes. The book remains a classic today and is considered by many to be the most evocative description of the Grand Canyon in print. Dutton's work was a significant factor in bringing attention to the wonders of what would later become one of America's premier national parks. Unfortunately, the pristine environment Dutton so eloquently portrayed with his words no longer exists in a totally undefiled condition.

Besides his work on the Colorado Plateau, Dutton studied volcanism in California, Oregon, and Hawaii; during this period he led a party to Crater Lake and determined its depth. Clarence E. Dutton retired from the army in 1891, resumed his interest in geology ten years later, and then passed away in New Jersey in 1912.

Trip Description: From the parking lot at 8,250 feet, the North Kaibab Trail begins the descent off the North Kaibab Plateau toward the head of Roaring Springs Canyon through thick ponderosa pine forest cover, which also includes lesser amounts of Douglas firs, Engelmann spruces, and aspens. The forest progressively lightens as the trail switchbacks down the slope on the way to Coconino Overlook, at 7,450 feet and 0.7 miles from the trailhead, offering the first unobstructed view toward the South Rim. The marvelous vista extends to the San Francisco Peaks in the distance, including 12,633-foot Humphreys Peak, the highest summit in the range.

View of the South Rim of the Grand Canyon from Bright Angel Canyon

Leaving the Toroweap Formation behind, the trail continues the zigzagging descent through the reddish hues of the Coconino Sandstone layer. At 2 miles and 6,800 feet is a composting toilet and a water fountain, just prior to where the trail passes through Supai Tunnel, a 20-foot-long, narrow passage blasted out of the rock of the Supai Formation by Civilian Conservation Corps crews in the 1930s.

Below the tunnel, the unrelenting descent continues through pinyon-juniper woodland, contrasting dramatically with the plants from the cooler and wetter environment above. Dropping into the Redwall Limestone layer, you cross Redwall Bridge at 0.6 mile from the tunnel. The bridge was built in 1966, after a devastating flood destroyed much of the previous route of the trail.

Now on the west side of the usually dry streambed, the trail makes a descending traverse across the canyon wall, down the Roaring Springs Fault, across the Redwall Limestone, eventually passing a large spire known as the Needle. Formerly, the route passed through a small tunnel referred to as the Eye of the Needle, but this feature recently broke away from the canyon wall. Impressive views are common along this section of trail, much of which is airy and exposed. Below the Needle, the trail remains high above the canyon floor on the way down through the Mauv Limestone and onto the Bright

Angel Shale layer, where the sound of rushing water becomes increasingly pronounced. Eventually the origin of this cacophony is seen across the canyon, where water from Roaring Springs gushes out of the far canyon wall. Snowmelt and rainwater high above on the North Kaibab Plateau percolate down through the rock layers to eventually burst forth from Roaring Springs, which is the water supply for both the North and South Rims; water from the springs is piped down Bright Angel Canyon, across the Silver Bridge over the Colorado River, and then up to Indian Garden, where a pump station pushes the water the rest of the way up to the South Rim. Continue down the canyon to a junction with the lateral to Roaring Springs Picnic Area, where drinking water, restrooms, and picnic tables are available.

Roaring Springs Pumphouse Where the trail comes near to the creek, you pass by the residence of the Roaring Springs pumphouse operator at 5.4 miles, a site formerly occupied by Bruce Aiken, his wife, and their three children. For three decades Aiken was a Park Service employee who lived in the canyon and tended the pumphouse. Along the way, he also became an accomplished artist, creating numerous paintings of the Grand Canyon area.

Beyond the junction, the North Kaibab Trail bends into Bright Angel Canyon and follows the course of tumbling Bright Angel Creek downstream into the Tapeats Sandstone layer, eventually drawing directly alongside the creek.

Just beyond the pumphouse residence, the trail crosses a bridge over Bright Angel Creek and continues downstream for another 1.4 miles to Cottonwood Campground.

With designated sites, vault toilets, and piped water, the campground provides the first legal camping on the trail. Although the 7 miles of downhill hiking from the North Rim is not physically taxing, your knees will probably appreciate not having to descend another 7 miles to the next legal camping at Bright Angel Campground. Although the area is named for the grove of cottonwoods lining the creek, shade at the individual campsites is a bit hard to find. If you need a place to beat the heat, plenty of shade is available, with picnic tables and running water, near the ranger station. Anglers may find the fishing to be good in Bright Angel Creek. With a free afternoon, many groups that camp at Cottonwood Campground day hike to Ribbon Falls, rather than doing so as a detour to their backpack down Bright Angel Creek on the way to the bottom of the Grand Canyon.

Side Trip to Ribbon Falls: The 0.3-mile side trip to Ribbon Falls should not be missed, as the red-rock amphitheater and picturesque falls are one of the prime scenic highlights of any rim-to-rim hike. From the junction, drop down to a bridge across Bright Angel Creek and follow gently graded tread downstream to the mouth of a side canyon. Work your way upstream to the base of the falls, where signs point the way up a path to a grotto of lush vegetation on the right, or a path bending around behind the falls on the left. Both routes are well worth the minimal time and effort, revealing two very different perspectives of Ribbon Falls. Water from the limestone canyon above carries deposits of calcium carbonate, which spills over the lip, precipitates, and forms the moss-covered travertine apron at the base. Hanging out in the cool amphitheater of the falls is especially pleasant during hot afternoons. Once you have thoroughly enjoyed the Ribbon Falls environs, retrace your steps to the main trail.

Away from Cottonwood Campground, you work your way down Bright Angel Canyon to a rise offering a fine view of the South Rim and Oza Butte to the northwest. Continue the descent through desert flora to a junction with the trail to Ribbon Falls, 1.2 miles from the campground.

From the Ribbon Falls junction, the North Kaibab Trail makes a short, steep climb over a hillside and then continues down Bright Angel Creek for a couple of miles, to where the walls of the gorge narrow and deepen and the creek adopts a more serpentine course, a part of the canyon known as the Box. The contrast of vegetation through this stretch is quite stark, with lush foliage lining a strip along the creek and arid desert plants peppering the dry soils beyond. Following the winding canyon downstream, you cross a number of bridges on the way to where the canyon starts to widen again, reaching a junction on the left with the Clear Creek Trail. A short stroll from the junction leads to cottonwood-shaded Phantom Ranch, where guests with reservations stay in dormitories or one of eleven rustic cabins. The air-conditioned Phantom Ranch Canteen serves meals to guests and provides cold beverages and assorted sundries to passersby.

Trail signs will direct you across a bridge to the Bright Angel Campground, below Phantom Ranch, 7.3 miles from Cottonwood Campground. Nestled along the west bank of the creek, Bright Angel Campground offers designated campsites with picnic tables and a restroom with flush toilets and running water.

Ribbon Falls, Grand Canyon National Park

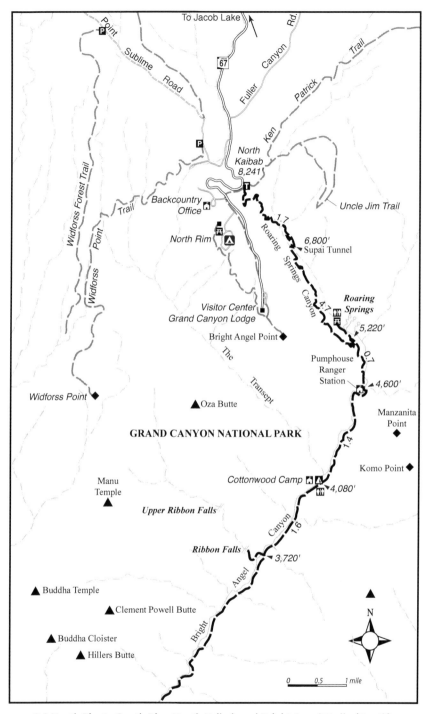

8.2 North Rim to South Rim: North Kaibab and Bright Angel Trails (North)

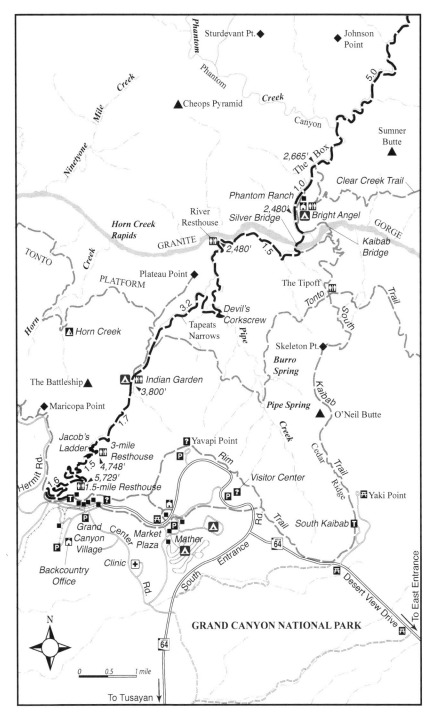

Phantom Pt. ◆ Sturdevant Pt. ◆   Johnson
                                      Point ◆

Phantom   5.0

Creek   ▲Cheops Pyramid   Creek

Mile Creek   Canyon   Sumner
                                            Butte ▲

Ninetyone   2,665' The Box

                              1.0   Clear Creek Trail

                    River   Phantom Ranch
        Horn Creek Resthouse 2,480'   GORGE
        Rapids   Silver Bridge ⚑▲ Bright Angel
TONTO   GRANITE   2,480'   Kaibab
                                    1.5   Bridge

Creek   Pipe   The Tipoff

        PLATFORM   Plateau Point ◆

Horn   3.2   Devil's   Tonto   South   Trail
        ▲ Horn Creek   Tapeats   Corkscrew
                        Narrows   Skeleton Pt. ◆
                                    Burro
The Battleship ▲   ▲⚑ Indian Garden Spring   Kaibab
                         3,800'   Pipe Spring   O'Neil Butte ▲
◆ Maricopa Point   Cedar

        Jacob's   1.7   Trail Ridge
        Ladder   ⚑ Yavapi Point   Rim
        3-mile P   Visitor Center
        Resthouse 1.5   P   Yaki Point
        4,748'   South Kaibab
Hermit Rd. ▲5,729'
        1.6 ⚑1.5-mile Resthouse Rd. Trail

              T   Entrance 64
        Grand Center Market   Mather
        Canyon Plaza P   64
        Village Clinic ✚
        P   South
Backcountry   Rd.
Office

                    GRAND CANYON NATIONAL PARK   Desert View Drive

        N   To East Entrance

        0   0.5   1 mile   64

        To Tusayan ↓

8.3 North Rim to South Rim: North Kaibab and Bright Angel Trails (South)

From Bright Angel Campground, walk toward the river and soon reach a junction. Veer right, cross a bridge over Bright Angel Creek, and follow the trail past some wood structures to the Silver Bridge over the Colorado River. On the far side of the bridge you meet the River Trail, turning right to follow this path through a nearly mile-long section of the Granite Gorge. Much of the tread crosses sand dunes, which makes for quite a slog during high temperatures. At the mouth of Pipe Creek Canyon, the trail leaves the river, turns upstream, and soon reaches the River Resthouse, with composting toilets, emergency phone, and a shaded porch. Just prior to the resthouse, you may notice Columbine Spring bubbling out of a cliff to the west of the trail, surrounded by lush vegetation.

Now a 4,400-foot climb to the South Rim begins, initially ascending moderately alongside Pipe Creek, up a narrow canyon through lush streamside

Side Trip Along the River Trail: While camped at Bright Angel Campground, a short loop trip (1.6 miles) incorporating the Silver and Black Bridges and a section of the River Trail offers a fine diversion for experiencing a stretch of the fabled Colorado River. From the campground, a short stroll leads to a junction—turn left here and pass above Boat Beach, where river runners often moor their boats. Immediately past the beach, the trail passes by some Native American ruins with interpretive signs and then traverses across the cliffs above the river toward the Black Bridge. Completed in 1928, the Black Bridge (also known as the Kaibab Suspension Bridge) provides a river crossing for both hikers and mules. On the far side of the bridge, you enter a short tunnel and make a brief climb to a junction between the River Trail and the waterless 6.3-mile South Kaibab Trail heading up to the South Rim.

At the junction, veer ahead on the righthand path and traverse across the south side of the river, with a grand vista of the Granite Gorge section of the Grand Canyon, as well as a fine view across the water of the delta and mouth of Bright Angel Canyon. A half-mile from the South Kaibab junction, you drop down and turn onto the Silver Bridge. Completed in the late 1960s, the hiker-only Silver Bridge actually carries more than just humans. In a major engineering marvel, the bridge also supports the transcanyon pipeline, which transports water from Roaring Springs to Indian Garden, from which the water is then pumped up to the South Rim. At the far end of the bridge, you follow the trail past several wood structures to a bridge over Bright Angel Creek and the close of the loop at the junction.

vegetation of willows and cottonwoods. After crossing the creek a few times, the trail veers away and attacks the cliffs of the Vishnu Schist layer via a set of switchbacks dubbed Devil's Corkscrew. Leaving the creek behind, a dramatic shift occurs from the riparian foliage near the creek to desert flora, including a variety of cacti. At the top of the switchbacks, the trail makes an ascending traverse, eventually leading into the canyon of Garden Creek. Follow the creek upstream through the scenic Tapeats Narrows on the way toward Indian Garden. Where the grade starts to ease, you reach a junction with the Tonto Trail on the left, 3.2 miles from the River Resthouse. Another half-mile of gently graded tread leads to the beautifully lush oasis of Indian Garden.

A number of springs bubble up above the impervious Bright Angel Shale to keep the picturesque foliage of Indian Garden well watered. Not surprisingly, this oasis has long been a gathering place for humans within the Grand Canyon. Nowadays, the area has a campground with designated sites, ranger station, restrooms with running water, and an emergency phone. The ranger station has a number of books one can borrow while enjoying a lengthy rest under the shaded porch or beneath a cottonwood. Also, the ranger on duty often presents daily programs. If you're camped at Indian Garden, or if you have the extra time, the 3-mile round-trip to Plateau Point offers a stunning view of the canyon.

Although Indian Garden is halfway by mileage between the Colorado River and the South Rim, you've gained only one-third of the elevation. Away from Indian Garden, the trail continues upstream along Garden Creek, ascending mildly to moderately across the upper Tonto Platform until reaching Jacob's Ladder, a set of switchbacks ascending a gap in the Redwall Limestone formed by the Bright Angel Fault. At the top of the switchbacks is a junction with the short lateral to the 3-Mile Resthouse, 1.7 miles from Indian Garden. This facility has running water, toilets, and emergency phone.

Beyond the resthouse, the trail continues a serpentine course beneath the massive cliffs on the west wall of Garden Creek Canyon. Along the ascent, the desert flora gives way to a scattered forest environment. Soon after crossing the creek, you reach 2-Mile Corner and a fine view. Beyond, the interminable ascent continues on a rising traverse before switchbacking to Mile-and-a-Half Resthouse, also equipped with composting toilets, running water, and emergency phone.

The final leg of the journey follows a lengthy upward traverse away from the resthouse before the trail resumes a zigzagging course up the canyon headwall, through pinyon-juniper woodland. Above a set of switchbacks, you pass through Second Tunnel and then follow long-legged switchbacks to First

Tunnel before eventually winding up the wall to the conclusion of the climb, at the Bright Angel trailhead on the South Rim near the Kolb Studio.

Possible Itinerary

Day	Camps and Side Trips	Distance (mi.)	Elevation (ft.)
1	North Kaibab TH to Cottonwood Campground	6.8	–4,150
2	Bright Angel Campground	7.3	–1,600
	Side trip to Ribbon Falls	0.6	+200/–200
	Side trip on River Trail	1.6	Negligible
3	Out to Bright Angel TH	9.3	+4,800/–100

Green Tips: Grand Canyon Association—grandcanyon.org

The Five Elements: Earth, Water, Air, Fire, and Salty Snacks The Colorado Plateau was one of the last significant areas of the American West to be explored. Coincidentally, the Grand Canyon represented the most glaring hole in my personal list of must-see places as well. Quite anxious to experience America's only representative of the Seven Natural Wonders of the World, Keith and I left Jacob Lake and drove to the wilderness office early on May 15, the opening day of the North Rim season. Without a reservation, we were hoping to secure a walk-in permit for our proposed rim-to-rim hike, but our countenances dimmed when we saw three groups already ahead of us in line. One by one, the groups were summoned into the office, where we watched them through the large window joyfully laughing and joking with the rangers. We kept hoping their revelry was not directed at the eventual misfortune of the suckers behind them in line. Thankfully, when our turn finally came, we were able to secure a permit for the next day.

During our interview with the rangers, they repeatedly reinforced the idea that we must continually eat lots of salty snacks during the cross-canyon hike. Over and over again, they recounted the possible disasters that could come from not heeding their advice. Due to these repeated warnings, we started second guessing the combined wisdom we had accrued from decades of backpacking experience, rationalizing this hard-gained knowledge away as having been obtained primarily in a mountain and not a desert environment. Clearly, without toting a twenty-five-pound bag of Corn Nuts, we were going to die, so off we went to the campground store. After gathering what salty snacks we could, we spent the day sightseeing along the North Rim and then found a place to spend the night.

Our trip down the North Kaibab Trail the next day proved uneventful, at least from a potential human disaster point of view. We arrived at Cottonwood Camp before midafternoon under clear skies and mild temperatures. The next day saw similar weather; by the time we reached Bright Angel Campground near the bottom of the canyon, the thermometer was slightly higher but nowhere near the intensely scorching heat we had been warned about. After day hiking the loop, using the two bridges over the river, we passed the afternoon lounging in the shade, sipping ice-cold lemonade from the Phantom Ranch Canteen. So far, the desperate need for the salty snacks we were warned about had yet to materialize. However, tomorrow was the climb out of the canyon up the exposed south-facing wall, which would surely present the ultimate test for anyone foolish enough to be without a sufficient supply of salty snacks.

That night, clouds moved in, and by the time we had packed up the next morning and started hiking, a mist and then a steady rain had developed. Clad in rain parkas and pants, we made the steady climb from the Colorado River up the south wall of the Grand Canyon in a nearly constant downpour. The rain came down the hardest on the way through Indian Garden, the tunnel-like enclosure of our parka hoods severely diminishing our ability to enjoy the otherwise lovely scenery. The rain ceased just before we topped out on the South Rim, where the combination of a stiff wind, cloudy skies, and very chilly temperatures created winter-like conditions. The usual crush of tourists on the South Rim didn't help the somber ambiance one bit.

We tried desperately to stay warm while restlessly awaiting the arrival of our van, which took us on a four-and-a-half-hour shuttle ride back to our car at the North Kaibab trailhead. Snow began to fall on the approach to the North Rim, and by the time we got to the parking lot, loaded our backpacks, and headed out again, a whiteout confronted us. As we drove away from the park, the highway was covered for several miles with a couple of inches of new snow before the eventual drop in elevation turned the precipitation into a cold rain in the lower altitudes. Hours later, upon reaching our motel in Kanab and the welcome prospect of a much needed shower and a hot meal, I put my car keys into my pants pocket, felt a crinkly plastic bag of unknown origin, and pulled out an unopened package of Corn Nuts. The life-saving salty snacks would have to wait to be consumed until our next backpacking trip to the Grand Canyon.

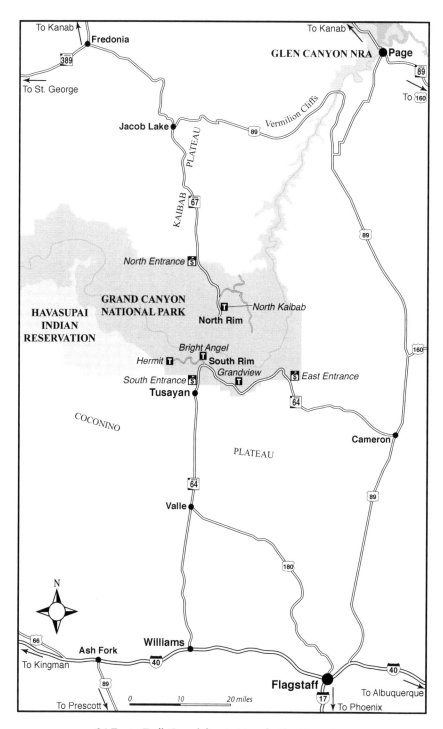

9.1 Tonto Trail: Grandview to Hermits Rest Location

—— TRIP 9 ——

Tonto Trail:
Grandview to Hermits Rest

You cannot see the Grand Canyon in one view,
as if it were a changeless spectacle from
which a curtain might be lifted, but to see it you have to
toil from month to month through its labyrinths.

—JOHN WESLEY POWELL

APPROXIMATELY TWO-THIRDS of the way from the South Rim of the Grand Canyon to the Colorado River below is the Tonto Platform, a broad 70-plus-mile-long terrace separating the inner gorge from the upper canyon. The Tonto Trail travels almost the entire distance from Garnet Canyon to Red Canyon, providing an alternative experience to the much more popular rim-to-rim hike in Trip 8. Rather than providing a view of the ever-changing rock layers on the way down to and back up from the Colorado River, as on a rim-to-rim journey, the Tonto Trail contours across the top of the platform, skirting the edges of side canyons along the way. The 50-mile route described here follows a section of the Tonto Trail between the Grandview and Hermits Rest Trails. Aside from at Indian Garden and Monument Creek Campgrounds, solitude is almost guaranteed. The scenery is always gorgeous.

A trip along the Tonto Trail is for experienced desert backpackers only. Unlike the rim-to-rim hike described in Trip 8, there are no resthouses, developed campgrounds, or running water except at Indian Garden. Away from Indian Garden, water and shade are both scarce, requiring a reasonable amount of planning and the ability to carry extra weight. The condition of the

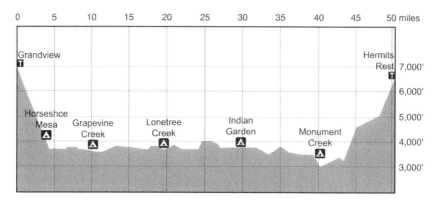

Tonto Trail: Grandview to Hermits Rest

trail is not as good either, but experiencing the vastness of the Grand Canyon without company is worth the inconvenience. Late winter to early spring offer the highest probability for acquiring water.

Days: 5–7

Distance: 49.4 miles

Type: Shuttle

Scenery: 10

Solitude: 7

Technical Difficulty: 5

Physical Difficulty: 7

Elevation Gain/Loss: +10,375'/–7,925'

Season: All year **Best:** April to May

Maps: USGS—Grandview Point, Cape Royal, Phantom Ranch, Grand Canyon; Earthwalk Press—*Grand Canyon National Park Hiking Map and Guide*

Resources: *Grand Canyon Grandview Trail Guide*, by the Grand Canyon Association; *Grand Canyon Hermit Trail Guide*, by the Grand Canyon Association

Contacts:

- Grand Canyon National Park
PO Box 129, Grand Canyon, AZ 86023
928-638-7864   www.nps.gov/grca

Permits: GCNP charges a $25 entrance fee for private vehicles, good for 7 days. The fee is $15 per person for those entering the park on foot, bicycle, motorcycle, or commercial bus. An annual pass is $50. The annual America the Beautiful interagency pass ($80) provides access to all national parks and national recreation areas, including Grand Canyon.

A valid wilderness permit is required for all overnight stays in the Grand Canyon backcountry. Competition for permits is perhaps higher for corridor trails at GCNP than for any other western park. Requests for advance reservations can be submitted by fax on the first day of the month, four months prior to the desired departure day (submitting a fax at one second past midnight on the first day of the appropriate month would not be too soon—provided you don't get a busy signal). The cost of an advance reservation includes a $10 permit charge and a $5 fee per person per night. Check out the park's website for additional information (www.nps.gov/grca). The backcountry office has a phone number (928-638-7875), but the phone traffic is at such a high volume, you shouldn't expect to get through easily. You may get a faster response using e-mail. Good luck!

Those without a permit reservation can show up at the South Rim Backcountry Office well before opening, stand in line, and wait their turn for a crack at any available reservations. Chances are fair for obtaining a backcountry permit, especially if your group is small and you can hang around for a day or two before departure. If you choose this option, be prepared to camp out, or find lodging (usually outside the park), for up to a few nights. Plenty of day hiking and sightseeing opportunities can fill up your days while you wait.

If you can't obtain a backcountry permit and don't mind the greater expense of a guided trip, several commercial enterprises are licensed to perform this service.

Regulations: Camping is exclusively limited to designated sites at campgrounds west of the South Kaibab Trail (Indian Garden, Horn Creek, Salt Creek, Cedar Spring, Monument Creek, and Hermit Creek). Campfires are not permitted.

Nearest Campgrounds: Mather Campground—near Grand Canyon Village

Nearest Airports:
- Grand Canyon Airport (GCN)—7 miles
- Flagstaff Pulliam Airport (FLG)—86 miles
- Phoenix Sky Harbor International Airport (PHX)—231 miles

Nearest Outdoor Retailers: Grand Canyon Village Market

Outfitters: More than twenty licensed outfitters provide guided backpacking trips into the Grand Canyon. Consult the park's website for a current list (www.nps.gov/grca).

Transportation Logistics: Due to the park's extreme popularity, many public transportation options have arisen for getting to the South Rim by airplane, bus, or train. The South Rim can be accessed by rental car from airports in Las Vegas, Phoenix, and Tucson. From the Nevada towns of North Las Vegas, Boulder City, and Henderson, three small airlines serve Grand Canyon Airport, where taxi and shuttle service is available to the South Rim (rental cars are not available). A free shuttle bus runs from the gateway town of Tusayan every 15 minutes between mid-May and early September. Once inside the park, three shuttle bus routes provide free access to the major destinations along the South Rim. From the town of Williams, Grand Canyon Railway offers four levels of service on train rides to the South Rim, which take two hours and fifteen minutes, with lodging packages also available. Consult their website at www.thetrain.com for more information.

Backcountry Logistics: (H, H2O, R, Su) Temperatures in the Grand Canyon are often extreme, especially during the summer, which makes spring the best time for a backpack on the Tonto Trail. Many summer visitors are forced to hike the canyon by headlamp during the cooler periods at night, which seems to defeat the purpose of coming all the way to see the canyon in the first place. Access to the South Rim is year-round.

Due to the heat and dryness of this desert climate, potential health hazards include heat exhaustion, heat stroke, and hyponatremia. With thousands of feet of elevation change, weather conditions can vary radically between the rims and the bottom of the canyon, which oftentimes requires backpackers to carry a wide range of clothing to avoid such conditions as hypothermia. During summer the Park Service recommends that hikers not travel during the hottest parts of the day, usually between 10 AM and 4 PM.

Drink plenty of fluids to stay hydrated—water is often scarce along the 51-mile route. Check with the rangers at the wilderness permit office for current reports. Cottonwood Creek (4.5 miles), Grapevine Creek (10 miles), Garden Creek (28.7), and Monument Creek (38.8) are perennial streams, where water should be available. (In dry years, there may be 9- and 10-mile stretches of the Tonto Trail where water is not available.) Santa Maria Spring (2.2 miles below Hermits Rest) is also a reliable water source. All water should be treated or filtered. Avoid drinking water from Horn Creek (radioactive) and

Salt Creek (highly mineralized). Also, the Park Service strongly encourages hikers to continually ingest plenty of salty snacks to replenish the body's salts lost through perspiration.

Although potentially wreaking havoc on one's knees, the descent down the Grandview Trail will be much less physically taxing than the climb up to Hermits Rest on the South Rim. Trekking poles are a near necessity. During the ascent out of the canyon, drink fluids, ingest salts, rest often, and go slowly. Medical emergencies are common enough in the Grand Canyon that emergency facilities and helicopter pads to facilitate evacuations are available. The closest such facility along the Tonto Trail is near Indian Garden.

Camping in the inner canyon along this section of the Tonto Trail is limited to six developed campgrounds west of the South Kaibab Trail. Of the six, demand seems highest for space at Indian Garden, which is arguably the prettiest setting. Except for Indian Garden, which offers shade, picnic tables, running water, and restrooms, camping areas are fairly primitive.

Amenities and Attractions: Grand Canyon Village on the **South Rim** of the canyon has much to offer the average tourist. The numerous lodging options are typically booked well in advance, and grabbing a bite to eat without reservations often requires a long wait as well. The nearby **Mather Campground** is often full, but space should be available in the backpackers' area at the start or completion of your hike. Free shuttle buses using three routes offer a convenient way to access the South Rim's major features, including Market Plaza (general store, bank, post office, Yavapai Cafeteria), the campground, vista points, and trailheads. Camper Services near Market Plaza conveniently offers a laundromat and showers.

For those who don't mind rubbing elbows with the masses, the elegant **El Tovar** is the premier place on the South Rim to spend a night, enjoy a meal, or sip a prickly pear margarita on the patio outside the bar. Additional lodging options include Bright Angel Lodge, Kachina Lodge, Maswik Lodge, Thunderbird Lodge, and Yavapai Lodge. Away from the village, **Desert View Drive** leads to many fine spots, including a glorious vista from **Lipan Point** as well as the **Watchtower**, a circular stone tower designed by Mary Colter on the South Rim's high point. Day hikers will have many excellent trails to choose from.

Overnighters not fortunate enough to have reservations inside the park will often stay in the gateway town of **Tusayan**, a half-mile-long strip of Highway 64 lined with motels, gas stations, and fast-food eateries. The town of **Williams**, which capitalizes on Route 66 fame, is a little over an hour south of the South Rim. The much larger city of **Flagstaff** is one and a half hours southeast, where the award-winning upscale **Cottage Place Restaurant** would be a fine way to reward oneself after a rigorous backpack through the Grand Canyon.

Directions to Trailhead: The gated Hermits Rest Road begins just west of Bright Angel Lodge. A valid wilderness permit includes the access code to open the gate, allowing you to drive 8 miles to Hermits Rest parking lot (restrooms, running water, picnic area, snack bar, gift shop) and then another quarter mile on gravel road to the backpacker parking area at the ending trailhead. Without a vehicle, the red shuttle bus route provides free access to Hermits Rest.

To reach the starting trailhead, follow Desert View Drive (Arizona Highway 64) east from the junction of the South Entrance Road for about 11 miles to the lefthand turn toward Grandview Point. Continue through the visitor parking area to the overnight lot (vault toilets). Note: Shuttle service does not extend to Grandview Point.

Mary Colter Aside from the creator of the landscape, no other being is so attached to the visual beauty of the Grand Canyon than architect Mary Colter, who designed many of the park's buildings. A bright, strong, and determined woman ahead of the times, she incorporated Hopi, Navajo, and Zuni motifs into her projects, using mostly native materials in the process. Colter became one of the driving architectural forces in the American style that came to be known as national park rustic. Her imprint on Grand Canyon can still be seen today at Hopi House, Hermits Rest, Phantom Ranch, Bright Angel Lodge, and the Watchtower.

The notion of a widowed mother sending her seventeen-year-old daughter across the country to attend art school as a viable means of eventual financial support might be met with quizzical expressions in our era, but this is exactly what Mary Colter's mother did way back in 1886. While Mary attended art school in San Francisco, she also apprenticed with an architect, the common practice at that time for those interested in the field, as few American schools of architecture existed in the late 1800s. Upon completion of her studies, Mary returned home to St. Paul, Minnesota, landing a teaching position in a neighboring community. The following year she began a fifteen-year career teaching at Mechanic Arts High School in St. Paul.

During a summer vacation to San Francisco, Mary made a contact with an employee of the Fred Harvey Company that would alter her destiny. Fred Harvey was something of an entrepreneurial visionary, creating and carrying out a plan to build high-quality eating houses and hotels along the route of the Santa Fe Railroad. Previously, without dining cars, railroad passengers were forced to pay inflated prices for substandard food at ramshackle roadhouses when the trains stopped for water. Harvey's penchant for quality and efficiency raised the standard for rail travel in conjunction with boosting tourist traffic to the American Southwest. Mary was hired one summer by the Fred Harvey Company to decorate the Indian Building next to the new Alvarado Hotel in Albuquerque, New Mexico, a short-term position that inaugurated a forty-year relationship with the company and the Santa Fe Railroad.

After the Santa Fe Railroad acquired and extended a rail line from Williams north to the Grand Canyon, the Fred Harvey Company commissioned the architect who had worked on the Alvarado Hotel to design the El Tovar on the South Rim. At the same time, the company commissioned Mary Colter to design an Indian building across from the hotel, which the company would use for sales of Indian arts. She designed the structure after a Hopi dwelling, and it became known as Hopi House. Much as she did upon completion of her job decorating the Indian Building, she returned home to St. Paul and resumed teaching after the Hopi House was built.

After the death of her mother, Mary and her older sister relocated to Seattle, Washington, where she worked for the Frederick and Nelson Department Store until a permanent position of architect and designer opened up with the Fred Harvey Company. Although based in Kansas City, Mary routinely traveled throughout the Southwest for business, and she also spent a fair amount of time in Southern California at a home she would purchase for her sister. During her years with Fred Harvey, she created numerous landmark hotels and commercial lodges, twenty-one projects in all. Although many consider the El Navajo Hotel (currently an Amtrak station) in Gallup, New Mexico, to be her masterwork, her most famous works remain those within Grand Canyon National Park. She passed away in 1958 at age eighty-eight.

Trip Description: You might want to prepare your legs for the drop into the canyon along the Grandview Trail by performing numerous lunges at the gym, or countless descents of stadium stairs, both while carrying an extra fifty pounds on your back. Otherwise, your legs will be screaming for the next couple of days after the stiff descent to Horseshoe Mesa. The trail drops off the Kaibab Formation at the rim in steep and unrelenting fashion via short-legged, rock-hard switchbacks. Fortunately, the views of the Grand Canyon are sweeping and glorious for most of the descent, as you pass through the Toroweap Formation and then the Coconino Sandstone. Along the way, the vegetation transitions from the ponderosa pine forest at the rim to the pinyon pine and juniper zone in the middle elevations, and then ultimately to the desert scrub community, which will be a nearly constant companion for the duration of the trip along the Tonto Platform. A couple of short-lived, not-as-steep traverses offer an all-too-brief respite from the precipitous plunge toward Horseshoe Mesa. You reach the unmarked Coconino Saddle at 6,236 feet on the divide between the canyons of Hance and Cottonwood Creeks, 2.2 miles from and 1,200 feet below the trailhead.

Away from Coconino Saddle, the trail continues its plunge through the Hermit Formation, the Supai Group, and then the Redwall Limestone. Eventually the grade eases where the trail gains the crest of a knoll and reaches a junction with a trail on the right, which leads shortly to Page Spring and the Last Chance Mine (also known as Grandview Mine). The Grandview Trail, constructed in 1893, was originally used by mule trains to transport copper ore from the mine, which ceased operations in 1907. An ominous-looking radioactive sign should discourage any notion of visiting the mine, which would be unsafe and illegal anyway. Vishnu Temple dominates the view across the gaping hole of the Inner Gorge.

Veer left at the mine junction and soon reach a second junction, signed COTTONWOOD CREEK, to the left. Nearby is an old stone ruin, formerly the mine's cookhouse. If your first night's camp is at Horseshoe Mesa, take the righthand path toward the designated campsites (the group site is 100 yards ahead) and three-sided privies. Any stay at Horseshoe Mesa would be incomplete without a walk out to the edge of the mesa for a supreme Grand Canyon view. For those with plenty of time, the path on the west side of Horseshoe Mesa leads to use trails accessing the entrance to Cave of the Domes, at 4,795 feet (for environmental concerns, the Park Service discourages, but does not prohibit, entrance into the cave).

From the junction to Cottonwood Creek, veer west a short distance past what must have been the cookhouse dump, evidenced by hundreds of rusty tin cans. Head down a gully on steep short-legged switchbacks, briefly interrupted by a traverse, to eventually reach the crossing of the creek bed, 800 feet below the mesa. The creek is usually dry at this elevation, but by continuing downstream you'll soon cross the now-running stream several times on the way to a junction with Tonto Trail, 5 miles from the trailhead. Nearby, the creek spills picturesquely over a low rock wall.

Heading westbound, the Tonto Trail makes an arc into a side drainage of Cottonwood Creek, where a spring usually provides a trickle of water and then returns to the rim above the main channel. Along the contour of the Tonto Platform, the trail follows the folds and creases of the main canyon, winding through a preponderance of blackbrush, the trademark shrub of the Tonto Platform's desert scrub community. In spring, this shrub is adorned with a profusion of tiny yellow flowers. The magnificent scenery along the North Rim includes the pyramidal Vishnu Temple, flanked by Krishna Shrine and Rama Shrine. Eventually, the mighty Colorado River makes its first appearance, coursing through the deep canyon below.

Turning southwest, you hike along the rim of Grapevine Creek on narrow, sometimes rocky, slightly undulating, and exposed tread. Grapevine Creek is the largest and most complex side canyon between the Grandview and Hermit Trails, and traversing the rim of this gorge will require two to three hours of steady hiking. The trail contours around numerous washes along the way. At 9.25 miles, the trail enters a side canyon, where a spring sends a trickle of water downstream. Eventually the trail drops to a crossing of Grapevine Creek, which usually offers a good flow of water and fine campsites nearby, 10.4 miles from the Grandview trailhead.

The extended walk you just completed along the northeast rim of Grapevine Creek to the crossing is repeated again on the return along the northwest side to Granite Gorge, again arcing into small side canyons, beneath Lyell Butte, along the way. Eventually, you leave Grapevine Canyon behind and climb a bit to a small bench (3,808 feet) overlooking Grapevine Rapids below. The view of the Colorado River is impressive, and a couple of view-packed, although dry, campsites will appear quite tempting to those in need of overnight accommodations.

The views of the Colorado continue for about the next mile, interrupted for a spell where the Tonto Trail arcs into a side canyon. After surmounting the northeast ridge of Lyell Butte (more river views and dry campsites), the trail bends into Boulder Creek Canyon, reaching the crossing of the creek in about half the time it took to reach the crossing of Grapevine Creek. The stream is typically dry at the Tonto crossing, but a spring up the south fork is usually reliable.

The journey out of Boulder Creek Canyon is relatively short, as the Tonto Trail cuts across a bench to an unnamed drainage. From there, you closely

A view of Granite Gorge from the Tonto Trail

follow the main canyon rim, arcing around the northeast ridge that spills down from Newton Butte before veering into Lonetree Canyon. Follow the rim of the canyon to the crossing of the creek, 3.1 miles from Boulder Creek. In the spring, Lonetree Creek usually has small amounts of water at the crossing and more about 0.3 mile downstream near a lone cottonwood tree. Overnighters may find a few good campsites near the crossing.

From the crossing, walk along the west rim of Lonetree Canyon for about 0.3 mile and then climb to the top of a low ridge (3,783 feet). A gently rising ascent leads across a side drainage and up to a knoll, where a short off-trail walk to the north leads to fine views of the Colorado River coursing through Granite Gorge. Beyond, a general descent arcs around the base of Pattie Butte and across a trio of usually dry washes into the Cremation Creek drainage and a crossing of the stream bed, 3.5 miles from Lonetree Canyon. Although the creek is usually dry, nearby campsites offer the possibility of a beautiful sunset glow on Zoraster Temple across the immense gulf of the Grand Canyon.

Work your way over to the middle channel of Cremation Creek and switchback steeply to the bottom, where there are a couple of campsites. Climb steeply out of the canyon and then repeat the same process 0.4 mile farther at the west fork. A half-mile gentle ascent leads past a dry campsite across from an overhanging rock, before a stiff 400-foot climb ensues. Beyond the climb, the grade eases, as you cross a couple of dry washes with a campsite in between. Pass by a couple of large cairns delineating the end of the at-large camping zone and then stroll easily for 0.75 mile to a junction with the South Kaibab Trail, 2.5 miles from Cremation Creek (restroom, phone). After days of probably few human encounters, you're apt to see plenty of day hikers and backpackers, and perhaps a mule train, using the popular South Kaibab Trail.

The westbound Tonto Trail departs from the South Kaibab Trail slightly uphill from the junction of the eastbound trail. The improved nature of the tread is immediately evident, as the trail arcs around the base of the ridge harboring the South Kaibab Trail above. Eventually, the trail nears the rim of Pipe Creek and dips into a side canyon choked with vegetation, well watered by Burro Spring. A use trail provides access to the spring above the main trail. At 2 miles from the South Kaibab junction, the Tonto Trail dips down to the crossing of cottonwood-lined Pipe Creek, which usually offers a good flow of water. Shady campsites and a splash of color from spring wildflowers create a fine overnight destination.

Away from Pipe Creek, the Tonto Trail contours generally northwest for a couple of miles across open and scenic terrain toward Garden Creek and a junction with the Bright Angel Trail. From there, a 0.3-mile jaunt leads through lush vegetation upstream to lovely Indian Garden. After 30-plus miles on the primitive Tonto Trail, the accoutrements at Indian Garden may seem quite luxurious. Running water, picnic tables, and a resthouse offer day-trippers and backpackers along the heavily used Bright Angel Trail an opportunity to relax and refresh. Designated campsites at the nearby campground are equipped with picnic tables, ammo cans for food storage, and steel bars for hanging backpacks, with composting toilets and running water nearby. A small stone building below the campground houses a visitor center, offering pertinent information about the Grand Canyon, as well as a library of books and playing cards for checkout. A nearby amphitheater is the site of evening ranger programs. As the campground is usually full and the Bright Angel Trail has a steady stream of hikers passing by, Indian Garden is not the place for solitude seekers, but the lush vegetation and gurgling stream create a true oasis in the desert.

Leaving the relative luxury of Indian Garden behind, the Tonto Trail crosses Garden Creek and then traverses above the stream back out into the open, reaching a junction with the spur trail to Plateau Point after 0.7 mile. If you haven't already hiked out to the point while camped at Indian Garden, the 1.6-mile round-trip hike on nearly level trail to the spectacular view from the

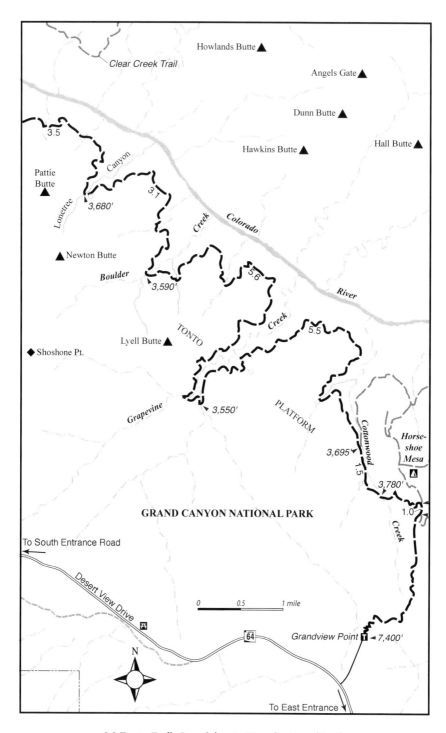

Clear Creek Trail

Howlands Butte ▲

Angels Gate ▲

Dunn Butte ▲

Hawkins Butte ▲

Hall Butte ▲

3.5

Canyon

Pattie
Butte
▲

Lonetree

3.7

3,680'

Creek

Colorado

▲ Newton Butte

Boulder

3,590'

5.6

River

TONTO

Creek

5.5

Lyell Butte ▲

◆ Shoshone Pt.

Grapevine

3,550'

PLATFORM

Cottonwood

Horse-
shoe
Mesa
▲

3,695'

1.5

3,780'

GRAND CANYON NATIONAL PARK

1.0

Creek

To South Entrance Road

Desert View Drive

0   0.5   1 mile

64

Grandview Point ▮ ◄ 7,400'

N

To East Entrance ▼

9.2 Tonto Trail: Grandview to Hermits Rest (East)

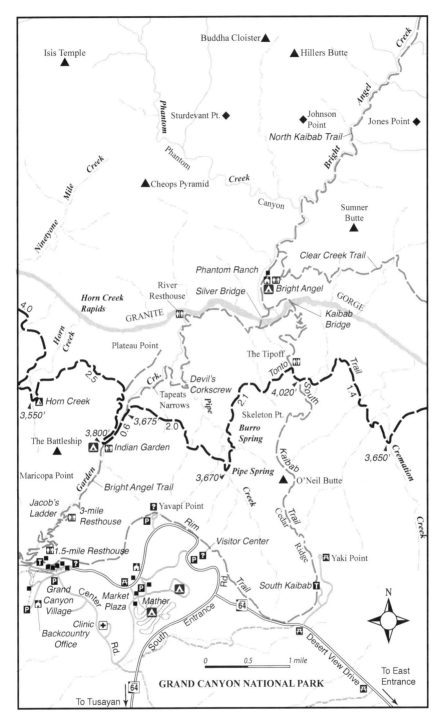

Isis Temple ▲

Buddha Cloister ▲

Hillers Butte ▲

Phantom

Sturdevant Pt. ◆

Johnson Point ◆

Jones Point ◆

North Kaibab Trail

Phantom

Mile

Creek

Creek

Canyon

Ninetyone

▲Cheops Pyramid

Sumner Butte ▲

Bright

Clear Creek Trail

Phantom Ranch

Horn Creek Rapids

River Resthouse

Silver Bridge

Bright Angel

4.0

Horn Creek

GRANITE

GORGE

Kaibab Bridge

Plateau Point

The Tipoff

Tonto

Trail

2.5

Crk.

Devil's Corkscrew

4,020'

South

1.4

▲ Horn Creek
3,550'

Tapeats Narrows

Pipe

2.1

Skeleton Pt.

The Battleship ▲

0.6

3,675'

2.0

Burro Spring

3,650' ▲

Cremation

3,800'

Indian Garden

3,670 ▾

Pipe Spring

O'Neil Butte ▲

Maricopa Point

Garden

Bright Angel Trail

Kaibab

Creek

Jacob's Ladder

3-mile Resthouse

? Yavapi Point

Rim

Visitor Center

Cedar

Trail

Yaki Point

1.5-mile Resthouse

Ridge

Creek

N

Grand Canyon Village

Center

Market Plaza

Mather

South Kaibab

Entrance

Clinic ✚

64

Rd.

Trail

Backcountry Office

South

Rd.

64

GRAND CANYON NATIONAL PARK

0   0.5   1 mile

Desert View Drive

To East Entrance

To Tusayan ↓

9.3 Tonto Trail: Grandview to Hermits Rest (Middle)

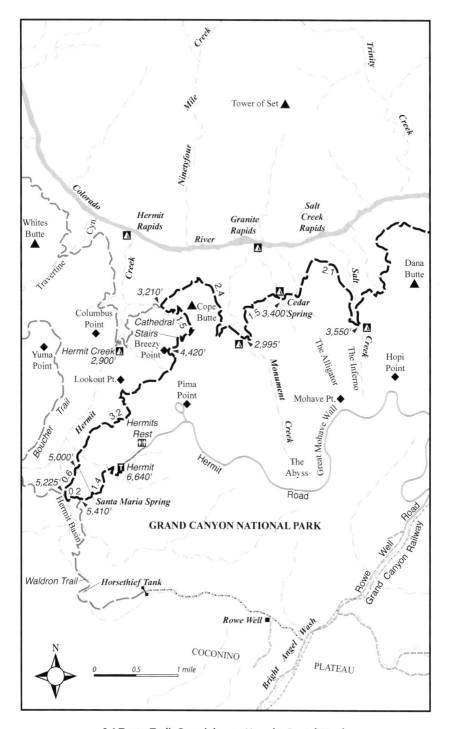

Creek

Trinity

Mile

Ninetyfour

Creek

Tower of Set ▲

Colorado

Hermit
Rapids
⚠

Granite
Rapids
⚠

River

Salt
Creek
Rapids

Whites
Butte
▲

Cyn.

Dana
Butte
▲

Travertine

Creek

3,210'

2.4

Cope
Butte ▲

2.7

Salt

⚠ Cedar
1.5 3,400' Spring

Columbus
Point
◆

Cathedral
Stairs
Breezy
Point

1.5

◆
⚠ 4,420'

⚠ 2,995'

3,550'

⚠

Creek

Yuma
Point ◆

Hermit Creek ⚠
2,900'

The Alligator

The Inferno

Hopi
Point
◆

Lookout Pt. ◆

Pima
Point
◆

Monument

Mohave Pt. ◆

Great Mohave Wall

Hermit

3.2

Trail

Boucher

5,000'

Hermits
Rest
🚻

Creek

The
Abyss

0.6

🚹 Hermit
1.4 6,640'

Hermit

5,225'

0.2

Santa Maria Spring
5,410'

Road

Rowe

Hermit Basin

GRAND CANYON NATIONAL PARK

Well

Road

Grand Canyon Railway

Waldron Trail

Horsethief Tank ◆

Rowe Well ■

COCONINO

Bright Angel Wash

PLATEAU

N

0   0.5   1 mile

9.4 Tonto Trail: Grandview to Hermits Rest (West)

On the Tonto Trail

top of the rock cliff is a highly worthwhile diversion. A section of iron railing may add a level of comfort to any acrophobes in your group.

Gently graded tread leads away from the junction, across the north base of the Battleship, until the Tonto Trail veers toward Horn Creek. At 1.8 miles from the Plateau Point junction, you descend to a crossing of the usually dry creek bed, where there is a designated campsite and pit toilet. The water in Horn Creek is radioactive and consequently not recommended for drinking, which would seem to considerably diminish the attractiveness of camping here.

Away from the Horn Creek crossing, you soon cross the west fork, climb out of the canyon, and then follow a rolling traverse below Dana Butte to the crossing of a dry wash. Beyond the wash, the trail climbs stiffly but briefly to the crest of a low ridge, where a fine view unfolds of the main canyon and the river. Continuing around the base of the ridge north of Dana Butte, the Tonto Trail follows a descending arc to the rim of Salt Creek canyon. A winding route ultimately leads down into the steep-walled canyon, aptly named the Inferno, and a crossing of the creek, 4 miles from Horn Creek. Similar to Horn Creek, a designated camp area and pit toilet are located nearby, but the Park Service recommends not drinking the highly mineralized water.

Climb out of the canyon and follow the rim back toward the main canyon around the nose of the Alligator, where you have partial canyon views before

The Colorado River from the Tonto Trail

angling away toward Cedar Spring. Continue across the first channel and over a low hump to the second channel, 2.1 miles from Salt Creek, where small amounts of water may be found a good distance downstream. The designated camp is also located a short distance downstream from the crossing on a sandy bench above the stream bed.

A stiff ascent leads out of the gorge of Cedar Spring and across a low ridge before a descent takes you along the rim of Monument Creek Canyon. Soon the namesake feature appears below, a distinctive sandstone spire rising more than 100 feet above the canyon floor. A set of steep, rocky, short-legged switchbacks leads through a gash in the east canyon wall down to the perennial stream, 1.5 miles from Cedar Spring. Several campsites are spread along the banks of Monument Creek, many partially shaded by mesquite trees. The area is quite popular, and oftentimes the campsites fill up quickly, which tends to create a feeling of congestion. A privy with three open-air toilets is located downstream on the hillside above the creek. Beyond the privy is arguably the best campsite, which is the group site, situated in the shade of a rock wall on a sandy shelf, well away from the hubbub of the main camp, and with a grand view of the canyon and the monument. Water is best acquired downstream from camp via a short side trail.

The Tonto Trail exits Monument Creek Canyon at a junction near the monument, where the trail ahead descends 1.3 miles to Granite Rapids on the Colorado River. The hike down to the river is a fine afternoon diversion for campers at Monument Creek, and the designated camp area is also a popular destination for backpackers departing from the Hermits Rest trailhead.

Veer left at the junction and climb steeply out of Monument Creek Canyon through a side canyon. About halfway up, the trail crosses the drainage and then follows an angling climb to the rim of the main slot of Monument Creek. Follow the rim for a while before a gentler climb heads for the top of a ridge (3,389 feet), offering a fine view of a stretch of the river. From there, a moderate descent leads downslope, followed by a gently graded jaunt over to a junction with the Hermit Trail, 1.7 miles from Monument Creek. To the right, the Hermit Trail leads 1.3 miles to Hermit Camp and then terminates at Hermit Rapids on the Colorado River.

Leaving the Tonto Trail, turn left at the junction and begin a moderate climb southeast toward Cope Butte on the Hermit Trail, which soon becomes a stiffer affair on numerous short-legged switchbacks. Beginning in the Bright Angel Shale, you soon climb through the greenish brown rock of the Mauv Limestone layer. Finally reaching the top of the first set of switchbacks, a long diagonal ascent slices across the west face of Cope Butte to the base of the

Cathedral Stairs, a second set of tight, rocky switchbacks winding up through a break in the Redwall Limestone. From the Tonto junction below, a route through this area seems totally inconceivable.

At the top of Cathedral Stairs, you've gained 1,200 of the 3,400 feet necessary to reach the Hermits Rest trailhead. A long traverse leads away from Cathedral Stairs to Breezy Point, 1.5 miles from the Tonto junction. The traverse continues, with minor ups and downs necessary to access ledges wide enough to carry the trail. A little over a mile from Breezy Point, the trail crests a narrow ridge trending north to Lookout Point, an excellent viewpoint for those who don't mind the short detour. The trail switchbacks away from Lookout Point, followed by another long traverse to the Santa Maria Spring resthouse, 4.8 miles from the Tonto junction. Water from the spring is piped into a trough adjacent to the resthouse. As with most water sources, the NPS recommends filtering the spring water, which is the last source available below Hermits Rest.

Shortly beyond Santa Maria Spring, a switchbacking ascent leads up through the Supai Group into Hermit Gorge, where the grade eases for a while before climbing again, through scattered trees of the pinyon-juniper forest and the rocks of the Hermit Formation, to a junction with the Dripping Springs Trail on the right (5,280 feet). A 0.3-mile moderate climb leads into Hermit Basin and a junction with the Waldron Trail heading south.

Continue ahead at the junction, soon beginning a steep, rocky ascent up the White Zig Zags through the Coconino Sandstone layer. At the top of the switchbacks, a lengthy rising traverse leads across the Toroweap Formation to the final cliff below Hermits Rest. A series of switchbacks, less steep than the previous set, ascends through the Kaibab Formation to the Hermits Rest trailhead, 2.2 miles and 1,640 feet from Santa Maria Spring. A cold drink or some ice cream from the Hermits Rest Snack Bar would be a fine reward at the end of your trip.

Possible Itinerary

Day	Camps and Side Trips	Distance (mi.)	Elevation (ft.)
1	Grandview TH to Horseshoe Mesa	3.5	+500/–3,100
2	Grapevine Creek	7.0	+1,350/–750
3	Lonetree Creek	8.7	+1,000/–625
4	Indian Garden	10.4	+1,325/–1,200
5	Monument Creek	10.7	+1,250/–800
6	Out to Hermits Rest TH	9.1	+4,950/–1,450

Alternates: If a permit can't be obtained for this section of the Tonto Trail, or if you'd like to extend the journey, the Jewels Route, a stretch of the Tonto between Hermits Rest and South Bass trailheads, would be a fine alternative or addition. The trail is more remote, water is even more of an issue, and transportation to the remote South Bass trailhead can be problematic. Without shuttles, you must drive your own high-clearance or four-wheel-drive vehicle to South Bass and pay a fee to cross reservation land en route. Further complicating matters, the road is often impassable following rainstorms. For those who scoff at such potential complications, however, the trip is quite rewarding.

Green Tips: Grand Canyon Association—grandcanyon.org

Three Days and the Condor Having previously completed a transcanyon hike on the popular South Kaibab and Bright Angel Trails, Keith and I looked forward to a more remote hike on the Tonto Trail between the Grandview and Hermits Rest trailheads. Although the rim-to-rim trip was stunningly beautiful, the hordes of people and developed campgrounds made for something less than a wilderness experience. We also noticed a corresponding scarcity of wildlife en route. The steady rain on the last day from the Colorado River up to the South Rim had also been a disappointment. On the Tonto we were hoping to enjoy similarly enchanting scenery, but with more solitude, better weather, and perhaps more animal life.

Although we were in decent shape, the nearly unrelenting descent from Hermits Rest on stone tread with fully loaded backpacks had a lingering effect on our legs for the next couple of days, despite the relatively gentle grade of the Tonto Trail. Once past Horseshoe Mesa, our expectation of solitude was easily met, as we saw no one for the next couple of days. The first night's camp at Cottonwood Creek provided us with plenty of water and beautiful scenery, particularly as the setting sun cast gorgeous desert hues on the surrounding landscape. We felt as if the whole canyon were our own personal domain.

The next day dawned bright and clear, with the mild mid-April temperatures well suited for hiking. We followed the Tonto on a westward contour, skirting into and weaving along the edges of side canyons between forays to the edge of the Inner Gorge. The Tonto Platform offers a view of the Grand Canyon uniquely different than the vistas from the rims above or the river below. The breadth and depth of the Granite Gorge seems enhanced from this perspective, especially where the trail runs close enough to the edge of the main canyon for the Colorado River to come into view. A campsite near Cremation Creek offered sanctuary for our second night on the trail; we were again grateful for free-flowing water, spectacular late-day scenery, and continued fine weather.

Similar to the previous days, day three offered clear skies, pleasant temperatures, and no one else on the trail—we couldn't ask for better conditions. But so far we hadn't seen much in the way of wildlife, just a few lizards and some small birds. As we worked our way around the west side of Cremation Creek Canyon and followed the rim around toward the Inner Gorge once more, something in the air caught our eyes. Traveling in our direction but slightly elevated was a pair of very large birds flying through the canyon. As they drew closer, we suddenly realized these mostly-black-with-a-touch-of-white birds were no ordinary creatures, but rather two rare specimens of California condor. We were transfixed; they held our gaze as we watched them glide effortlessly through the canyon, eventually becoming small dark specks before completely disappearing out of sight. Although we had heard of condors flying over to the Grand Canyon from the Vermilion Cliffs, we didn't hold out much hope of actually seeing one, let alone two. Thrilled beyond belief, our hope of seeing some wildlife was exceeded beyond measure by the sight of the condors, a truly transcendent experience.

PART IV

NEW MEXICO

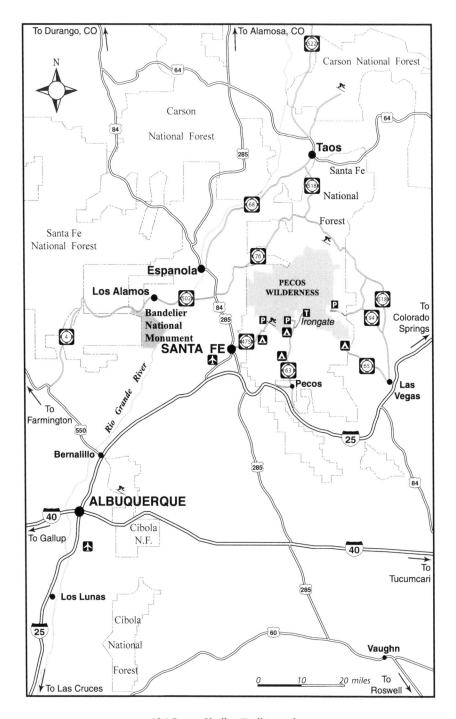

10.1 Pecos Skyline Trail Location

Pecos Wilderness
Santa Fe National Forest

Pecos Skyline Trail

I think the loss of quiet in our lives
is one of the great tragedies of civilization,
and to have known even for a moment the silence of the wilderness
is one of our most precious memories.

—Sigurd F. Olson

Although popular and well known in New Mexico, Pecos Skyline Trail, the unquestioned highlight of the impressive Pecos Wilderness, has not yet received the national attention it so richly deserves. The mountain scenery, wildlife, wildflowers, and other attractions are outstanding, and they are only rarely any better in the more famous hiking areas of the American West. Nonetheless, out-of-state license plates remain an oddity here, and that's just fine for those who tire of cumbersome permit processes and prefer to share the scenery with knowledgeable locals instead of the legions of hiking tourists that crowd more famous hiking destinations. And what fine scenery to share! Rugged 13,000-foot peaks, sparkling trout-filled lakes, vast meadows carpeted with wildflowers, and miles of view-packed ridges—in short, all the attributes that mountain-loving backpackers crave are here in abundance. So set your sights away from the more famous trails in the Colorado Rockies, the Teton Range, or Glacier National Park, and consider heading south. You'll soon discover that New Mexico, the aptly named Land of Enchantment, includes plenty of great mountain trails, and arguably the best of these high-elevation routes is the Pecos Skyline Trail.

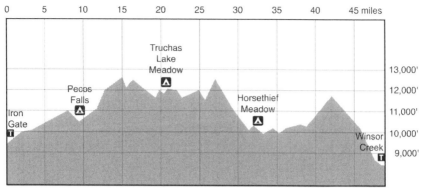

Pecos Skyline Trail

Days:	4–6
Distance:	47.6 miles (excluding the road walk but including side trips)
Type:	Loop or Shuttle
Scenery:	8
Solitude:	6
Technical Difficulty:	4
Physical Difficulty:	6
Elevation Gain/Loss:	+9,350'/–10,250' (excluding the road walk)
Season:	Mid-June to late October **Best:** July
Maps:	USFS—Pecos Wilderness
Resources:	*Aldo Leopold's Southwest*, by Aldo Leopold (a collection of his Southwest essays)

Contacts:

• Santa Fe National Forest
Pecos/Las Vegas Ranger District
PO Drawer 429, Pecos, NM 87552
505-757-6121

Permits: No permits are required.

Regulations: Camping is prohibited in any of the wilderness's lake basins. Maximum group size of fifteen people and fifteen stock.

Nearest Campgrounds: Iron Gate Campground—at Iron Gate trailhead

Nearest Airports:

• Santa Fe Municipal Airport (SAF)—67 miles
• Albuquerque International Sunport (ABQ)—122 miles

Nearest Outdoor Retailers:

- REI Santa Fe—68 miles
500 Market St., Ste. 100, Santa Fe, NM 87501
505-982-3557

Outfitters: None.

Transportation Logistics: There are no public transportation options to reach the trailhead, so you'll need your own vehicle(s).

Backcountry Logistics: (A, L, St) Afternoon thunderstorms are an almost daily occurrence from early July through early September. Plan your hike so that you are off the high ridges by about 2 PM.

Amenities and Attractions: There are a few small stores and businesses in the town of Pecos (don't expect to be overwhelmed), but for the full range of services, your best bet is **Santa Fe**. This charming old city not only has everything you could reasonably need in terms of food, accommodations, and supplies, it also features a wealth of history. The town proudly boasts of being the oldest state capital in the United States and has a number of interesting museums worth visiting. (The tour of the state capitol is especially recommended.) If you prefer art, Santa Fe has a thriving arts community, with dozens of excellent galleries and artist fairs. In the unlikely event that you can't find anything you want in Santa Fe, even larger Albuquerque is only another fifty-minute drive away.

Directions to Trailhead: From Albuquerque, drive about 74 miles north on Interstate 25, passing exits for Santa Fe after 57 miles, until you reach Exit 299 for Glorieta. Leave the freeway here and go east on State Highway 50 for 6.1 miles to a junction in the town of Pecos. Turn left on Highway 63, a winding paved road that travels north into the Santa Fe National Forest. After 18.4 miles you come to a junction with Forest Road 223, angling off to the right, signed for Iron Gate Campground.

If you are doing this trip as an "almost" loop (with a relatively short car shuttle or hike between the two trailheads), then turn right on FR 223 and slowly drive this very rough gravel and dirt road, which is not suitable for low-clearance vehicles (when wet, four-wheel drive may be necessary). After 0.6 mile, you bear right at a fork, and then drive past numerous summer homes for another 2.6 miles to a parking area on the left for Geronimo Trail. The official trailhead is still a bit farther up the road, but if you plan to walk between trailheads, this is a reasonable place to park, since it saves you from having to drive the last section of very rough road. Road 223 continues another mile to Iron Gate Campground and the trailhead at the north end of the small car campground. Hikers are asked to park only in slots for wilderness users rather than those for campers.

If you have a second vehicle, then leave it at the Winsor Creek trailhead. To reach this spot, return to the junction with Highway 63, and then turn north on that winding paved road for 1.2 miles to a prominent junction. Turn left onto Forest Road 121, a single-lane paved road that almost immediately passes Cowles Campground before continuing another 1.3 miles to the road-end trailhead along Winsor Creek.

Aldo Leopold Born in Burlington, Iowa, on January 11, 1887, Aldo was the oldest of four children. He displayed an interest in the outdoors from a very early age and eventually achieved an advanced degree from the newly founded Yale Forestry School. Upon graduation, he joined the US Forestry Service in 1909 and was assigned a position with the Apache National Forest in Arizona Territory. Two years later he was transferred to the Carson National Forest in northern New Mexico. His experience as a ranger in the Southwest would begin to shape the developing ecological ethic that would ultimately make him a household name.

Leopold came to realize that the current human-centric policies of killing off predators and allowing the overgrazing of cattle were detrimental to the overall environmental health of the region he was managing. The advent of automobile travel and the subsequent increase in road construction also became a significant concern. By the 1920s, he began advocating for a more holistic and preservationist approach to land management, including setting aside wilderness areas. His efforts culminated in the establishment of the Gila Wilderness in 1924, the first designated wilderness area in the nation of significant size. Such notions contradicted the more widespread utilitarian views of the day promoted by such famed naturalists as Gifford Pinchot and Theodore Roosevelt. The same year Gila became a wilderness area, Leopold, somewhat unexplainably, left the Southwest to accept a position as associate director of the US Forest Products Laboratory in Madison, Wisconsin. After four years with the lab and nineteen total with the Forest Service, Leopold left the employ of the Forest Service in 1932.

The next part of Leopold's career would be spent with the Sporting Arms Ammunition Manufacturers' Institute, at least until the Great Depression dried up funding four years later. Jobs were in short supply, including forestry positions, which allowed him some unscheduled free time to work on his *Game Management* manuscript, eventually published by Scribner's in 1933. Later that year, he accepted what would be a long-running post with the University of Wisconsin as professor of game management, the first such professorship in the country.

With a paid position and a platform for conservation ethics, Leopold was able to spread his ideals more widely. Along with Bob Marshall, he and a small group of like-minded conservationists founded the Wilderness Society in 1935. At this time, an 80-acre parcel of land was purchased that would provide the foundation for *A Sand County Almanac*. His masterpiece was completed shortly before his death in 1948, when he sustained a heart attack while helping fight a neighbor's wildfire. Although hailed as a critical success, *A Sand County Almanac* was not initially a hit with the public. A new version published during the growing environmental movement of the 1970s became a surprise bestseller, catapulting the name of Aldo Leopold into America's consciousness. Today the book is regarded as one of the most important pieces of American environmental literature, alongside such notable works as Thoreau's *Walden* and Rachel Carson's *Silent Spring*.

Trip Description: From the Iron Gate trailhead, the popular and somewhat dusty trail takes off through a lovely forest of quaking aspens and true firs, with an increasing number of ponderosa pines as you gain elevation. The path almost immediately goes through a gate in a wood fence, and then climbs at a moderate pace for the next 0.25 mile before coming to a junction atop a ridge. Go left on Hamilton Mesa Trail 249 and follow this well-maintained path along the ridgetop to the north, reaching a junction at 0.5 mile. Keep left, still on Hamilton Mesa Trail, and steadily but not too steeply ascend along the ridge in a forest of oaks, firs, aspens, and pines. Along the way are frequent good views of rounded and heavily forested Spring Mountain to the east.

At 1.3 miles you go through a gate in another wooden fence (please close the gate behind you), and less than 100 yards later, you reach the lower meadows of Hamilton Mesa. This open, rolling grassland offers continuous excellent views to the north and west of Pecos Baldy, Truchas Peak, Pecos River Canyon, and the rest of the scenic country you will explore in the days to come. The mesa is also home to a wide variety of colorful wildflowers, including blue iris, paintbrush, vetch, yarrow, dandelion, flax, wallflower, yellow lupine, lomatium, and cinquefoil, among many others. The hiking for the next two miles crosses Hamilton Mesa and remains gentle, easy, and delightful throughout.

At 3.1 miles is another fork, where Larkspur Trail 260 goes left, but you keep right and cross more of the lovely meadows on Hamilton Mesa. You soon pass a nice spring, where you can camp if cattle haven't trampled and befouled the area too badly. The trail now climbs, eventually leaving the meadows for a spruce and fir forest on the way to a four-way junction with Bob Grounds Trail 270. Turning left here would take you down to the Pecos River at popular Beatty's Flats (no camping allowed).

You go straight at the junction, sticking with the Hamilton Mesa Trail, which stays on or near the slowly ascending top of a rounded ridge. The ridge is mostly forested but does go through a couple of fairly large meadows, which provide nice, if not spectacular, views to the east. About a mile from the Bob Grounds Trail junction, you may notice an unsigned trail angling off to the left, an old trail that has been abandoned. You could follow this as a slightly shorter route to Pecos Falls, but the Forest Service does not encourage use of this abandoned path and no longer maintains the route.

At about 7.9 miles is a junction. The shortest route to the high country and the one with the fewest ups and downs goes right but misses lovely Pecos Falls. The recommended course is to turn left on Gascon Trail 239 and steadily descend through a mature evergreen forest. After losing almost 600 feet in a mile, you go straight at a junction with the abandoned trail mentioned above (not shown on most maps) and 50 yards later reach a signed junction, about 20 yards before the trail crosses the Pecos River, which is more akin to a creek at this spot. To see Pecos Falls, take the 0.15-mile steep, dead-end scramble trail that follows the stream's eastern bank to a good viewpoint beside the tall, segmented falls. There is a posted "no camping or campfires" zone all around Pecos Falls, so do not plan to spend the night in this vicinity.

After visiting Pecos Falls, you rock-hop the river, then briefly climb a grassy hillside to another junction. Turn right on Pecos River Trail 456, which heads upstream, traveling across open slopes carpeted with grasses and wildflowers, with a particular abundance of false hellebores (corn lilies). If you need a campsite, there are some good choices amid the patches of evergreens and willows growing near the stream. Not quite 1.8 miles upstream from Pecos Falls, you come to a dilapidated fence and a well-established campsite just before the trail crosses what's left of the Pecos River. **Warning:** This stream is your last reliable on-trail water for about 7.5 miles. Be sure to fill your water bottles here.

Once across the river, you begin a stiff climb that gains about 950 feet over the next mile. The climb is often steep, and the trail is sometimes obscured by deadfall and game trails, but getting off course here is difficult. About 850 feet into the climb, you come to a small and possibly waterless little alpine basin, and then complete the climb to the top of an open ridge just a little below timberline.

The trail effectively disappears here, but if you make your way a little to the left and uphill, you will come to a tall and prominent post that marks the route of the Skyline Trail. Turn left (uphill), and about 80 yards later, look for a little-used path that branches to the right, crossing over to the east side of the ridge.

If you have an extra day, this side trail makes an excellent detour, allowing you to explore more of this lovely high terrain. The trail stays near, contouring over to the high basin of Rincon Bonito. From there it goes over a minor ridge before reaching scenic and rarely visited Middle Fork Lake, which sits beneath a long steep ridge. The hike to the lake is about 2.3 miles one way on sometimes sketchy tread, but it's well worth the effort for possible elk sightings, little-used lakeside campsites, and superb high country scenery.

The main Skyline Trail goes straight at the unsigned junction with the path to Middle Fork Lake and climbs steadily along or near the top of an increasingly exposed ridge. The few trees get smaller as you climb, and they eventually disappear entirely, leaving an alpine landscape of grasses, wildflowers, rocks, and snowfields. A grand consequence of this change in vegetation is that nothing obstructs the outstanding views, extending southwest over the Pecos River valley to the deserts beyond and taking in peaks both rounded and craggy in almost every direction. It's a real "top of the world" kind of feeling. Of course, this is also no place to be in a thunderstorm, and since that kind of weather occurs almost every afternoon for much of July and August, plan to hike the next several miles in the morning hours. Even without thunderstorms, the winds are usually strong, so have your windbreaker handy and cinch your hat down tightly. As you climb, the tread often fades away amid the rocks, snow, and tundra, but occasional large cairns help to keep you on course.

The climb up the ridge tops out near 12,550 feet on the southwest shoulder of an unnamed 12,626-foot peak. The trail may be hard to find on the ground, but it goes northeast along a mostly above-timberline ridge toward distant Jicarita Peak.

Your route turns left to follow the Santa Barbara Divide. The first section along this divide is a steep and rocky downhill of 0.6 mile to a windswept pass and a four-way junction. The trail to the left goes back down to Pecos Falls, while a route down Middle Fork Rio Santa Barbara goes right. (**Note:** Rio is

Spanish for "river" and will show up in the names of many of the streams in this area.)

You keep straight and begin an extended section of gradual ups and downs along the view-packed Santa Barbara Divide. About 2 miles from the last junction is another saddle, this one right beside the strikingly colorful cliffs of Chimayosos Peak. From this pass, the trail contours around the southeast side of Chimayosos Peak, where you come to a signed junction with Beattys Trail 25. Go straight, still on Skyline Trail, and travel generally downhill through an open high-elevation forest for 0.6 mile to a signed junction.

The trail that angles to the right (uphill) goes over a high viewpoint on Santa Barbara Divide (well worth the 1.6-mile round-trip), but you keep left. Still going a little downhill, you come to a scenic rolling basin, in the middle of which is a signed junction with a very faint trail coming in from the left.

Keep straight on the main trail, make a brief climb, and then look for a small cairn marking an unofficial boot trail, which goes to the right and climbs to a tiny but scenic pond on the east side of North Truchas Peak. The Skyline Trail continues straight at this cairn and 0.2 mile later comes to a tiny spring-fed creek, which represents the first on-trail water since the Pecos River. There are a couple of mediocre campsites just beyond this little creek, below the trail and on the left. Keep an eye out in this area for small herds of Rocky Mountain bighorn sheep, which are common along this divide. The sheep are fairly accustomed to seeing people, so they may allow you to get close enough to take photographs. No matter how close they get, however, never feed the animals and always keep dogs restrained to avoid unnecessarily disturbing the wildlife.

Just 150 yards after the first little creek, you come to some good camps a little before hopping over a slightly larger creek. You then walk another 0.3 mile up and down to Truchas Lake. This scenic lake, which offers good fishing, is backed by the steep slopes of Truchas and North Truchas Peaks, both of which top out at more than 13,000 feet. As is true for all the lakes in the Pecos Wilderness, rules prohibit camping in the lake's immediate basin. A possibly unsigned trail goes to the right along the east shore of the lake on the way over a pass and on to North Fork Rio Quemado.

Go straight at the unsigned junction beside Truchas Lake, cross the lake's outlet, and follow the scenic trail along the south shore. The path turns left (downhill) just before it comes to an old earthen dam, which keeps the lake's level a little higher than nature intended. After 0.2 mile of downhill hiking, you reach a small meadow with an equally small creek and a possible campsite. The trail forks here.

Truchas Lake

You bear right, staying on the Skyline Trail, which takes you through forest and past a couple of lush meadows before reaching the tip of a shallow pond. The trail immediately climbs away from this pool, and then for the next 1.5 miles, it travels beneath the rocky crags and talus slopes of Truchas Peak. An unsigned trail goes left about 2 miles from Truchas Lake, but keep right and ascend for 0.3 mile to a junction in a rolling, grassy saddle. There are good views from here in all directions, but particularly south to Pecos Baldy and Santa Fe Baldy peaks.

You go left at the saddle junction and ascend open view-packed slopes to the windy top of Trailrider's Wall, a long steep drop-off just a few yards to the east, initially unseen from the trail. What you can see are fine vistas that extend over nearly all the Pecos Wilderness and beyond to distant mountains and deserts. This glorious high-country hike through open meadows continues for almost 2 miles as you walk south atop the wall. At the south end are particularly outstanding views back to the north along the length of Trailrider's Wall to Truchas Peak.

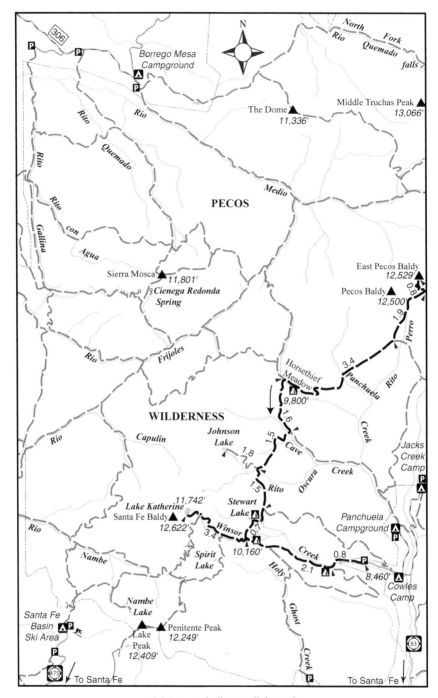

306

P   P

North Fork

Rio Quemado

falls

Borrego Mesa
Campground

N

P

Rio   *Rio*

The Dome ▲
11,336'

Middle Truchas Peak ▲
13,066'

Rito

Quemado

Medio

PECOS

Rito

con

Agua

Gallina

Sierra Mosca ▲ *11,801'*

East Pecos Baldy ▲
12,529'

♀ *Cienega Redonda
Spring*

Pecos Baldy ▲
12,500'

0.8

1.9

Perro

Rito   *Frijoles*

3.4

Panchuela

Rito

Horsethief
Meadow
▲
9,800'

WILDERNESS

Capulin

Johnson
Lake
▲

1.6

1.5

1.8

Cave

Creek

*Jacks
Creek
Camp*

P
▲

Rito

1.5

Oscura   *Creek*

Rito

Lake Katherine *11,742'*
Santa Fe Baldy ▲
12,622'

Stewart
Lake
▲

3.4

.7

0

Winsor

*Panchuela
Campground* ▲
P

Rio

Nambe

*Spirit
Lake*

10,160'

Creek   0.8

2.1

P

8,460'

▲

*Cowles
Camp*

Ghost

Holy

Santa Fe
Basin
Ski Area

▲P

Nambe
Lake
▲

Lake ▲ Penitente Peak
Peak   *12,249'*
12,409'

Creek

63

P

475

↓ To Santa Fe

To Santa Fe ▼

10.2 Pecos Skyline Trail (West)

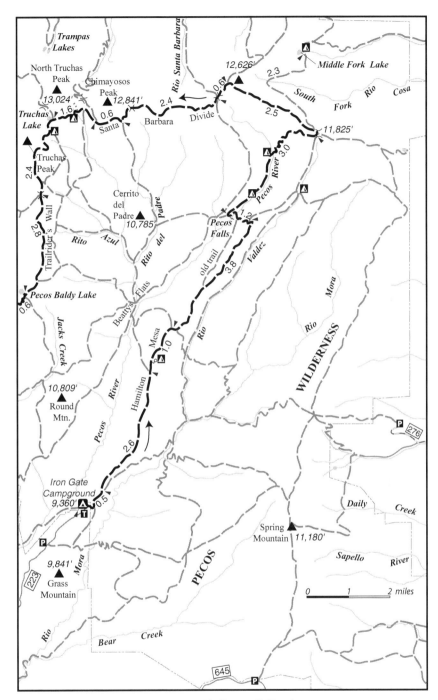

Trampas Lakes

North Truchas Peak
▲ 13,024'

Chimayosos Peak
▲ 12,841'

Truchas Lake
▲

Truchas Peak

Rio Santa Barbara

12,626' ▲

Middle Fork Lake
▲

2.3

South Fork

Rio Cosa

0.6

1.6
▲
0.6
Santa Barbara Divide

2.4

2.5

2.4

11,825'

Cerrito del Padre ▲
10,785'

Pecos River 3.0
▲

▲

2.4

Trailrider's Wall

Pecos Falls
1.2

2.8

Rito Azul

Rito del Padre

old trail

Rio Valdez

3.8

Pecos Baldy Lake
0.6

Jacks Creek

Beatty's Flats

Hamilton Mesa

1.0
▲

Rio

Rio Mora

WILDERNESS

10,809'
▲
Round Mtn.

Pecos River

2.6

P 276

Iron Gate Campground
9,360'
▲
T
0.5

Daily Creek

Spring Mountain ▲ 11,180'

P

Sapello River

223
9,841'
▲
Grass Mountain

Mora

PECOS

0   1   2 miles

Rio

Bear Creek

645

P

10.3 Pecos Skyline Trail (East)

View north along Trailrider's Wall

The trail finally descends from Trailrider's Wall into increasingly forested terrain to a merger with Jacks Creek Trail 257. From here you keep going downhill for another 0.5 mile to a junction in the bottom of a basin. Trail 257 leaves your route here and goes left. The Skyline Trail, your route, goes straight. Before heading that way, however, make a 150-yard side trip to the right to visit Pecos Baldy Lake, which sits directly beneath the hulking mass of East Pecos Baldy peak. The lake's water level tends to drop considerably as the summer progresses, but the setting is still very scenic. As with all other lakes in this wilderness, camping is not allowed in the immediate lake basin.

Back on the Skyline Trail, you finish walking across the flat basin of Pecos Baldy Lake, and then make a short but steep climb with two switchbacks to a narrow pass and a junction on the southeast shoulder of East Pecos Baldy peak.

The Skyline Trail goes straight at the junction with the trail up East Pecos Baldy and almost immediately begins a long downhill run. At 0.7 mile from the pass, you come to small Rito Perro, and then parallel this creek for 0.2 mile before hopping across the flow and resuming downhill on a forested hillside. At about 1.9 miles from the pass is a junction. You go right, follow

Side Trip to East Pecos Baldy Peak: From the junction, a signed trail goes to the right and in 0.8 mile climbs to the top of East Pecos Baldy Peak. From there you'll enjoy expansive vistas that encompass most of northern New Mexico.

the contours for a while, and then return to the long descent, although this section is more gradual. The next couple of miles pass through a forest with lots of beetle-killed trees, so deadfall is a real problem before the trail maintenance is completed.

About 1.4 miles from the last junction, you hop over Panchuela Creek. From here you gain about 300 feet, walk around the end of a small ridge, and then start to once again lose elevation. Near the bottom of this descent, you make two switchbacks and reach the lower end of long and narrow Horsethief Meadow. There are some very good campsites here among the trees near Horsethief Creek.

The trail goes upstream to a junction near the upper (west) end of Horsethief Meadow. You veer left, cross the creek, and begin climbing heavily forested side drainage. After gaining about 400 feet, the trail levels off for about 0.4 mile, and then passes a pretty but waterless meadow. Just past this meadow, you descend a series of tight short switchbacks on rocky tread until you meet the welcome flow of Cave Creek. You then follow this creek downstream for 0.3 mile to a junction with Cave Creek Trail 288.

Turn right, still on Skyline Trail 251, immediately cross Cave Creek, and gradually climb two long, lazy switchbacks to the crossing of another small creek. From here you slowly climb for another mile to a junction with Johnson Lake Trail 267, just below a lush meadow.

Go straight on Skyline Trail, cross fairly good-sized Rito Oscura and a second smaller creek just beyond. From there you'll make good progress because the trail is gentle for the next 1.4 miles, until reaching a large swampy meadow with a nice view up to Santa Fe Baldy. At the south end of this meadow is a junction with Trail 271, which angles to the left (uphill). This is a slightly shorter alternate exit route, but you miss some pretty lakes that way.

The recommended route is to go straight at the junction, still on Skyline Trail, and 0.1 mile later reach a campsite beside a small but very pretty meadow-rimmed lake. Just 0.2 mile later is much larger Stewart Lake, where an earthen and rock dam helps keep the water level high. Again, wilderness rules prohibit camping and campfires in this lake basin. Beyond Stewart

Lake, you walk mostly on the level for 0.4 mile to a junction beside cascading Winsor Creek.

After returning from your side trip to Lake Katherine, go left at the junction beside Winsor Creek, rock-hop its flow, immediately pass a nice campsite, and walk 0.4 mile to a fork in the trail. The new trail, which is much longer but has a gentler grade, goes right. The older trail goes left (downhill) and has a sign saying TRAIL NOT SUITABLE FOR PACK AND SADDLE STOCK. Backpacker's without the encumbrance of livestock should take the shorter, older trail, which is not shown on the newer maps but is easy to follow and receives a lot of use. The trail is no longer regularly maintained, so expect some deadfall across the path. The trail is rocky but not particularly steep on a steady descent of a forested hillside down to Winsor Creek. From there, follow the stream to a campsite just 0.1 mile before meeting back up with the new trail. The merged routes then go downstream for 0.1 mile to a creek crossing. Shortly thereafter you cross the wilderness boundary and then wander gently downhill along Winsor Creek through a lovely open forest of quaking aspens and white firs for 0.7 mile to the well-developed trailhead. From here, you have either a car shuttle or a moderate road walk of 6.7 miles to the Iron Gate Campground and trailhead.

Side Trip to Lake Katherine The junction beside Winsor Creek is the turnoff for an excellent but tiring side trip to large and scenic Lake Katherine. To visit this beauty, turn right at the junction and begin climbing beside the rushing waters of Winsor Creek. After less than 0.3 mile, the trail diverges from the water and ascends in switchbacks and traverses on a partly forested slope, rapidly taking you into a high-elevation environment. After passing a turnoff to Spirit Lake, you continue uphill, gathering increasingly impressive views of Santa Fe Baldy as you go. At about 3 miles from the start of your side trip is a junction, where the Skyline Trail goes left on the way to the Santa Fe Basin Ski Area. To reach the lake, turn right, pass a small pond, and then make a short uphill jog to the shore. Lake Katherine sits in an impressive bowl, surrounded by the rugged cliffs, talus slopes, and rocky pinnacles of Santa Fe Baldy. Not only the largest lake in the Pecos Wilderness, Lake Katherine is also one of the highest, at 11,742 feet. With reasonably easy access from a trailhead at the Santa Fe Basin Ski Area, this lake is quite popular; don't expect to be alone, especially on weekends. As always, camping is not allowed in the lake basin.

Possible Itinerary

Day	Camps and Side Trips	Distance (mi.)	Elevation (ft.)
1	Iron Gate TH to above Pecos Falls	9.5	+2,100/−800
2	Meadow below Truchas Lake	10.6	+3,000/−2,000
3	Horsethief Meadow	10.6	+1,400/−3,200
	Side Trip to East Pecos Baldy	1.6	+650/−650
4	Out to Winsor Creek TH	8.5	+1,200/−2,600
	Side trip to Lake Katherine	6.8	+1,600/−1,600

Alternates: For greater solitude, consider starting your trip from any of several trailheads on the north side of the wilderness. There are a multitude of possible itineraries. Of particular note is an excellent high route that starts from the Santa Barbara trailhead, climbs to the ridge north of Jicarita Peak, goes south to the Skyline Trail, follows that route west to near Truchas Lake, and then returns via a trail along West Fork Rio Santa Barbara.

Green Tips: New Mexico Wilderness Alliance—www.nmwild.org

Up in Smoke

The summer of 2011 was a difficult year for firefighters in New Mexico. Of course, this is nothing new in the Land of Enchantment. After all, the original Smokey Bear was from this state, famously rescued as a cub in the spring of 1950 from a fire in the Lincoln National Forest of central New Mexico. Forest fires have a long and storied history in this part of the country. But this isn't a history piece, it's a personal story, and 2011 was the year I chose to do a bit of long-anticipated backpacking in the mountains of this state.

It seemed like a great idea in the planning stages. I was aware that the Southwest had been in the grips of a long-term drought, and that the previous winter's snowpack was well below average once again. With the high country snow-free much sooner than normal, I planned on hitting the trails of New Mexico as early as mid-June, thus saving the prime mountain hiking months of July and August for snowier ranges farther north. Hiking early in the season also provided the added advantage of avoiding the thunderstorms so common to the Southwest in midsummer. Now I wouldn't have to worry about lightning strikes threatening my afternoon travels along the high ridges. Without any lightning, there shouldn't be any lightning-caused fires either. I happily pored over maps and guidebooks, planning out the premier trails in this exciting state.

In May, my plans hit a bit of a snag, with news reports of large fires in Arizona and the Gila Wilderness of southern New Mexico. This was worrisome because the Gila was my first planned destination in the state. Further research led to more concerns, as I discovered that several of the trails I had hoped to hike were included in a partial closure of that wilderness area. As my trip drew nearer, the flames continued to scorch tens of thousands of acres of the Gila's dry terrain, despite the heroic efforts of firefighters to combat the blaze. Fortunately, there were no reports of any significant fires in northern New Mexico. I therefore assumed that, if necessary, I could always forgo the Gila and head directly to the Pecos Wilderness instead, ensuring that my trip would not be a complete waste of time.

Two days before my trip, the fires were finally put out in the Gila, although the trails did not officially reopen for travel until the day I reached the area. During my hike I saw thousands of recently burned snags, and there was plenty of ash around, but the river levels were low (very important when I had to ford the rivers literally hundreds of times during my hike), and the Gila's scenery was wonderful. Scared off by the fires, few other hikers were on the trails, so solitude was another bonus.

Feeling quite fortunate, I completed my trip in the Gila and headed north to the Pecos for my next backpacking adventure, where conditions were looking great as well. As anticipated, there was amazingly little snow on the high peaks, more like what you would expect in late July or early August rather than mid-June, and even the highest elevation trails had been open for snow-free travel for several weeks already. There were a few tiny forest fires in scattered locations nearby, but nothing terribly concerning. I happily packed up my gear and hit the trail with a satisfied smile on my face, not only in anticipation of a fun adventure, but content that my careful planning seemed to be paying off.

For the next few days I climbed the Pecos's scenic ridges, walked through acres of colorful wildflowers, took lots of pictures, enjoyed great views, saw plenty of interesting wildlife, and generally had my usual grand time in the back-country. I had occasionally smelled smoke on the trip, but the winds always seemed to be pushing most of the smoke away from my location. Everything seemed to be going well.

By the evening of the third day, conditions took a turn for the worse. I was camped in lovely Horsethief Meadow when I noticed large plumes of smoke rising ominously over the ridge to the west. Well, I thought, *that* can't be good, but my luck has been great so far, so let's just see what happens. Upon reflection, I did find it odd that I had yet to see a single person during the course of my trip, despite the lovely scenery and the seemingly good conditions.

The next morning dawned with a lot more smoke. I packed up camp and headed on my way, with ever-denser smoke obscuring the nearby peaks, hiding

Pecos Wilderness closed because of fire in 2011

much of the scenery and irritating my lungs. Finally deciding that perhaps my luck was running out, I decided to forgo a planned side trip to Lake Katherine, since I could plainly see huge towers of smoke rising above the peak behind the lake. Instead, I reluctantly turned downhill and headed back toward civilization. When I got to the Winsor Creek trailhead, I was surprised to find not a single car at this popular wilderness access point. Puzzled but undeterred, I hiked down the trailhead spur road to the Pecos River and found a large sign explaining the situation.

Apparently, my timing had not only been fortuitous but extraordinarily so. Only hours after I began my hike, Santa Fe National Forest officials had closed the entire Pecos Wilderness to travel because of the extreme fire danger. I found out later that they had even sent a ranger up looking for me to pull me out of the wilderness. I walked the lonely road back toward my parked car, noticing for the first time smoke plumes rising now from several directions. Eventually I discovered that the Forest Service had even locked a gate across the road behind my car to keep people out. I was forced to knock on doors of what turned out to be mostly deserted vacation cabins to find someone with a key to unlock the gate and allow me to drive out to safety.

I ended up having a terrific time in New Mexico. The scenery was superb, and I had the trails all to myself. I'm certain you'll love this state too. However, checking on the fire conditions first might be a wise idea, lest your plans go up in smoke.

— Doug

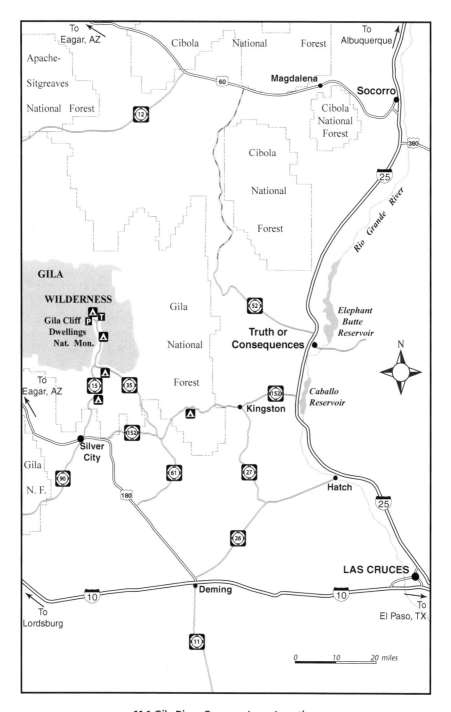

11.1 Gila River Canyons Loop Location

Gila Wilderness
Gila National Forest

─────────────── **TRIP 11** ───────────────

Gila River Canyons Loop

The wilderness and the idea of wilderness
is one of the permanent homes of the human spirit.
The desire to experience that reality rather than destroy it drew
to our shores some of the best who have ever come to them.
If we do not preserve it, then we shall have diminished
by just that much the unique privilege of being an American.

—JOSEPH WOOD KRUTCH

THE GILA WILDERNESS was the country's (and the world's) first officially designated wilderness area. In fact, its protected status goes all the way back to 1924, when the dedicated advocacy of the legendary Aldo Leopold, among others, paid off with the creation of this new idea in land management. Despite its long and distinguished history, the wilderness remains relatively unknown and is never crowded (except during elk hunting season)—perhaps what Leopold envisioned in the first place. Although this huge wilderness offers diverse wildlife, stately ponderosa pine forests, and excellent high viewpoints, arguably the main attractions are the two dramatically scenic canyons of the middle and west forks of the Gila River. These deep, parallel defiles both offer impressive displays of cliffs, forests, wildlife, and tall pinnacles, which makes deciding which canyon to hike a difficult choice. Fortunately, no such decision is necessary, as traveling a wonderful loop hike up one canyon and down the other is relatively simple. The southerly latitude (only about 90 miles north of the Mexican border) means these canyons are sometimes open to hiking all year, but spring (late March to mid-June) is probably ideal

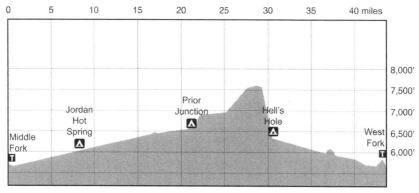

0	5	10	15	20	25	30	35	40 miles

8,000'
7,500'
7,000'
6,500'
6,000'

Middle Fork
Jordan Hot Spring
Prior Junction
Hell's Hole
West Fork

Gila River Canyons Loop

for avoiding the heat and flooding thunderstorms of summer. Thus, the Gila is an excellent backpacking destination when trails in the higher mountains to the north are still buried under several feet of snow.

The only significant downside to this wilderness trip is that bridges are deemed an unnecessary luxury, and with almost 180 stream crossings along the way, this lack has consequences. During a heavy spring runoff, or after large summer thunderstorms, the stream crossings can be dangerous. Most of the time, however, the crossings are generally easy and usually less than knee-deep fords. You can even rock-hop many of the crossings when the water is particularly low. Still, you should plan to hike for long distances in wet feet.

Note: All the stream crossings, as well as the often sandy tread, tend to slow you down. Most hikers will do well to average 1.5 miles per hour instead of the usual hiker's norm of 2 or 2.5 miles per hour. Plan your days accordingly.

Days: 4–6

Distance: 43.7 miles (excluding 2.1-mile road walk but including side trip)

Type: Loop

Scenery: 7

Solitude: 8

Technical Difficulty: 6

Physical Difficulty: 5

Elevation Gain/Loss: +3,700'/−3,700'

Season: March to November **Best:** April to mid-June and October

Maps: USFS—Gila Wilderness

Resources: *Hiking New Mexico's Gila Wilderness*, by Bill Cunningham and Polly Burke

Contacts:

- Gila National Forest Wilderness Ranger District
  Gila Visitor Center
  Route 11, Box 100, Silver City, NM 88061
  505-536-9461

Permits: Permits are not required.

Regulations: The usual "leave no trace" rules are in place, but other restrictions are minimal.

Nearest Campgrounds: Upper and Lower Scorpion Campgrounds—0.5 mile

Nearest Airports:

- El Paso International Airport (ELP)—210 miles
- Albuquerque International Sunport (ABQ)—285 miles

Nearest Outdoor Retailers:

- Gila Hike and Bike—45 miles
  103 E. College Ave., Silver City, NM 88061
  505-388-3222
- Rough Country Outdoor Gear—45 miles
  1874 Highway 180 E, Silver City, NM 88061
  505-534-0540
- REI Albuquerque—285 miles
  1550 Mercantile Ave. N.E., Albuquerque, NM 87107
  505-247-1191

Outfitters:

- Gila Wilderness Ventures
  HC 61, Box 296, Glenwood, NM 88039
  866-677-2008
  (Strictly for horseback trips, but great fun)

Transportation Logistics: There are no public transportation options to reach the trailhead, so you'll need your own vehicle. The paved road into the trailhead is wildly scenic but also very winding, with many steep drop-offs, so take it slow.

Backcountry Logistics: (FF, H, PI, R, St, Su) Get used to wet feet, because if I counted right, this loop requires 179 (!) unbridged river crossings, and depending on water levels, almost all of these result in wet feet. Wear old boots that you don't mind getting soaked and bring a pair of lightweight shoes to change into at the end of the day. Fortunately, only during particularly heavy spring runoff or after occasional thunderstorms in the summer are these stream crossings potentially dangerous.

Rattlesnakes are fairly common, so watch where you step. Summer temperatures can be quite hot, so spring and fall are better times to visit.

Poison ivy is common along the canyon trails. Know how to identify this plant and avoid contact.

Meningitis, which is spread by an amoeba that sometimes lives in warm waters, is a potential hazard for those who soak in hot springs in the Gila Wilderness. The parasite typically enters via mouth and nasal passages, so avoid submerging your head or splashing water on your face.

Amenities and Attractions: Silver City, which is 45 miles south of the trailhead, is a growing town with a wide array of restaurants, motels, shopping, and other amenities. You should be able to find almost any last-minute supplies you would reasonably need.

As the name implies, Silver City is a historic mining town with many interesting old buildings. The town center is worth walking through, and be sure to set aside an hour or so to tour the **Silver City Museum** (312 W. Broadway, 505-538-5921). Another interesting stop (although not exactly scenic) is the overlook of the enormous open-pit **Chino Mine** a few miles east of town. The gaping hole of this copper mine is about 1.7 miles across and more than 1,000 feet deep, so it's quite a sight.

Right beside the upper trailhead is not-to-be-missed **Gila Cliff Dwellings National Monument**, where a 1-mile loop trail leads up a side canyon to an exceptionally well-preserved set of Native American ruins set back into caves on the canyon wall.

Directions to Trailhead: First make your way to bustling Silver City, which is located in southwestern New Mexico, about 156 miles northwest of El Paso, Texas. From El Paso, take Interstate 10 to Deming, then north on US 180. If you're coming from Albuquerque, drive 164 miles south on Interstate 25, then go 76 miles west on scenic but slow and winding State Highway 152.

Once in Silver City, go north from a traffic light in the northeast part of town onto Pinos Altos Road (State Highway 15). Follow this paved, winding, and very scenic mountain road for 25.8 miles to a junction with State Highway 35. Go left, still on Highway 15, and continue north on a slow and curving road for 17.4 miles, past several fine viewpoints, to a junction with the turnoff to Gila Visitor Center.

To reach the West Fork trailhead, where this trip ends, you go left at this junction and drive 1.6 miles, passing Upper and Lower Scorpion Campgrounds along the way, to the road-end parking lot near the trailhead for Gila Cliff Dwellings National Monument.

To reach the Middle Fork trailhead, the recommended starting point, you go straight at the Gila Visitor Center junction, past the visitor center, and then continue on a one-lane paved road that loops around the left side of the center to the trailhead parking area, 0.5 mile from the junction.

Lucky Seven? Seven is usually considered a lucky number. If you are visiting Las Vegas, it will win you lots of money at the craps table. Surveys show that more Americans consider seven to be their personal lucky number than any of the other literally infinite possibilities.

In genetics, however, seven can be a perilously tiny number. During the late 1980s and early 1990s, seven was all biologists had to work with from the miniscule founder population of Mexican gray wolves. Why only seven? Well, very nearly, this was all that was left.

Mexican gray wolves (or lobos) are a subspecies of the gray wolf, which is still fairly common in Canada, Alaska, and a few areas in the northern United States. In historical times, tens of thousands of this southern subspecies roamed over a huge area of forests, deserts, and scrublands in the American Southwest and northern Mexico. They were long-eared, thick-necked, and quite small by wolf standards, weighing in at only about sixty to eighty pounds (about the size of the typical German shepherd), with males tending to be somewhat taller and heavier than females. They were mostly light gray in color, almost never displaying the very dark gray or even black phases that were common in their northern cousins. Like other wolves, they hunted in packs and generally fed on large ungulates—mostly deer and elk—although when those large prey species were unavailable, the wolves would eat javelinas, rabbits, squirrels, or even mice.

Unfortunately, for both wolves and ranchers, these efficient predators also occasionally attacked a new food source brought in by people—livestock, which provided nice, plump, and relatively slow targets of opportunity. In addition, like wolves everywhere, the animals were saddled with long-held prejudices, as well as silly and absolutely fictional stories about North American wolves preying on people. So, the slaughter began. Ranchers, recreational hunters, trappers, and government agents all got in on the act, and by the 1950s the Mexican gray wolf was extinct in the United States. In 1976 the Mexican wolf was placed on the endangered species list—a classic case of too little too late—where it has remained ever since. By the 1980s only a tiny remnant population of a few individual wild wolves survived in Mexico. Additionally, there were a handful of wolves in captive breeding programs north of the border.

With a mandate under the Endangered Species Act, the US Fish and Wildlife Service came up with a recovery plan for the Mexican wolf, which involved developing a captive breeding program and releasing the animals back into the wild. The original goal was to have at least one hundred wolves living in two or more wild populations by 2006. The usual political controversies and some understandable opposition from ranchers and other stakeholders cropped up, but these obstacles were eventually overcome, and on a cold and snowy day in late March of 1998, biologists released eleven wolves into the Blue Range of eastern Arizona.

Since this initial release, progress for the species has been agonizingly slow. Several wolves have been illegally shot, and extended drought conditions have affected the wolves' food supply, but there have also been some tentative successes. As of 2013 there were about seventy-five wild Mexican gray wolves in several closely related packs in the United States— a decent start, but still well short of the program's goal. This population is centered in Arizona's Apache National Forest, although a few packs and wandering animals are also in New Mexico's Gila National Forest.

The Mexican gray wolf remains the world's most endangered type of wolf. In 2012 only six breeding pairs lived in the wild, although even that low number was up from just two or three the year before. An additional 350 or so animals are in the almost fifty captive breeding programs scattered around the United States. Scientists agree that the wild population needs several dozen more animals, and at least one more area with a wolf population, to ensure a tenuous but sustainable recovery for the species. The current wild wolves simply lack enough genetic diversity to thrive. In addition, the fledgling population is currently vulnerable to a localized disaster, such as forest fires or disease.

While hiking in the Gila Wilderness, you are right in the heart of a huge wild area that stretches across two states. The hope of many conservationists is that, eventually, this will serve as the core habitat for a large and self-sustaining population of wolves. As of 2013, the animals are seen in the Gila Wilderness only on rare occasions, but with luck and continued support both from the public and from government organizations,

Hoodoos in Middle Fork Canyon, below Jordan Hot Springs

there is reason to believe that this will change. So, even though you probably won't see one today, perhaps in the future a descendant of those original seven founders will lope across the trail in front of a delighted backpacker.

Now, wouldn't that be lucky?

Trip Description: The initially wide trail starts in a low-elevation area that was partially burned in the large Miller Fire of 2011. Until the land recovers from this fire, you can expect lots of dead snags, deadfall, and blackened terrain for the next 2.5 miles. The path drops less than 30 feet to the clear waters of Middle Fork Gila River, with its relatively lush riparian strip of willows, cottonwoods, and other greenery. The surrounding rocky hills are home to junipers and a few ponderosa pines. Wildlife is present as well. This entire wilderness area is part of the Mexican wolf reintroduction and recovery zone, so keep an eye out for these extremely endangered animals. Sure, the odds of seeing one of the seventy-five or so wolves surviving in the wild (as of 2013) are extraordinarily remote, but think of the thrill if you succeed!

After 0.15 mile you make your first of what will be several dozen stream crossings. The river is typically less than knee deep, but you will still be forced to hike long distances in wet shoes. During spring runoff of heavy snow years or after summer thunderstorms, the water can be swift, deep, and dangerous. Call ahead about the latest conditions. The canyon is relatively shallow at first, and the walls aren't very steep, so the scenery, while good, does not compare to the drama ahead. At 0.7 mile, and shortly after the second crossing, you pass small Middle Fork Hot Spring, a popular day hike destination.

Immediately after Middle Fork Hot Spring, you enter the Gila Wilderness. Campsites begin just 0.2 mile later, with a nice site immediately after the third river crossing. Campsites will remain plentiful for the next several miles. The river's permanent water has the benefit of attracting a wide range of wildlife. Look for numerous colorful songbirds, turkeys, various lizards, mule deer, rabbits, Rocky Mountain elk, squirrels, and rattlesnakes, among many other species. The Gila has several species of rattlers, and they are fairly common from April to October, so watch your step and be careful of where you sit down to rest.

At 1.5 miles, just after river crossing number six, is a junction with the trail to White Rocks. Go straight on Middle Fork Trail, immediately passing another fine campsite. The main canyon gradually becomes grander, as cliffs and bluffs of tan and yellow with dark streaks of desert varnish rise 200 to 300 feet on either side of the twisting stream. In addition, interesting caves can often be found at the base of the cliffs. Your neck will soon start to get a workout with so much time spent staring upward at the canyon walls.

After two dozen crossings, or nearly 5 miles, you come to a lush little spring-fed meadow backed by tall rock pinnacles. This is where the really fine canyon scenery starts, as you pass beneath an endless series of colorful colonnades, cliffs, pinnacles, and hoodoos for the next several miles.

At 6 miles you come to a spacious and attractive campsite immediately before the junction with Little Bear Canyon Trail. This trail is a popular shortcut for hikers heading for Jordan Hot Springs. During the full backpacking loop, the Little Bear Canyon Trail makes an excellent side trip, especially for the first mile or so, where the route passes through a very narrow (nearly a slot) canyon. **Warning:** Little Bear Canyon is prone to dangerous flash floods during the summer rainy season, so avoid it if thunderclouds are in the area.

At 8 miles (or forty-four river crossings, if keeping track), you pass a particularly large campsite, and then make a brief uphill to Jordan Hot Springs. Here a large cascading spring feeds a deep pool of warm (not really "hot")

Rock pinnacle below Jordan Hot Springs

water that is ideal for soaking. Don't expect privacy, as this spot is one of the most popular backcountry destinations in the Gila Wilderness.

Above Jordan Hot Springs the trail continues with its previous pattern of crossing and recrossing the ever-smaller stream countless times as you proceed past impressive rock formations on either side of the narrow canyon. Most of the cliffs and pinnacles are so close that photographing their splendor is challenging, but your eyes can take it all in with delight. Campsites are less numerous along this section, but there are still a couple of good spots for those who want to spend the night.

About 6.4 miles above Jordan Hot Springs you come to the Meadows, a generally open expanse where the canyon widens considerably, and small Indian Creek flows in from the right (north). The trail here can be hard to follow because of myriad elk trails (the elk droppings are everywhere, and with any luck, you will probably see some of these magnificent animals) and some minor fire damage. Just keep going upstream on the right (north) side of the river and you can't get lost. If it is late in the day, you will find several possible campsites in the Meadows. Beavers are active on the stream here, with lots of chewed-off trees and a couple of large dams.

Dramatic-looking pinnacle in Middle Fork Canyon below the Meadows

In the middle of the Meadows is a signed junction. Continue straight on the Middle Fork Trail and wander upstream through a lovely parkland of ponderosa pines, Gambel oaks, and some Douglas firs near the river (now the size of a modest creek). The canyon remains fairly wide for the next 0.5 mile, but then it tightens up again into a narrow chasm featuring the tallest cliffs and pinnacles seen thus far. The narrow confines and the twisting watercourse force the trail to constantly cross and recross the stream, often as many as fifteen times per mile. Despite the fine scenery, the trail above the Meadows gets far less use than it does in the lower canyon, so you can expect plenty of solitude. On the downside, the route is also brushier (including some poison ivy), and campsites are infrequent.

About 2.4 miles above the Meadows, the trail detours about 100 feet uphill to pass around a rocky chute and small sliding falls on the river. After just 0.1 mile, you switchback back down to the water and continue hiking upstream. The canyon opens up above this point, with fewer stream crossings. The scenery remains excellent, as the slopes above the river are often peppered with hundreds of oddly shaped pinnacles and spires. Anglers should note that the stream here is home to some very large trout, which tend to hide in the deeper pools. As you gradually ascend, the canyon becomes more heavily forested, with views less frequent.

At just over 7 miles from the Meadows, you make one last crossing of Middle Fork Gila River (that's 123 since the trailhead), then come to a good campsite just before an important junction.

This is the recommended place to leave the Middle Fork Canyon for the traverse over to the West Fork Canyon. So turn sharply left (uphill), following signs to Prior, and climb away from the river on six well-graded switchbacks. These are followed by some rolling ups and downs before you begin an extended gradual uphill through an open ponderosa pine forest. About 1.5 miles from the Middle Fork junction, you pass just above some rocky outcroppings that provide fine views of the rugged Middle Fork Gila River Canyon.

The trail tops a rounded ridge, and then contours for about 0.3 mile along a partially forested hillside. Look to the west along this section for some good views of Mogollon Baldy peak, which at 10,770 feet is the second highest point in the Gila Wilderness.

The trail now descends slowly to a crossing of the usually dry watercourse in the upper reaches of Chicken Coop Canyon, turns downstream along this gully of about 150 yards, and then curves to the right up a dry side canyon for 0.2 mile to a signed junction. The trail to Jackson Mesa goes sharply right.

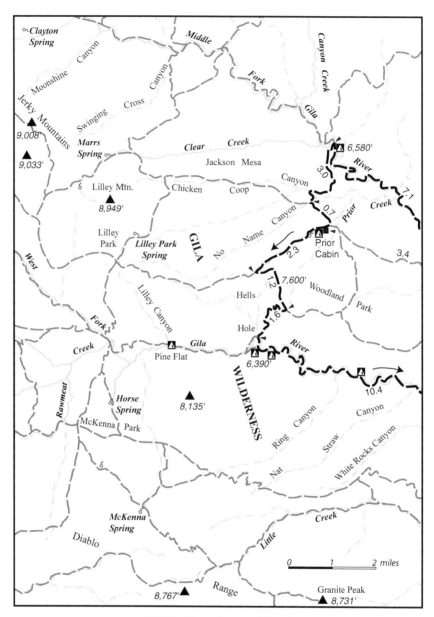

11.2 Gila River Canyons (West)

You keep straight, still heading toward Prior, and go gently up and down for 0.7 mile to a metal water cistern (not available for the use of hikers) and a possibly unsigned junction beside log Prior Cabin. This tiny structure is occasionally used by employees of the New Mexico Department of Fish and Wildlife and is not open to hikers. You can camp in the vicinity, with water

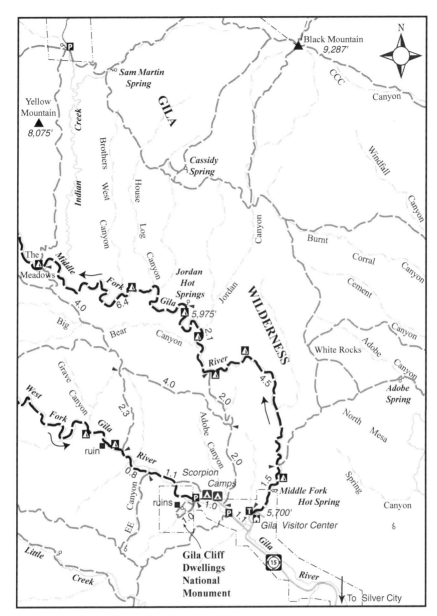

11.3 Gila River Canyons (East)

hopefully available from either the tiny green strip of Prior Creek just below the cabin (in dry years, the creek will have no water) or a nearby intermittent spring.

You go straight at the cabin, picking up the sometimes faint path that initially goes up the right (north) side of Prior Creek. At 0.25 mile above the cabin, you pass a small spring that usually provides at least a trickle of water in all but the driest years. Above this point, the trail goes back and forth across the dry and shallow gully of Prior Creek in a long and very gradual ascent. About 2.3 miles from Prior Cabin is an unsigned junction with an obvious and well-used trail that angles across your route. You go sharply left and very soon reach the views from the top of the drop-off above Hells Hole Canyon.

From here you can see all the way down into the depths of the West Fork Gila River Canyon. You will be going down there shortly, but first the trail loops around the north and east sides of Hells Hole, staying high on the ridge with its open forest of ponderosa pines. After 1.2 miles you turn right at a junction, walk on the level for about 0.15 mile, and reach the lip of Hells Hole Canyon. The often-rocky trail now descends into this canyon using twenty-eight switchbacks to descend 1,000 feet in 1.4 miles. At the bottom is a junction with the West Fork Gila River Trail.

You turn left (downstream) and almost immediately make the first of what will be many crossings of the clear and fairly small West Fork Gila River. The trail stays on the right (south) side of the stream for 0.2 mile, passing a couple of fine campsites, to a junction. You may notice intermittent fire scars in this area, especially on the south side of the trail. These are from the 2011 Miller Fire. Get used to these blackened remains, because for most of the rest of the hike, fire scars will be common. The crews used the river and trail here as a fire line to combat the blaze.

You go straight at the junction and continue down the canyon. Like the similar Middle Fork Canyon, the West Fork's defile is extremely scenic, with cliffs and pinnacles galore. Which canyon is more impressive is a matter of opinion, but both are unquestionably terrific. Objectively, the trail along the West Fork includes more ups and downs, has slightly fewer stream crossings (there are still plenty), and much fewer campsites than you found on the Middle Fork. There are also, for some unexplained reason, more biting flies in this canyon, which can be quite bothersome. Poison ivy is common in both canyons.

The scenery remains little changed as you work your way down the canyon, with plenty of good views and occasional burn scars. About 4 miles below Hells Hole, you pass a good campsite, and then climb a bit for the next 0.4 mile, staying on the hillside well above the water. Here you'll enjoy fine canyon views, and for the time being, you won't need to worry about stream crossings. The dry-footed interlude ends when you return to river level and another crossing. From this point on you will spend long stretches without crossing the river, which is a welcome difference from the Middle Fork Canyon. At about 8.3 miles from Hells Hole (and forty-two river crossings), you pass Grave Canyon coming in from the left and reach another good campsite. At 9.2 miles from Hells Hole, look upstream at yet another river crossing to see two large caves in the canyon wall about 25 feet above the stream. In the smaller of these caves is an ancient cliff dwelling. After crossing the stream, it is possible to walk up to the ruins, but, as always, do not disturb this important site.

Shortly below the ruins, the canyon begins to open up and get sunnier, drier, and hotter. At 10.3 miles from Hells Hole is a junction. Go straight, still on the West Fork Trail, cross the river again, climb a bit, and then walk across a badly fire-scarred bench well above the south side of the river. At 0.8 mile from the last junction, you go straight at the junction with the trail to Little Creek, and then descend to make another crossing of the river to yet another junction, where the horse trail to TJ Corral goes left.

To reach the trailhead at Gila Cliff Dwellings, turn right and almost immediately enter national monument land. This trail crosses the river twice more in the next 0.5 mile (for a total of fifty-six along this stream) before you arrive at the parking lot for the West Fork Trail. Just above the adjacent lot is the path up to the fascinating Gila Cliff Dwellings (a 1-mile loop that is well worth doing). It's a relatively easy, but often hot, 2.1-mile road walk from the Gila Cliff Dwellings parking lot to the Middle Fork trailhead.

Possible Itinerary

Day	Camps and Side Trips	Distance (mi.)	Elevation (ft.)
1	Middle Fork TH to Jordan Hot Springs	8.1	+500/–200
2	Middle Fork at Prior junction	13.5	+1,000/–400
3	West Fork at Hells Hole	9.0	+1,400/–1,600
4	Out to West Fork TH	12.1	+600/–1,300
	Side trip to Gila Cliff Dwellings	1.0	+200/–200

Green Tips: New Mexico Wilderness Alliance—www.nmwild.org

Best Trips by Season

Late March

   5. Salt Creek Canyon and Chesler Park Traverse

April

   4. Coyote Gulch and the Escalante River Country

   5. Salt Creek Canyon and Chesler Park Traverse

   7. Buckskin Gulch and Paria River Canyon

   9. Tonto Trail: Grandview to Hermits Rest

 11. Gila River Canyons Loop

Mid-April

   6. Grand Gulch and Bullet Canyon Traverse

      All trips listed under April

May

   2. Under-the-Rim Trail

   4. Coyote Gulch and the Escalante River Country

   5. Salt Creek Canyon and Chesler Park Traverse

   6. Grand Gulch and Bullet Canyon Traverse

   7. Buckskin Gulch and Paria River Canyon

   9. Tonto Trail: Grandview to Hermits Rest

 11. Gila River Canyons Loop

Mid-May to early June

   3. Zion Park Traverse

   5. Salt Creek Canyon and Chesler Park Traverse

   6. Grand Gulch and Bullet Canyon Traverse

   7. Buckskin Gulch and Paria River Canyon

   8. North Rim to South Rim: North Kaibab and Bright Angel Trails

 11. Gila River Canyons Loop

Mid-June

   2. Under-the-Rim Trail

   8. North Rim to South Rim: North Kaibab and Bright Angel Trails

 11. Gila River Canyons Loop

June

   2. Under-the-Rim Trail

July

 10. Pecos Skyline Trail

Late July to mid-August

   1. Highline Trail

September

   2. Under-the-Rim Trail

   5. Salt Creek Canyon and Chesler Park Traverse

Mid-September through end-October

   4. Coyote Gulch and the Escalante River Country

   6. Grand Gulch and Bullet Canyon Traverse

   7. Buckskin Gulch and Paria River Canyon

Early to mid-October

   8. North Rim to South Rim: North Kaibab and Bright Angel Trails
      All trips listed under October

October

   2. Under-the-Rim Trail

   5. Salt Creek Canyon and Chesler Park Traverse

 11. Gila River Canyons Loop

Index

Page numbers in **bold** indicate illustrations.

Abajo Mountains, 77
Abbey, Edward, 95–96
Agua Canyon, 30
Agua Canyon Connecting
    Trail, 30
Aiken, Bruce, 141
All American Man, 83
Alligator, 165, 167
Anasazi culture and ruins:
    Canyonlands, 82, 83, 85;
    Grand Gulch Primitive
    Area, 97, 105–106, 108;
    history of, 102–104
Ancestral Puebloans, 87,
    102–104
"Ancient Ones," 102–104
Anderson Pass, **6**, 13
Angel Arch, 85, 86, 94
Angel Arch Camp, **74**, 85, 94
Angel Arch Trail, 85
Angels Landing, 50, 52
Angels Landing Trail, 41, 50
Angka-ku-wass-a-wits, 28
Apache National Forest, 196
Archaic People, 87, 102–104
Archaic Period, 108
Arches National Monument,
    79
Arches National Park, 77
architecture, 156–157
Ashley National Forest, 8

Basketmaker Period, 108
Battleship, 165
Beatty's Flats, 178
Beatty's Trail 25, 180
Beef Basin Road, 78
Big Pocket, 82
Big Ruins, 82, 94
Big Spring (Vermilion Cliffs),
    114, 126, 128
Big Springs Canyon (Canyon-
    lands), 94
Big Springs Canyon Trail
    (Canyonlands), 91
black bears, 77

Black Bridge, 146
Blue Creek, 41, 47
Blue Range, 196
Bob Grounds Trail 270, 178
Boulder Creek Canyon, 159
Boulder Mail Trail, 71
Box, 142
Brave Cowboy, The (Abbey),
    96
Breezy Point, 168
Bright Angel Campground,
    132, 136, 142, 146, 148, 149
Bright Angel Canyon, **140**,
    141–142, 146
Bright Angel Creek, 135, 141,
    142, 146
Bright Angel Fault, 147
Bright Angel Lodge, 156
Bright Angel Point Trail, 137
Bright Angel Shale, 140–141,
    147, 167
Bright Angel Trail, **130**, **132**,
    141–148, 161, 207, 208
Bright Angel trailhead, **132**,
    138, 148
Broken Bow Arch, 60
Brook Lake, **6**, 11, 19
Bryce Amphitheater, 21
Bryce Canyon: history of,
    26–28
Bryce Canyon City (UT), 25
Bryce Canyon National
    Monument, 28
Bryce Canyon National Park:
    creation of, 28; Under-the-
    Rim Trail, 21–26, 29–35,
    207, 208
Bryce, Ebenezer and Mary, 26,
    27–28
Bryce Point, **23**, 31, 35
Buckskin Gulch, **112**, 113–
    117, 119–124, 128, 207, 208
Bullet Canyon, 108–110
Bullet Canyon trailhead, **99**,
    100, 102, 110
Bullet Canyon Traverse. **See**

Grand Gulch and Bullet
    Canyon Traverse
Bundu Bus, 24
Bureau of Reclamation, 63, 80
Burnt Mountain, 44
Burro Springs, 161
Butterfly campground, 7

Cabin Spring, 50
cairns: Highline Trail, 8, 10,
    11, 16, 20
Calf Creek Campground, 59
Calf Creek Falls, 59
California condors, 117–119,
    170
Camp BS1, 94
Camp CP1, 93
Camp EC1, 93
Camp EC2, 91, 93
Camp EC3, **74**, 91, 93, 94
Camp SC1, **74**, 81, 94
Camp SC2, 81
Camp SC3, 83
Camp SC4, 85
Camp SQ2, 90
Camps CP3–5, 93
Camps LC1–3, 90
Canyonlands National Park:
    beauty of, 78–79; creation
    of, 79–80; Salt Creek
    Canyon and Chesler Park
    Traverse, **72**, 73–78, 81–95,
    207, 208
Cape Royal, 137
Castle Dome Café, 42
Casto Canyon, 25
Cathedral Butte, 78
Cathedral Butte trailhead, **74**,
    78, 94
Cathedral Stairs, 168
Cave Creek, 185
Cave Creek Trail 288, 185
Cave of Domes, 158
Cedar Mesa, 97
Cedar Spring, 167
Chepeta Lake, 5

Chepeta Lake trailhead, **6**, 19
Chesler Park, 76, 91, 92–93, 94
Chesler Park Traverse. *See* Salt
  Creek Canyon and Chesler
  Park Traverse
Chicken Coop Canyon, 201
Chimayosos Peak, 180
Chino Mine, 194
Chocolate Drops, 95
Circle D Restaurant, 59
civil disobedience: Edward
  Abbey and, 96
Civilian Conservation Corps,
  140
Claim Jumper, 9
Clear Creek Trail, 142
Cliff Arch, 67
Coconino Overlook, 139
Coconino Saddle, 158
Coconino Sandstone, 140,
  158, 168
Colorado Plateau, 62, 79, 139
Colorado River, 43, 61, 63, 95,
  131, 146
Colorado River Canyon, 77
Colter, Mary, 138, 155,
  156–157
Columbine Spring, 146
condors, 117–119, 170
Connector Trail (Zion Park
  Traverse), 46
Cope Butte, 167
Cosmos Club, 63
Cottage Place Restaurant, 156
Cottonwood Camp, **132**
Cottonwood Campground,
  132, 136, 141, 148, 149
Cottonwood Canyon Narrows,
  116–117
Cottonwood Canyon Road, 25
Cottonwood Creek, 154,
  158–159, 169
Cottonwood Creek Canyon,
  158
Cowboy Blues Restaurant, 59
Cowles Campground, 176
Coyote Canyon, 106
Coyote Gulch, **54**, 55–61,
  64–71, 207, 208
Coyote Gulch–Harris Wash
  Traverse, 71
Coyote Natural Bridge, **56**, 67,
  68, 71
Coyote Shuttle, 76
Coyote Spring, 100, 106

Crack in the Wall, 70–71
Crater Lake, 17, 139
Cremation Creek, 160, 170
Cremation Creek Canyon, 170
Crescent Arch, 86–87
Crescent Lake, 11

Dana Butte, 165
Davis Lake, 12
Dead Horse Lake, **6**, 8, 17, 19
Dead Horse Pass, 17, 18
Dead Horse Point State Park,
  77
Dean Lake, 18
Dellenbaugh, Frederick S., 43
De Motte Park Campground,
  136–137
Desert Solitaire (Abbey), 96
Desert View Drive, 138, 155,
  156
Devil's Corkscrew, 147
Devils Garden Outstanding
  Natural Area, 59
Dick's Uinta Drive Inn, 9
Divide Lake, 11
Divide Pass, 11
Double Arch Alcove, 41
Dripping Springs Trail, 168
Druid Arch, 79, 90, 91, **92**,
  93, 94
Dry Fork Coyote Gulch, 64
Dry Fork Road, 60
Dutton, Clarence Edward,
  138–139

Earth First movement, 96
East Fork Duchesne River, 18
East Fork Pinto Lake Trail, 18
East Fork Salt Creek, 81
East Pecos Baldy, 184, 185, 187
ecotage, 96
Egypt Loop, 71
Elephant Canyon, 76, 90, 91,
  93, 94
Elephant Hill, 94
El Navajo Hotel, 157
El Tovar, 138, 155, 157
Escalante (UT), 59
Escalante Interagency Visitor
  Center, 59
Escalante River Canyon, 58, 69
Escalante River Country, **54**,
  55–61, 63–71, 207, 208
Explorer Peak, 17
Eye of the Needle, 140

Fall Creek, 17
Fence Canyon, 71
Fins, 95
Fire on the Mountain (Abbey),
  96
Firepit Knoll, 46
First Tunnel, 147–148
Fisher Towers, 77
Fisheye Arch, 83
Flagstaff (AZ), 138, 156
flash floods: Buckskin Gulch
  and the Paria Narrows, 113,
  116, 121; Coyote Gulch and
  Escalante River Country,
  55, 58–59; Grand Gulch and
  Bullet Canyon, 100–101;
  Little Bear Canyon, 198;
  Lost Canyon, 90
Food Town, 9
forest fires of 2011, 187–189,
  197, 204
Fortymile Ridge, 69
Fortymile Ridge Road, 58,
  60, 61
Four Faces pictograph, 83
Four Lakes Basin, 18
Fox Lake, 11
Fox Queant Pass, 11
Fred Harvey Company, 157
Fremont people, 83
frost wedging, 27

Game Management (Leopold),
  177
Garden Creek, 135, 147, 154,
  161
Garden Creek Canyon, 147
Garfield Basin, 13, 16
Garnet Canyon, 151
General Store (North Rim,
  Grand Canyon), 137
Geronimo Trail, 175
Gila Cliff Dwellings National
  Monument, 194, 205
Gila National Forest: Mexican
  gray wolves, 195–197. *See
  also* Gila River Canyons
  Loop
Gila River Canyons Loop, **190**,
  191–195, 197–205, 207, 208
Gila Visitor Center, 195
Gila Wilderness: forest fires
  of 2011, 187–188; Gila
  River Canyons Loop, **190**,
  191–195, 197–205, 207,

208; Aldo Leopold and, 176; Mexican gray wolves, 195–197
Gilbert Creek, 12
Glen Canyon, 63
Glen Canyon Dam, 131
Glen Canyon National Recreation Area. *See* Coyote Gulch; Escalante River Country
Goosenecks State Park, 101
Grand Canyon: Mary Colter and architecture, 156–157; Clarence Edward Dutton and, 138–139; overview and description of, 131; John Wesley Powell and, 61–62, 63; rim-to-rim hiking, 131–132; Roaring Springs Pumphouse and Bruce Aiken, 141
Grand Canyon Airport, 154
Grand Canyon Lodge, 137
Grand Canyon National Park: amenities and attractions, 136–138, 155–156; backcountry logistics, 135–136, 154–155; on hiking and salty snacks, 148–149; North Kaibab and Bright Angel Trails, 138, 139–148, 207, 208; permits, 133–134, 152–153; regulations, 134, 153; rim-to-rim hikes, 131–132; size of, 131; Tonto Trail, **150**, 151–170, 207; transportation logistics, 134–135, 154
Grand Canyon Railway, 135, 154
Grand Canyon Village, 137
Grand Gulch, 104–106, 108
Grand Gulch and Bullet Canyon Traverse, 97–102, 104–110, 207, 208
Grand Gulch Primitive Area: Anasazi culture and ruins, 97, 102–104, 105–106, 108; Grand Gulch and Bullet Canyon Traverse, 97–102, 104–110, 207, 208
Grand Staircase–Escalante National Monument, 29. *See also* Coyote Gulch; Escalante River Country
Grandview Mine, 158

Grand View Point (Canyonlands), 77
Grandview Point (Grand Canyon), 156
Grandview Trail, 138, 157–159
Grandview trailhead, **152**, 168
Grand Walsh Cliff, 131
Granite Gorge, 146, 159, **160**, 169–170
Granite Rapids, 167
Grapevine Canyon, 159
Grapevine Creek, **152**, 154, 159, 168
Grapevine Rapids, 159
Grave Canyon, 205
gray wolves, 195–197
Great West Canyon, 47
Green Mask Panel, 108, **109**, 110
Green Mask Spring, 100, 108
Green River, 61
Gregory Butte, 45
Grosvenor Arch, 25
Grotto Picnic Area, **38**, 50, 52
Gunsight Pass, 13

Hackberry Canyon, 128
Hamilton Mesa, 177, 178
Hamilton Mesa Trail 249, 177–178
Hance Canyon, 158
Hanksville (UT), 95
Harding, Warren G., 28
Harris Wash, 71
Harvey, Fred, 157
Hat Shop, 35
Hayden Pass, 5
Hayden Pass trailhead, 6, 19
Heber City (UT), 9
Hells Canyon (Grand Canyon), 131
Hell's Hole Canyon (Gila Wilderness), **192**, 204, 205
Henry Mountains, 93
Henrys Fork trailhead, 6
Hermit Basin, 168
Hermit Camp, 167
Hermit Formation, 158, 168
Hermit Gorge, 168
Hermit Rapids, 167
Hermit Trail, 138, 167
Hermits Rest, 168, 169
Hermits Rest Road, 156
Hermits Rest Snack Bar, 168
Hermits Rest trailhead, **152**, 168

Highline Trail, **4**, 5–20, 208
Highline trailhead, 19
High Uintas Wilderness. **See** Highline Trail
Hole (box canyon), 126–127
Hole-in-the-Rock Road, 58, 59–60
Holmes, William Henry, 139
Hoodoos, **197**
Hop Valley, 38, 41, 45–46
Hop Valley Trail, 45–46
Hop Valley trailhead, 41, 46
Hopi House, 157
Hopi Indians, 103
Horn Creek, 154, 165
Horse Pasture Plateau, 38, 50
Horseshoe Mesa, 138, **152**, 158, 168, 169
Horsethief Creek, 185
Horsethief Meadow, 174, 185, 187, 188
House Rock Valley Road, 116
Humphrey, J. W., 28
Humphreys Peak, 139
Hurricane Wash, 66–67
Hurricane Wash trailhead, 60

Indian Building, 157
Indian Creek (Canyonlands), 78
Indian Creek (Grand Canyon), 199
Indian Garden, 146, 147, 151, **152**, 155, 161, 168
Indian Garden Campground, 132, 136
Inner Gorge, 158, 170
Iron Gate Campground, 174, 175, 176, 186
Iron Gate trailhead, 177, 186, 187
Iron Spring, **23**, 29

Jacks Creek Trail 257, 184
Jackson Mesa, 201
Jacob Hamlin Arch, 61, 67
Jacob Lake, 138
Jacob Lake Inn, 136
Jacob's Ladder, 147
Jailhouse Ruin, 108
Jailhouse Spring, **99**, 100, 108, 110
Jasper Canyon, 95
Jewels Route, 169

Jicarita Peak, 187
Jobs Head, 46
Johnson Lake Trail 267, 185
Jordan Hot Springs, **192,**
    198–199, 205
Judd Hollow Pump, 126
Junction Ruin, 105
Junction Spring, 105

Kaibab Formation, 158, 168
Kaibab General Store, 136
Kaibab Lodge, 136
Kaibab Suspension Bridge, 146
Kaibab Trail parking lot, 138
Kamas (UT), 9
Kane Gulch, **99,** 100, 104, 110
Kane Gulch Ranger Station,
    99, 102
Kidney Lakes, 12
Kings Canyon, 131
Kings Peak, 5, 6, 13
Kirk's Arch, 82
Kirk's Cabin, 81, 82
Kodachrome Basin State
    Park, 25
Kolb Studio, 148
Kolob Arch, 38, 45
Kolob Arch junction, **38,** 44,
    45, 52
Kolob Canyons, 37–38, 43, **44**
Kolob Terrace Road, 38, 46
Krishna Shrine, 159

Lake Fork River canyon, 16
Lake Katherine, 186, 187
Lake Mead, 131
Lambert Meadow, **6,** 16, 19
Larkspur Trail 260, 178
La Sal Mountains, 77, 88, 94
Last Chance Mine, 158
Lava Point Campground,
    41, 50
La Verkin Creek, 40, 41, 44,
    45, 46
La Verkin Creek Canyon, 45
La Verkin Creek Trail, 37–38,
    43–44
Ledge Lake, 18
Lee Pass, 37, **38,** 44, 52
Lees Ferry, 128, 131
Lees Ferry trailhead, 127
Leopold, Aldo, 176–177, 191
Lincoln National Forest, 187
Lipan Point, 138, 155
Little Bear Canyon Trail, 198

Little Creek, 205
Little Siberia Canyon, 50
Lonetree Canyon, 160
Lonetree Creek, **152,** 160, 168
Lookout Point, 168
Lost Canyon, 76, 87, 90
Lower Buckskin Gulch, **114**
Lower Reader Lake, 10
Lower Scorpion Campground,
    195
Lyell Butte, 159

Market Plaza, 155
Marshall, Bob, 177
Mather Campground, 137, 155
Mauv Limestone, 140, 167
Maze, 79
Maze District, 95
Meadows, 199, 201
meningitis, 194
Mexican gray wolves, 195–197
Middle Fork Gila River,
    197–201
Middle Fork Gila River
    Canyon, 197–201
Middle Fork Hot Spring, 198
Middle Fork junction, 201
Middle Fork Lake, 179
Middle Fork Rio Santa
    Barbara, 179
Middle Fork Trail, 198–201
Middle Fork trailhead, **192,**
    195, 205
Mile-and-a-Half Resthouse, 147
Miller Fire, 197, 204
Mirror Lake, 6, 19
Mirror Lake Scenic Byway, 8, 9
Moab (UT), 77
Mogollon Baldy Peak, 201
Monkey Wrench Gang, The
    (Abbey), 96
Monticello (UT), 101
Monument Creek, **152,** 154,
    167, 168
Monument Creek Canyon, 167
Moon Lake trailhead, 16
moqui holes, 91
Moran, Thomas, 139
Mount Majestic, 50
Mud Canyon Overlook, 30
Mukuntuweap National
    Monument, 43

national park rustic style, 156
Natural Bridge campsite, 30

Natural Bridges National
    Monument, 100, 101, 102
Naturalist Basin, 6, 18, 19
Navajo Indians, 103
Navajo Mountain, 29
Neagle Ridge, 44
Needle (Grand Canyon), 140
Needles (Canyonlands), 90
Needles Visitor Center
    (Canyonlands), 78
New Mexico: forest fires of
    2011, 187–189
Newton Butte, 160
North Fork Ponderosa
    Canyon, 30
North Fork Rio Quemado,
    180
Northgate Peaks, 47, 52
Northgate Peaks Trail, 40, 47
North Guardian Angel, 47
North Kaibab Plateau, 139
North Kaibab Plateau Visitor
    Center, 136
North Kaibab Trail, **130, 132,**
    139–141, **144–145,** 149,
    207, 208
North Kaibab trailhead, **132,**
    148
North Pole Pass, **6,** 11
North Rim, 137
North Rim Campground, 137
North Rim Visitor Center, 137
North Sixshooter Peak, 88
North Star Lake, 13
North Truchas Peak, 180

Owachomo Bridge, 101
Oweep Creek, 16
Owl Creek–Fish Creek Loop,
    110
Oza Butte, 142

Packard Lake, 19
Page Spring, 158
Painter Basin, **6,** 12, 13, 19
Paiute Indians, 28
Panchuela Creek, 185
Paria Canyon Information
    Center, 115
Paria Narrows, 128
Paria River, 27, 125, 127
Paria River Canyon, **112,** 114–
    117, 124–128, 207, 208
Pasture Wash, 31
Pattie Butte, 160

Paunsaugunt Plateau. *See*
Under-the-Rim Trail
Pecos (NM), 175
Pecos Baldy Lake, 184
Pecos Baldy Peak, 181
Pecos Falls, 174, 178, 187
Pecos River, 178
Pecos River Trail 456, 178–179
Pecos Skyline Trail, **172**,
173–187, 208
Pecos Wilderness: forest fires
of 2011, 187–189; Skyline
Trail, **172**, 173–187, 208
Peekaboo Camp (Canyon-
lands), **74**, 87, 94
Peek-a-boo Canyon (Es-
calante River Country),
59–60
Peekaboo Spring (Canyon-
lands), 87
Peekaboo Window (Canyon-
lands), 87
Perfect Kiva Ruin, 108
petroglyphs and pictographs:
Canyonlands, 83, 87; Green
Mask Panel, 108, **109**
Phantom Ranch, 132, 142
Phantom Ranch Canteen,
142, 149
Phinney Lake, 18
Pine Valley Peak, 46
Pink Cliffs, 30
Pinos Altos Road, 194
Pipe Creek, 146–147, 161
Pipe Creek Canyon, 146
Plateau Point, 161
Plateau Point Junction, 165
Point Imperial, 137
Point Roosevelt, 137
poison ivy, 194
Pole Creek Lake camp-
ground, 7
Ponderosa Canyon, 29
Porcupine Pass, **6**, 8, 13, 16
Potato Hollow Spring, 50
Pour-off Pool, 105
Powell, John Wesley, 43,
61–63
Prior Cabin, 202–203
Prior Creek, 203–204
Prior Junction, **192**, 205
Pueblo Indians, 103

Rabbit Hole, 123
Rainbow Lake, 12

Rainbow Point, 31
Rainbow Point trailhead,
23, 29
Rama Shrine, 159
rattlesnakes, 76–77, 194, 198
Reader Creek, 10
Reader Lakes, 20
Red Butte, 44
Red Canyon, 25, 151
Red Knob Pass, **6**, 16, 17
Red Knob Peak, 17
Red Rock Grill and Lounge, 42
Redwall Bridge, 140
Redwall Limestone, 140, 158,
168
Red Well, **56**, 60, 64, 71
Refrigerator Canyon, 50
Ribbon Falls, 141, 142, **143**,
148
Right Fork Swamp Canyon
campsite, 30
Right Fork Yellow Creek, 33
Right Fork Yellow Creek
campsite, 33
rincon, 126
Rincon Bonito, 179
Rito Oscura, 185
Rito Perro, 184
River Resthouse, 147
River Trail, 146, 148
Roaring Springs, 141, 146
Roaring Springs Canyon, 139
Roaring Springs Fault, 140
Roaring Springs Picnic Area,
141
Roaring Springs Pumphouse,
141
rock art. *See* petroglyphs and
pictographs
Rock Creek, 18
Rock Creek Lakes, 18
Rockville (UT), 41
Rocky Mountain big horn
sheep, 180
Rocky Mountains. *See* Highline
Trail
Rocky Sea Pass, **6**, 18
Roosevelt (UT), 9
Ruby's Inn General Store,
24, 25
Russell Gulch, 47

Salt Creek, 81, 83, 85, 86, 87,
155
Salt Creek Canyon, 165

Salt Creek Canyon and
Chesler Park Traverse, **72**,
73–78, 81–95, 207, 208
Salt Creek jeep road, 87
Salt Creek Trail, 85
Salt/Horse at-large backpack-
ing zone, 85
Sand County Almanac, A
(Leopold), 177
San Francisco Peaks, 139
San Juan River, 110
Santa Barbara Divide, 179–181
Santa Barbara trailhead, 187
Santa Fe (NM), 175
Santa Fe Baldy, 181, 185, 186
Santa Fe National Forest: for-
est fires of 2011, 187–189;
Pecos Skyline Trail, **172**,
173–187, 208
Santa Fe Railroad, 157
Santa Maria Spring, 154, 168
Sawmill Spring, 50
Scouts Lookout, 50
Scudder Lake, 19
Second Tunnel, 147
Shale Creek, 11
Sharlee Lake, 10
Sheep Creek campsite, 30
Sheep Creek Connecting
Trail, 30
Sheiks Canyon, 106, 108
Shower Springs, 127
Shuntavie Butte, 44
Silver Bridge, 141, 146
Silver City (NM), 194
Silver City Museum, 194
Silver Falls, 71
Sipapu Bridge, 101
Skutumpah Road, 26
Skyline Trail, 179–187. *See also*
Pecos Skyline Trail
Slate Creek Fee Station, 7, 10
Slide Rock Arch, 128
Smiths Fork Pass, 13
Smokey Bear, 187
South Bass trailhead, 169
South Entrance Road, 138
South Fork Horse Canyon, 95
South Kaibab Trail, 146, 161
South Rim, 155
Split Level Ruin, 105
Spooky Canyon, 59–60
Springdale (UT), 41
Spring Mountain, 177
Squaw Canyon, 76, 87, 90–91

Squaw Flat Campground A, 78, 95
Squaw Flat Campground B, 95
Squaw Flat trailhead, **74**, 94
Squaw Pass, 16
Stevens Arch, 69
Stewart Lake, 185
St. George (UT), 41
Stimper Arch, 105
Straight Cliffs, 64
Subway Top-Down Route, 47
Summit Inn Pizza and Ice Cream, 9
Supai Formation, 140
Supai Group, 158, 168
Supai Tunnel, 140
Swamp Canyon, 30
Swamp Canyon campsite, 30
Swamp Canyon Connecting Trail, 30

Taft, William, 43
Tapeats Narrow, 147
Tapeats Sandstone, 141
Taylor Creek Trail, 41
Taylor Lake, 11
Telephone Canyon Trail, 50
Tertiary History of the Grand Canyon District (Dutton), 139
3-Mile Resthouse, 147
Thumb, 106, **107**
Timber Creek, 38, 43–44
Timber Top Mountain, 45
Todie Canyon, **99**, 105, 110
Todie Spring, 100, 105
Tonto Platform, 147, 151, 158, 159, 169
Tonto Trail, 147, **150**, 151–170, 207
Toroweap Formation, 140, 158, 168
Trail 043 (High Uinta Wilderness), 12
Trail 044 (High Uinta Wilderness), 12
Trail 054 (High Uinta Wilderness), 13
Trail 059 (High Uinta Wilderness), 13
Trail 061 (High Uinta Wilderness), 16
Trail 103 (High Uinta Wilderness), 16
Trail Rider Pass, 12–13

Trailrider's Wall, 181, 184
Transcanyon Shuttle, 135
Transept Trail, 137
Truchas Lake, 180, 181
Truchas Lake Meadow, 174, 187
Truchas Peak, 180, 181
Tungsten Lake, **6**, 13, 19
Tungsten Pass, 13
Turkey Pen Ruin, 105
Tusayan, 138, 155
2-Mile Corner, 147

Udall, Stewart, 79, 80
Uinta Mountains, 5
Uinta River Trail, 12
Uinta–Wasatch–Cache National Forest. *See* Highline Trail
Under-the-Rim Trail, 21–26, 29–35, 207, 208
United States Geological Survey, 63
Upper Jump waterfall, 83, 85
Upper Reader Lake, 11
Upper Scorpion Campground, 195
Utah National Park, 28

Valley of the Gods, 101
Vermilion Cliffs condor viewing site, 117
Vermilion Cliffs National Monument: Buckskin Gulch and Paria River Canyon, **112**, 113–117, 119–128, 207, 208; California condors, 117–119
Vernal (UT), 9
Village Loop Drive, 138
Virgin River, 37, 50, 61
Vishnu Schist, 147
Vishnu Temple, 158, 159
Vista Encantada, 137

Waldron Trail, 168
Walhalla Overlook, 137
Walters Wiggles, 50
Wasatch National Forest, 18
Watchtower, 138, 155
Wave formation, 117, 119
Wedding Ring Arch, 82–83, 94
West Fork Blacks Fork, 17
West Fork Gila River, 204–205
West Fork Gila River Canyon, 201, 204–205

West Fork Gila River Trail, 204–205
West Fork Rio Santa Barbara, 187
West Fork trailhead, **192**, 195, 205
West Rim, **38**
West Rim Trail, 50–52
West Rim trailhead, 41
White House trailhead, **114**, 117, 125, 128
Whiteman Connecting Trail, 30
White Rocks, 198
White Zig Zags, 168
Wildcat Canyon, 38, **38**, 41, 47, 50, 52
Wildcat Canyon Trail, 40, 47, 50
Wildcat Canyon trailhead, 41
Wildcat Spring, 47
Wilderness Lake, 12
Wilderness Society, 177
Williams (AZ), 135, 138, 154, 155–156
Willis Creek, 30
Willis Creek Canyon, 26
Willow Gulch, 60
Wilson, Bates, 79–80
Winsor Creek, 186
Winsor Creek trailhead, 174, 176, 187, 189
Wire Pass, 119–120
Wire Pass trailhead, **114**, 116, 119, 128
wolves, 195–197
Wrather Arch, 125, 127, 128
Wrather Canyon, **114**, 127, 128

Yellow Creek, **23**, 31, 32
Yellow Creek campsite, 32
Yellow Creek group campsite, 22, 33
Yellowstone Creek, 13

Zion Canyon, 37, 38, 43, 50–52
Zion Lodge, 52
Zion National Park: creation of, 43; Zion Park Traverse, **36**, 37–53, 207
Zion Park Lodge, 42
Zion Park Traverse, **36**, 37–53, 207
Zoraster Temple, 160

About the Authors

Doug Lorain began hiking at age four and until recently had always managed to hike his age in miles in a single day. (Upon turning forty-one several years back, he switched to kilometers.)

His first backpacking trip was at age twelve with his father—a miserable mosquito-infested affair about which the nightmares have yet to subside—and he has since logged well over thirty thousand trail miles pursuing his favorite activity all around the American and Canadian West.

Over time, he has been charged by grizzly bears (*twice!*), been bitten by a rattlesnake, gotten stuck in quicksand, suffered through a nasty bout of giardia, been shot at once by a hunter, been nearly washed away in river fords, and survived enough Pacific Northwest storms to turn the Sahara into a rainforest, but he has also been blessed to see some of the most beautiful scenery on Earth.

He is the national-award-winning author of nine previous hiking and backpacking guidebooks, with plans for several more, assuming his knees hold out. Although he considers his real home to be on the trail, those days he is forced indoors he spends in Hamilton, Montana, with his wife, Becky Lovejoy.

Mike White grew up in Portland, Oregon, from where he began adventuring in the Cascade Range. He obtained a BA from Seattle Pacific University, where he met and married his wife, Robin. The couple lived in Seattle for two years before relocating to Reno, Nevada, where Robin had been accepted to medical school. For the next fifteen years, Mike worked for a consulting engineering firm, journeying to the Sierra Nevada and other areas of the West as time permitted. During that time, the couple had two sons, David and Stephen, and Robin completed school and residency, and then went into private practice as a pediatrician. Upon leaving the engineering firm, Mike became a full-time writer, eventually authoring or contributing to numerous outdoor guides, as well as articles for magazines and newspapers. A former community college instructor, Mike is also a featured speaker for outdoors and conservation organizations.